"Increasingly visible through the enveloping fog of political turmoil, economic uncertainty, social unrest and ecological decline is a new energy; one that is challenging old assumptions, is life-affirming, regenerative and ecologically passionate. It is profoundly aware relationally, and determinedly hopeful that humanity can yet win a safe and secure future for people and nature. In this endeavor, the vision and practice of education is being widely reclaimed, reconceived, and repurposed by communities of educators and learners motivated to make a decisive and positive difference. *Prioritizing Sustainability Education* is part of this vital movement, and will offer any educator the knowledge, skills and spirit to join this critically important and timely wave of renewal."

— **Stephen Sterling**, *Professor Emeritus of Sustainability Education, University of Plymouth, UK*

"Humane sustainability education that rewilds hearts and heads is sorely needed. *Prioritizing Sustainability Education* could well be a game-changer for creating an ethic of care, resilience, and optimistic activism. This book belongs in classrooms worldwide."

— **Marc Bekoff**, *Ph.D. author of* Rewilding Our Hearts *and co-author of* The Animals' Agenda

"This book uplifts mind, heart, and soul. It offers the possibility and necessity for a profound shift in sustainability education, unveiling new opportunities for hope. It is a grounded and visionary book, mapping the terrain that lies ahead and the wisdom and skills needed to transform these unsustainable times."

— **David Hicks**, *former Professor, School of Education, Bath Spa University, UK*

"If you want a holistic and pragmatic approach to the concept of sustainability education, this book is a solid choice. The authors are diverse, skilled, and respected. They infuse the dimensions of comprehensive sustainability education with global developments and offer practical pathways for the transformation of minds and practice."

— **Akpezi Ogbuigwe**, *Former Head, Environmental Education & Training, UNEP; Adviser, UNU-RCE Africa; Member, Group of Experts in SDGs and Higher Education (GUNi)*

T0384243

PRIORITIZING SUSTAINABILITY EDUCATION

Prioritizing Sustainability Education presents theory-to-practice essays and case studies by educators from six countries who elucidate dynamic approaches to sustainability education. Too often, students graduate with exploitative, consumer-driven orientations toward ecosystems and are unprepared to confront the urgent challenges presented by environmental degradation. Educators are prioritizing sustainability-oriented courses and programs that cultivate students' knowledge, skills, and values and contextualize them within relational connections to local and global ecosystems. Little has yet been written, however, about the comprehensive sustainability education that educators are currently designing and implementing, often across or at the edges of disciplinary boundaries.

The approaches described in this book expand beyond conventional emphases on developing students' attitudes, knowledge, and behaviors by thinking and talking about ecosystems to additionally engaging students with ecosystems in sensory, affective, psychological, and cognitive dimensions, as well as imaginative, spiritual, or existential dimensions that guide environmental care and regeneration.

This book supports educators and graduate and upper-level undergraduate students in the humanities, social sciences, environmental studies, environmental sciences, and professional programs in considering how to reorient their fields toward relational sustainability perspectives and practices.

Joan Armon is Professor of Education at Regis University, USA.

Stephen Scoffham is Visiting Reader in Sustainability and Education, Canterbury Christ Church University, UK.

Chara Armon is Lawrence C. Gallen Fellow in the Humanities and Assistant Professor at Villanova University, USA.

PRIORITIZING SUSTAINABILITY EDUCATION

A Comprehensive Approach

Edited by Joan Armon, Stephen Scoffham and Chara Armon

Routledge
Taylor & Francis Group
LONDON AND NEW YORK

earthscan
from Routledge

First published 2020
by Routledge
2 Park Square, Milton Park, Abingdon, Oxon OX14 4RN

and by Routledge
52 Vanderbilt Avenue, New York, NY 10017

Routledge is an imprint of the Taylor & Francis Group, an informa business

© 2020 selection and editorial matter, Joan Armon, Stephen Scoffham and Chara Armon; individual chapters, the contributors

British Library Cataloguing-in-Publication Data
A catalogue record for this book is available from the British Library

Library of Congress Cataloging-in-Publication Data
A catalog record for this book has been requested

ISBN: 978-1-138-39129-1 (hbk)
ISBN: 978-0-367-07643-6 (pbk)
ISBN: 978-0-429-02180-0 (ebk)

Typeset in Bembo
by Apex CoVantage, LLC

CONTENTS

FIGURES

TABLES

FOREWORD

Jeannette Armstrong

As humanity remains gridlocked by massive inequities linked to worldwide environmental and other challenges, we experience the loss of hope. Prioritizing sustainability education may be the only path for pursuing a change of course. Our current reality is that all communities are facing escalating degradation in the environments they occupy as they confront political, cultural, and economic disruptions. Greater imbalances have become the norm as competing interests intensify efforts to contain chaotic conditions now arising.

Daly (1996), recognized for the foundational framing of ecological economics, concluded that a major obstacle to living sustainably is the contemporary difficulty with advancing a strong environmental ethic within society. Without a society-wide, accessible mechanism to advance a logic grounded in the understanding and belief in the *rightness* of a regenerative interaction with nature, as well as a counteractive logic regarding the *wrongness* of a destructive view of the utility of nature, society will not change.

As authors in this volume delineate, sustainability education must serve as an accessible mechanism to promote society's commitment to regenerative interactions with nature and to eschew destructive interactions. Such a shift requires a thought community to contemplate and enact the issue from multiple viewpoints. I add my thinking from my perspective and experience as an Indigenous person of the Okanagan Valley in British Columbia, Canada, connected to this place of my ancestors by the knowledge that nurtured their lives sustainably for millennia.

Shifting the contemporary paradigm demands that we locate the origin of the problem. In my research and from my view as a Syilx Okanagan person, I have come to discern that an ethically charged dichotomy exists in the way one relates to the place in which one lives. This has resulted in the dangerous political chasm between "Indigenous" and "nonindigenous". This chasm can be ameliorated by community leaders and sustainability educators who recognize that "being in place" means knowing intimately that the human responsibility is to the living system, and "being out of place" means having little or no knowledge of it as a living system that requires reciprocal relationship and care.

Indigenous and indigeneity

For our purposes in this volume, I frame the concept of "Indigenous" as a society-wide knowledgeable adaption to the ecological conditions of place rather than as political ethnicity or race. This allows us to consider "Indigenous" knowledge and practices through the lens of "Indigeneity" as a social construct accessible to all. I position Indigenous knowledge as adapting nature's sustainability acumen into human principles. Knowledge of the necessity for normalizing nature's integration into humanity's daily life and its full regeneration is still the predominant Indigenous reality. Indigenous people's sustainable practices emerged from a knowledgeable interaction shaped by and required by the "place" being occupied. These practices are grounded in "traditional ecological knowledge" or "Indigenous knowledge" that provide foundational guiding principles for appropriate decision-making.

I offer thoughts on learning situated toward "re-indigenizing" to frame an approach for creating "communities of ecological hope." In defining the term "re-indigenizing," the Seneca scholar, the late John Mohawk, explained: "It's not necessarily about the Indigenous Peoples of a specific place; it's about re-indigenizing the peoples of the planet. It's about us looking at the whole thing in the broadest of possible ways" (Mohawk, Cajete, & Rivera, 2008, p. 259).

As an Indigenous person, I have knowledge that allows me to prioritize coexistence and cooperation with other living things. I have had the opportunity to experience the process of claiming the Syilx Okanagan ethic and living it, despite lifelong pressures by the education system and other institutions of society concerned with the unsustainable practices of our contemporary reality. My Syilx Okanagan education transferred knowledge through community and family as an essential foundation for embracing my relationship with other beings on my land.

The practical process of sustainably harvesting roots, berries, fish, and meat all my life didn't just give me access to food; it gave me knowledge of direct accountability to learn their needs as Indigenous beings that need to regenerate themselves so that I can continue to harvest their gift of life to us. The practise of engaging physically, intellectually, and emotionally with them in all aspects of our Syilx Okanagan knowledge systems opens the space for glimpsing, as a form of spiritual insight, the significance of the reciprocally intimate relationship with the living beings that gave us life for the millennia we have been in this place. It allows me to see that I am only here digging the beautiful roots or picking the sweet berries of the land because their gifts to us bind us to a covenant of human responsibility through our society's land ethic. The same ethic demands that we are accountable to know not to allow any one of them to become extinct or to destroy their place for unnecessary needs.

Communities of hope

Understanding the loss of an indigenous relationship has immense potential in sustainability education. Finding concrete ways to create a paradigm shift by introducing "Indigeneity" as a new social construct requires a knowledge relationship with place. Learners can begin prioritizing sustainability education to re-indigenize a place through collaborations with its Indigenous peoples in an authentic, respectful, and reciprocal process of restoration and protection work. Such an educational process in itself would create new communities of hope steeped in the quest for knowledge needed in that particular place.

It is incumbent on humans to learn to cooperatively and equitably share nature's gifts and to celebrate the lives of other living beings. Learning in this way requires a process of continuously infusing a community with hope that its members can continue to celebrate the health that they deserve as living beings of this land. Indigenous, to me, means you must know a profound level of cooperation with the land within a community with whom you are sharing cooperative practices, with hope at the deepest core, driving the choices we make.

For a willing shift toward re-indigenizing humans to the places they occupy, the idea of alienation from nature needs correction. We must identify the core issue as a disassociation from the knowledge that is necessary for a regenerative interdependence within a place. Directing the concept of "sustainability education" toward a focus on the creation of "communities of ecological hope" means restoring knowledge of community being "in place" rather than "out of place." Building community as part of nature should focus on learning that restores humans to living sustainably within all the places they live. Places need their human inhabitants to enact this knowledge of being "in place."

Re-framing the concept of restoration of an environment to one that prioritizes restoring human community to live with nature establishes the need to create new life-ways that will be sustainable in the long-term. In this age of freedom to co-create, we continuously generate new customs and so initiate values that change societal decision-making and produce new life-ways. Advancing an Indigeneity-based learning approach to prioritizing sustainability education allows for co-imagining the building of knowledgeable communities of ecological hope in the places we live, no matter how small or how large.

Without the Syilx Okanagan knowledge of our community that we are relatives of the living beings that sustain us with food, medicine, clothing, and shelter, I would not be. The meaning that this has for me amplifies the reality of being unable to protect that land, being unable to stand alone between the extinguishment of these living beings from the land and those responsible for that destruction. The depth of love and understanding that is required to continue to receive that gift of knowing myself as a relative of those living beings that sustain me drives my need to find sound ways to educate others in the gift of being in community with land in that way with me.

Learning new ways to care for our environment together is a way to restore community by building communities of ecological hope. Hope and solutions are possible through supporting and empowering new relationships to place. Such relationships require implementation of practical, socially and environmentally sustainable ways to actualize communities of ecological change. The work of these communities must be beneficial in concrete and visible ways that contribute to the well-being and wholeness of living beings as part of an environment in which they live. Creating communities of ecological hope must begin by prioritizing projects that deliver immediate tangible benefits to people in need of community and food security while focusing on strategic long-term outcomes for specific places.

Constructing a clear hope of long-term security, stability, and well-being together as a community of place is necessary to develop principles of reciprocity, cooperation, and harmlessness to each other and the environment. In the current absence of food security and employment stability, and the reality of social isolation for an increasing many as an everyday norm, new approaches to reversing those trends are necessary. Creating a solidarity of purpose in being of one mind as a part of the living beings of each place is Indigeneity in practice. This is a required ethic for developing and maintaining principled living within the places where we live in a community.

New stories

Expanding approaches to learning for "re-indigenizing" requires us to create new stories by which we inform and are informed. Stories connect us to a different way of human knowing about the requirements of sustainability in a place. Stories provide a way of knowing by which one constructs and confirms the common text of societal responsibility to live by, and the ethical boundaries required within "place" in the real world.

Knowledge expressing specialized nature-perception through language is an essential survival science for Indigenous people. It requires as much exactness of sensorial and active detail as is possible for those who have depended on harvesting the land. Science is the human ability to observe, understand, and explain nature for human endeavor, and, whether revealed through a microscope or abstract theory, science is nature's intelligence translated by the human mind in a variety of ways. Organizing what appears as chaos into cognizant patterns is critical to human intelligence, whether through mathematical formulae or through story. The fundamental difference between science and story, however, is story's accessibility to more people through both intellectual and emotional intelligence, while access through the various languages of science is limited to those educated in its rules. Society endorses and enacts ethical conduct through the common text of its people in general. People must not only understand the logic of an ethic but also must feel that it is *right* in order to follow its tenets.

We can educate through story to engage the emotions and immerse the intellectual imagination in knowledge, which makes sustainability principles visible in the real world. The shift in values and views requires the story about living beings and their continuous requirements in regenerating themselves. The relationship of telling and building community reveals that story is about binding people to values they collectively hold. Community is the outcome produced by story. Prioritizing sustainability education for re-Indigenizing places must include exploring Indigenous story and the languages of a place. Reconnecting, remembering, or relocating the human into each place requires the language and story of place to embed knowledge. This knowledge will contextualize the human story gained over long periods of being in that same community.

Conclusion

Indigeneity as a socially conscious placement within a landscape of sustainable thought and action requires:

- An intellectual dialogue about indigenizing place and the need for Indigeneity as a new social construct;
- Prioritizing sustainability education that is informed by Indigenous knowledge to guide decision-making and active participation in communities;
- Reimagining education through stories embracing Indigenous knowledge and collaborative engagement in restoration projects intended to build community;
- Creating strategic collaborations foundational to building ecological communities of hope through deliberate planning. Conceptual and experiential educational models of engagement can promote restoration through indigenizing community principles in relation to the specific place in which people reside.

Prioritizing sustainability education toward a collective purpose, when actualized in the concept that "WE are this place," is the greatest hope for an ecologically sound paradigm shift.

References

Daly, H. E. (1996). *Beyond growth: The economics of sustainable development*. Boston, MA: Beacon Press.
Mohawk, J. C., Cajete, G., & Rivera, J. C. (2008). Re-indigenization defined. In M. K. Nelson (Ed.), *Original instructions: Indigenous teachings for a sustainable future* (pp. 252–265). Rochester, VT: Bear & Company.

CONTRIBUTORS

Chara Armon, Ph.D. is an Associate Teaching Professor and Gallen Fellow in the Humanities at Villanova University, US, where she teaches interdisciplinary courses in the area of humanities and ecology. She holds degrees from Colorado College and Cornell University. Her research and teaching interests include humanities and ecology, spirituality and ecology, sustainable and justice-oriented agriculture, transformative sustainability education, and comprehensive sustainability education.

Joan Armon is a Professor at Regis University in Denver, Colorado, US. Justice and sustainability concepts and practices are foundational to her teacher preparation courses and transdisciplinary core courses taught with colleagues in Fine and Performing Arts, History, and Peace and Justice disciplines. Evolving as comprehensive sustainability education, these courses have taken place in classrooms as well as in school and university gardens, community spaces, and on urban, suburban, and rural farms, particularly where food deserts exist. Her research focuses on sustainability, relational, and justice orientations that drive transformative learning in conducive contexts.

Jeannette Armstrong, Syilx Okanagan, is Associate Professor in Community, Culture & Global Studies and Canada Research Chair at the University of British Columbia Okanagan, Canada. Her research, focused in Syilx and Settler ecosystem research collaborations, is engaged in recovering Syilx knowledge. She is a recipient of the EcoTrust USA Buffett Award for Indigenous Leadership, and recently the George Woodcock Lifetime Achievement Award. Her social transformation work and publishing in the past decade includes work such as dialogue with the Centre for Ecoliteracy in Berkerly, CA, and Bioneers in Santa Fe, NM, as well as extensively in community practice and graduate student mentoring.

Zanagee Artis is a 19 year old from Clinton, Connecticut, US, and a co-founder of the youth climate justice organization Zero Hour. Zanagee became involved in the climate movement because he grew up on the coast of Connecticut and became passionate about mitigating plastic pollution and climate change that impact our oceans. He organized the Zero Hour Youth Climate March in Washington, D.C., in 2018, and alongside other Zero Hour organizers hosted the Zero Hour Youth Climate Summit in Miami, Florida, from July 12–14, 2019. He is majoring in environmental studies and political science at Brown University and plans to attend law school after graduating.

Polly Bolshaw is a senior lecturer in Early Years at Canterbury Christ Church University, UK, where she teaches predominantly in the B.A. (Hons) Early Childhood Studies programme. Prior to this, she completed the New Leaders in Early Years programme at CCCU and worked as an Early Years Professional in a Sure Start Children's Centre. Her research interests include research methods for undergraduate students, the experiences of people who work with young children and study early childhood, early childhood education for sustainability, and services within the UK that aim to support children and their families. She is also co-author of the blog Contemplating Childhoods https://contemplatingchildhoods.com/

Patty Born, Ed.D., is an assistant professor of environmental and STEM education at Hamline University in St Paul, Minnesota, US. She has a background in preK-6 teaching in classrooms and nonformal settings such as parks and museums. She is program director for Hamline's Master of Arts in Environmental Education, which is a member of the United Nations Global University Partnership for Environment and Sustainability network. Her research interests include ecopedagogy, culturally-sustaining pedagogies, critical animal studies, and urban environmental education.

Arielle Martinez Cohen is a 17-year-old singer, songwriter, producer, and activist from Los Angeles, California, US. Arielle is the Partnerships Director for Zero Hour and an organizer with Youth Climate Strike Los Angeles. In 2018, her song, "Two Minutes to Midnight" was used by The Bulletin of the Atomic Scientists in their announcement of the Doomsday Clock. She was selected by Instagram and Good Morning America for their #captureconfidence campaign. In 2018, Arielle was featured in LA Works' The Power of Women in the Music Industry and the UN-affiliated Youth Creating Global Change concert. In 2019, she was a lead organizer for the Class of 0000 Campaign and spoke at her high school graduation to demand climate action.

A D Nuwan Gunarathne is a Senior Lecturer in the Department of Accounting, University of Sri Jayewardenepura, Sri Lanka. He is a member of both the Chartered Institute of Management Accounting (UK) and the Institute of Certified Management Accountants of Sri Lanka. He has an M.B.A. and a degree in business administration from the University of Sri Jayewardenepura. He has authored and co-authored many publications in different spheres of management accounting, sustainability accounting, integrated reporting, and accounting education. Nuwan is a committee member of the Environmental and Sustainability Management Accounting Network (EMAN) Asia Pacific (AP) and country representative of the Sri Lanka Chapter of EMAN-AP.

Thomas R. Hudspeth is Professor Emeritus of Environmental Studies and Natural Resources and Affiliate, Gund Institute for Environment, at the University of Vermont, US. He serves as co-coordinator of Greater Burlington Sustainability Education Network, a Regional Center of Expertise in Education for Sustainable Development recognized by United Nations University. His scholarly interest in sustainability applies insights of behavioral sciences to help people live more sustainably. Tom taught service-learning courses in Sustainability Education, Creating Environmentally Sustainable Communities, Place-based Landscape Analysis, Environmental Interpretation, and 18 travel-study courses to Latin America – Belize, Costa Rica, Ecuador, Honduras, Brazil – addressing ecotourism as a tool for sustainability.

Ivy Jaguzny grew up on Vashon Island, Washington, US. In 2017, she joined the Legislative Youth Advisory Council for Washington State to fight for youth civic engagement and representation of environmental issues in youth legislation. She is a frequent visitor to Olympia, where she testifies on legislation for pollution management, environmental education, and clean energy. In fall 2017, she met Jamie Margolin, who became the co-founder and executive director of Zero Hour. Ivy joined the press team of Zero Hour later that year in order to uplift the voices of the Zero Hour directors and marginalized youth. She hopes to study physics and become an environmental engineer who bridges the gap between policy and science.

Nicola Kemp is a senior lecturer in Early Childhood at Canterbury Christ Church University, UK, where she leads the M.A. Early Childhood Education. She also works across the University as Education for Sustainable Development (ESD) lead. A geographer by background, Nicola's interests include children's experiences of the natural environment and she has developed the 'Connecting Children and Nature Network for Kent, which brings together staff, students, and a range of local organizations to explore and develop this agenda through research, knowledge exchange, and curriculum development. Research interests include Forest School, home education, alternative curricular, and Education for Sustainable Futures.

Kendall Kieras is a 16-year-old environmental and LGBT activist from Seattle, Washington, US. They currently serve on the communications team for Zero Hour National, as well as serving as the Executive Director for Zero Hour Seattle. They are also a performing slam poet and singer-songwriter, and truly believe in the power of stories to change the world.

Heila Lotz–Sisitka, Professor, holds a Tier 1 South African National Research Foundation Chair in Global Change and Social Learning Systems, and is a Distinguished Research Professor in Education at Rhodes University, South Africa. She has published widely, and has served on numerous national and international scientific and policy committees in Education and Sustainability, including the international reference group for the UN Decade on Education for Sustainable Development. She regularly presents keynote contributions and has edited numerous journals and books, with a recent co-edited book, '*Critical Realism, Environmental Learning and Social-Ecological Change*' (Routledge, 2016) being awarded the Cheryl Frank Memorial Prize.

Dan McKanan is the Emerson Senior Lecturer at Harvard Divinity School, US, where he has taught since 2008. His scholarship focuses broadly on religion and social transformation, and specifically on intentional community, environmentalism, the anthroposophical movement, and Unitarian Universalism. He is the author or editor of seven books, including *Eco-Alchemy: Anthroposophy and the History and Future of Environmentalism* (University of California Press). Currently he is completing a book on generational transitions in the Camphill movement.

Florence Monsour is a professor and chair of Teacher Education at the University of Wisconsin River Falls, US. She teaches courses in educational psychology for education majors and coordinates the Principal Licensure/Director of Instruction Program. She was trained in the first Sustainability Across the Curriculum workshop in 2011, and since then has taken a leadership role co-chairing the Sustainability Faculty Fellows Committee. Florence co-led the second annual "Kinnickinnic Project" in 2012 and participated in the Sustainability Learning Outcomes subcommittee. She has presented at over five AASHE Conferences focusing on the integration of sustainability within K-12, (early years, primary, and secondary) lesson plans for teacher candidates.

Victor Tichaona Pesanayi (late) obtained his Ph.D. at Rhodes University, South Africa on 11 April 2019. He sadly passed away on 17 April 2019. Prior to obtaining his Ph.D., he worked as Regional Programme Manager for the Southern African Development Community's Environmental Education Programme. He was also the serving Secretary General of the Environmental Education Association of Southern Africa at the time of his passing. Shortly before his passing, his work in advancing sustainable agriculture and co-learning was recognized in a national Mail and Guardian Greening the Future Award, and the Vice Chancellors Award for Community Engagement.

Sasith Rajasooriya is a lecturer in the Department of Mathematics, University of Dayton, Ohio, US. He obtained his Ph.D. in statistics from the University of South Florida, Florida, US. He has an M.Sc. in mathematics from Georgia Southern University, Georgia, US, and a degree in business administration from

University of Sri Jayewardenepura, Sri Lanka. Sasith is also an attorney-at-law in the Supreme Court of Sri Lanka. He has authored and co-authored several publications in the area of cybersecurity and statistical modelling.

Stephen Scoffham is a Visiting Reader in Sustainability and Education at Canterbury Christ Church University, UK, where he has worked for many years as a teacher educator. His research interests include sustainability, global learning, geography education, and creativity. Stephen has explored these themes through research and publications – his latest books are *Leadership for Sustainability in Higher Education* (Bloomsbury Academic, 2018) and *Teaching Geography Creatively* (Routledge, 2017, 2nd edn.). Stephen is also the author/consultant for a wide range of school atlases, an active member of local social and environmental groups, and the elected President of the UK Geographical Association (2018–19).

Soul Shava holds a Ph.D. in Environmental Education from Rhodes University, South Africa, and is currently an Associate Professor in Environmental Education in the Department of Science and Technology Education at the University of South Africa. Soul's main research interests are in environmental sustainability education processes in Southern Africa, Indigenous epistemologies, and decoloniality. He also has research interests in community-based natural resources management (CBNRM); socio-ecological resilience; climate change education; green economy; cultural heritage; sustainable agriculture; traditional agrobiodiversity conservation; Indigenous food plants; and food security and sovereignty.

Arran Stibbe is a Professor of Ecological Linguistics at the University of Gloucestershire, UK. He has an academic background in both linguistics and human ecology and combines the two in his research and teaching. He is the founder of the International Ecolinguistics Association, and is author of *Animals Erased: Discourse, Ecology and Reconnection With Nature* (Weslyan University Press) and *Ecolinguistics: Language, Ecology and the Stories We Live By* (Routledge). He was awarded a National Teaching Fellowship by the Higher Education Academy for teaching excellence and has published widely on ecolinguistics and education for sustainability.

Sangion Appiee Tiu is the Director for the Research & Conservation Foundation, a not-for-profit non-governmental organization in Papua New Guinea. She also teaches part-time at the University of Goroka through a partnership arrangement with the university's Division of Indigenous, Environment and Development Studies. Sangion holds a Ph.D. from the University of Waikato in New Zealand. Her research interests are in the areas of Environment and Sustainability Education, Bio-culture Education, and Traditional Ecological Knowledge for natural resource management.

Simon Wilson is a Senior Lecturer at Canterbury Christ Church University in the UK, where he teaches on both undergraduate and postgraduate programs, and is also a member of the Institute for Orthodox Christian Studies at Cambridge, UK. He has published widely on a variety of topics, including, most recently, ecology and paranormal phenomena, in *Greening the Paranormal*, edited by Jack Hunter (2019). He has also written on the Grail, René Guénon, colour symbolism, the visionary architecture of the Facteur Cheval, and the imaginal history of a Cambridge college. With Angela Voss, he is the editor of *Re-enchanting the Academy* (2017).

Mary Wright is a Professor of Literacy Education at the University of Wisconsin River Falls, US, with 30 years of educational experience, including thirteen years as a classroom English teacher. Her pedagogies are grounded in arts-based transdisciplinary methods bridging socially engaged inquiry-based learning with mindful participatory engagement with place. As the founding coordinator of the UWRF Sustainability Faculty Fellows committee in 2011, she started an annual sustainability curriculum workshop to support faculty in integrating sustainability in coursework. She serves on the UWRF Sustainable Justice Program steering panel. Her research interests include arts-based teaching and learning, sustainability and mindfulness, and peace education.

INTRODUCTION

Joan Armon

The purpose of *Prioritizing Sustainability Education* is to disseminate and invite discussion of sustainability-oriented initiatives developed by educators from several global regions. In theory-to-practice essays and case studies, authors conceptualize comprehensive sustainability education as it applies to particular circumstances. They interpret its significance in the context of escalating environmental degradation and associated challenges, and suggest educational approaches designed to empower students and enhance their prospects for thriving. The aim toward planetary thriving, however, demands holistic systems thinking that informs humanity's choices with both short- and long-term impacts in view.

The cover of this volume shows students approaching a fork in the pathway ahead of them, preparing to choose one path or the other. Speth aptly frames the implications of humanity's choices along the pathway ahead. One path leads toward an abyss of severe planetary degradation; the other leads to a bridge over the abyss where humanity arrives after having chosen a shift in consciousness toward valuing the well-being of all lives and the natural world (2008).

Here authors write with a keen awareness of challenges confronting humanity, including the challenge of mindfully discerning which path to choose at each fork in the pathways ahead. What makes this book particularly distinctive is:

- The concept of sustainability education as a holistic approach that balances the values, attitudes, and behaviors of Earth care; the knowledge and skills of resilience and regeneration; and the actions arising from advocacy for life's flourishing.
- References to (a) the Earth Charter and (b) the Sustainable Development Goals (SDGs) in all chapters to situate authors' ideas in a global context of environmental assessment and action.

- Acknowledgment of recent school strikes, Zero Hour, and Extinction Rebellion, which provide current responses to a rapidly evolving debate.
- Examples from six countries, bringing together international perspectives, indigenous knowledge, and traditional wisdom.
- A broad basis in both time (past/present/future) and space (North America, Europe, Africa, and Asia).
- A focus on a form of ecological consciousness that unites cognitive, affective, imaginative, and spiritual perspectives.

While the term "comprehensive sustainability education" is used here to denote a relational, holistic, participatory, and systemic approach, other terms have evolved to describe related educational practices. These range from environmental education to place-based education, education for sustainable development (ESD), environmental and sustainability education (ESE), ecojustice education, global learning, and others. Each of these initiatives seeks to explore conceptual and practical variations of engaging students with concepts and applications educators may select according to their purposes, participants, and contexts. What differentiates comprehensive sustainability education is educators' openness not only to cognitive aspects of developing and acting on an ecological consciousness, but also to the sensory, imaginative, aesthetic, intuitive, and spiritual facets that inform thought and action regarding environmental challenges. Such experiences contribute to an environmental education paradigm that occurs in and outside of classrooms, provides opportunities to analyze the underlying drivers and manifestations of unjust and escalating degradation in local and global contexts, and develops human-human and human-nature relationships (Sterling, 2017).

Too many universities and colleges continue to base their policies, curricula, and operations on unsustainable rather than sustainable assumptions. Higher education too often pursues unbridled rather than sufficient economic growth, unquestioned allegiance rather than challenges to consumerism, and an unlimited rather than equitable quest for wealth. Educators who promote sustainability education thus work against the institutional grain and are perceived as nonconformists to be merely tolerated (Orr, 2017b). The authors in this volume question the mindset that orients students toward exploitation of the Earth and its myriad lives rather than toward a relational and "intimate human rapport with the Earth community" that can guide regeneration and care of degraded environments and lives (Berry, 1999, p. 19). As British economist E.F. Schumacher emphasized, the education system's bias toward industry and technology fosters competition, injustice, and "minds unchecked by the heart," which diminish capacities to establish nonviolent relationships with others and the natural world (1998, p. 192). Similarly, Kenyan environmental activist and Nobel Prize Laureate Wangari Maathai declared that humanity must heal deep wounds it has inflicted upon the Earth community and develop a reimagined consciousness that acknowledges our place in the whole community of life (2010). Within the larger systems of which they are a part, educators, students, and community members can take a role in cultivating a reimagined consciousness in an ecological form developed through transformative learning that is participatory, appreciative, synergistic, and collaborative (Sterling, 2014).

Authors in this volume convey path-breaking efforts that are largely unknown across disciplinary boundaries even though some college and university educators are engaging students in developing an environmental consciousness imbued with hope. Considering the pace of escalating environmental degradation and its associated challenges, dissemination of educators' and students' innovative efforts is urgently needed so that the significance of an ecological consciousness can gain wide acceptance. This ecological consciousness evolves as students, educators, and community members collaborate to develop attitudes, knowledge, and behaviors not only by thinking and talking *about* environmental challenges and the injustices associated with them, but also by integrating relational, reflexive, systemic, and action-oriented approaches to *engage with* the whole Earth community that includes human and other-than-human lives. Transformative learning is a notable aim as educators guide students to critique popular assumptions and standard operating procedures (Wals & Blewitt, 2010).

What matters, as David Orr reminds us, is ensuring that students possess not only resolve and stamina to confront increasingly deadly storms, seas, and heat, but also clear thinking and some measure of humor to analyze challenges and respond mindfully. Additionally, students must develop capacities to buoy their hearts and souls while strengthening community bonds amidst unfamiliar perils (2017a). Now is the time to continually ask whether our educational approaches are meeting these needs and, if they are not, to shift them rapidly.

Global context

To situate comprehensive sustainability education in a global context and provide coherence among chapters, contributing authors refer to two international documents. The Sustainable Development Goals (SDGs) consist of seventeen voluntary goals that all 193 member states of the U.N. agreed upon in 2015. Each goal is supported by a set of targets to be achieved by 2030. The SDGs offer policy orientations that balance social, economic, and environmental factors with an overall emphasis on economic well-being that is essential to global sustainability objectives.

The Earth Charter was authored by the independent, nongovernmental Earth Charter Commission charged with facilitating the work of more than five thousand citizens from around the world (2001). Importantly, the charter focuses on the human dimensions of culture and diverse lives. It fills a void found too often in varying approaches to environmental and sustainability education, namely, acknowledgement of environmental racism and associated injustices (Agyeman,

Schlosberg, & Matthews, 2016). As a practical plan for a sustainable future, it underscores interlaced issues of justice, peace, and environment that are central to addressing global challenges (Tucker, 2008).

While both documents have shortcomings, they very effectively support educators' shifts toward comprehensive sustainability education, as the authors in the following chapters show. The documents complement each other; reading them together provides a rounded sense of sustainability aims and challenges. The SDGs, for example, stress an end to poverty and emphasize equal rights to economic resources for the poor and vulnerable, as stated in the first Goal. The Earth Charter accentuates respect and care for every life form irrespective of its value to humans, and freedom to advance the common good, as articulated in the first Principle. Together, the Sustainable Development Goals and the Earth Charter signal humanity's desire to establish relationships with and regeneration of the Earth community, now and into the future.

Dimensions of comprehensive sustainability education

The three crucial dimensions of comprehensive sustainability education brought together in this book are:

- cultivating an ethic of care,
- fostering resilience and regeneration, and
- advocating for life's flourishing.

Focusing on just one of these dimensions on their own may introduce students to sustainability on a superficial level that is necessarily fragmented and incomplete. Bringing the three dimensions together is essential if students are to develop the deep understanding of sustainability which will bring about a fundamental shift in their thinking.

Cultivating an ethic of care

An Ethic of Care emerges as educators support students' values, attitudes, and behaviors. This dimension builds upon notions of relational awareness, reciprocity, and caring toward self, others, plants, and animals, as well as things and ideas (Noddings, 1992). Principle 2 of The Earth Charter expresses this concept as "Care for the community of life with understanding, compassion, and love." The American forester and environmentalist Aldo Leopold described relational awareness when he observed that "We can be ethical only in relation to something we can see, feel, understand, love, or otherwise have faith in" (1949, p. 214). To spark relational awareness and affiliation, evolutionary biologist Marc Bekoff advocates imagining the viewpoints of animals, plants, rocks, and other elements of nature, perceiving and interacting with them from a mindset of empathy, compassion, and peace (2014). Perceiving the lives and elements of the

Comprehensive Sustainability Education

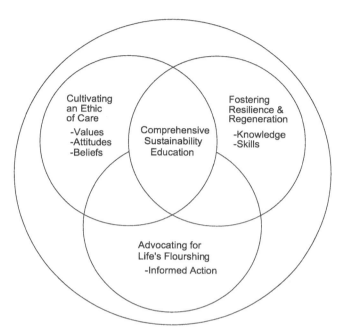

FIGURE 0.1 Comprehensive sustainability education cultivates an "Ethic of Care," "Resilience and Regeneration," and "Advocating for Life's Flourishing." It brings these three dimensions together holistically as represented by the outer circle

natural world from a mindset of affiliation and care can contribute to students' transformative shift toward environmental care, particularly when educators offer classroom discourses grounded in students' nature experiences as well as scientific studies (Barlett, 2008).

Encountering Indigenous traditions of reverent rapport with the Earth community has the potential to deepen students' insights into relational awareness. Tewa Pueblo educator Gregory Cajete, for example, explains that relational awareness emerges from awareness of kinship with all lives, lands, and waters and contributes to understanding how to address twenty-first century environmental challenges (2001). Additionally, ancient knowledge teaches gratitude that forms cultures of reciprocal relationship among all that exist, as Potawatomi environmental biologist Robin Wall Kimmerer articulates (2013). Underscoring these perspectives, Wals, Weakland, and Corcoran assert that intentional as well as Indigenous communities that express ontologies comprised of relationally and spiritually oriented lifeways, ethics, and values may provide guidance as humanity aims for a future that is sustainable (2017).

Fostering resilience and regeneration

Increasingly, educators recognize the need for fostering resilience so that students possess the knowledge and skills to recover some measure of stability amidst turbulence. Resilience involves the against-all-odds resolution and stamina accompanied by a clear mind capable of identifying problems and knowing how to respond. It is the capability of absorbing disruption while maintaining structure and function, or identity, so that individuals and systems can adapt to unexpected change (Post Carbon Institute, 2015). In SDG 13.1, the aim is to "Strengthen resilience and adaptive capacity to climate-related hazards and natural disasters in all countries." As an example, Tidball's and colleagues' research explores if and how citizens' past opportunities to engage in acts of ecological restoration, care, and regeneration might serve as crucial experiences for forming and maintaining resilience amidst future complex change (2010). Furthermore, in times of disruption, leadership and new stories drawing upon a society's history and values have the potential to stimulate revised assumptions and innovative problem-solving that promote resilience, collaboration, and perceptions of problems as opportunities (Hopkins, 2010; Speth, 2008).

Regeneration may emerge in tandem with altered assumptions and creative problem-solving linked to resilience. Potentially, students perceive the need for restoring, renewing, strengthening, and perpetuating ecosystems, cultures, institutions of value, and natural abundance for current and future generations (Thayer, 2012). Much can be learned from those Indigenous communities that rely on their regenerative ways of being and acting in the world guided by wisdom traditions which have withstood the test of time throughout ecological, political, economic, and cultural disruption, often in the context of devastating colonization (Greenwood, 2014). However, educators integrating Indigenous wisdom traditions are not implying that they serve as panaceas for complex, contemporary problems stemming from worldwide ecosystem crises, conflict, and inequalities in economic and social arenas. Rather, traditional relational ontologies provide alternative visions with guidelines for contributing to life's flourishing (Grim, 2001).

Advocating for life's flourishing

Advocacy opportunities in classrooms involve students' action informed by investigations of the structural problems fuelling climate change and its impacts. Increasingly, however, students are not waiting for educators to orchestrate opportunities but are taking initiative to conduct their own advocacy campaigns. Students from Zero Hour outline such advocacy initiatives in chapter two of this volume. Furthermore, at the time of writing, students in varying countries are following the lead of Swedish activist Greta Thunberg to boycott school on Fridays with demands that politicians and others enact immediate responses to climate change. SDG Goal 13 accords with students' activism: "Take urgent action to combat climate change and its impacts." Within an advocacy framework, students and educators examine contributors to climate change impacts, engage in dialogue, and focus on issues that align with their own values, attitudes, and understanding, and accordingly, discern which advocacy and action they choose to take (Barlett & Chase, 2013).

Additional values, knowledge, and skills to expand human-nature relationships and ameliorate environmental degradation can emerge at the intersection of an ethic of care, resilience, and regeneration, and advocacy for life's flourishing. At this intersection, educators and students learn deeply, experience the Earth community fully, and collaborate in and beyond their communities, wherever the need for restoration, regeneration, and reciprocal care is most urgent.

Conclusion

As educators contributing to this volume re-envision and reorient courses, programs, institutions, and communities through a comprehensive sustainability education lens, they are spurred not only by their own sense of urgency about complex challenges, but also by students' despair, fear, and hopelessness about damaged futures they feel powerless to repair. Educators who recognize hopelessness as "hope that has lost its bearings" immerse students in education that dispels despair and inaction while inspiring hope and action (Freire, 1994, p. 8).

The following chapters convey dynamic approaches to providing opportunities for action and hope through comprehensive sustainability education in and across the humanities and sciences. There are two sections: Comprehensive Sustainability Education Perspectives and Theory to Practice. Contributing authors capture topics that are critical to students' grasp of both ecological degradation and of regeneration via skills and values that empower students to relate to and transform lives and places. The authors provide course content guides as examples that educators can adapt to their own distinctive contexts, students, and communities.

A relational turn toward the thriving of all lives and living Earth systems signals higher education's awakening to its role in cultivating humanity's ecological consciousness and dedication to the larger Earth community. Undaunted by the scale of the task, educators worldwide go forward assuming that every collaborative step toward care, resilience, regeneration, and flourishing matters.

References

Agyeman, J., Schlosberg, L., & Matthews, C. (2016). Trends and directions in environmental justice: From inequity to everyday life, community, and just sustainabilities. *Annual Review of Environment and Resources, 41*, 321–340.

Barlett, P. F. (2008). Reason and reenchantment in cultural change. *Current Anthropology, 49*(6), 1077–1098.

Barlett, P. F., & Chase, G. (Eds.). (2013). *Sustainability in higher education: Stories and strategies for transformation*. Cambridge, MA: Massachusetts Institute of Technology.

Bekoff, M. (2014). *Rewilding our hearts*. Novato, CA: New World Library.

Berry, T. (1999). *The great work: Our way into the future*. New York: Bell Tower.

Cajete, G. (2001). Indigenous education and ecology: Perspectives of an American Indian educator. In J. Grim (Ed.), *Indigenous traditions and ecology: The interbeing of cosmology and community* (pp. 619–638). Cambridge, MA: Harvard University Press.

The Earth Charter. (2001). Earth Charter International Secretariat. Retrieved from www.earthcharter.org

Freire, P. (1994). *Pedadgogy of hope: Reliving pedagogy of the oppressed*. New York , NY: Continuum Publishing Company.

Greenwood, D. (2014). Culture, environment, and education in the Anthropocene. In M. P. Mueller et al. (Eds.), *Assessing schools for generation r (responsibility)* (pp. 279–292). Dordrecht, Netherlands: Springer.

Grim, J. (2001). Introduction. In J. Grim (Ed.), *Indigenous traditions and ecology: The interbeing of cosmology and community*. Cambridge, MA: Harvard University Press.

Hopkins, R. (2010). What can communities do? In R. Heinberg & D. Lerch (Eds.), *Post carbon reader: Managing the 21st century's sustainability crises*. Healdsburg, CA: Watershed Media.

Kimmerer, R. W. (2013). *Braiding sweetgrass: Indigenous wisdom, scientific knowledge, and the teachings of plants*. Minneapolis, MN: Milkweed Editions.

Leopold, A. (1949). *A sand county almanac and sketches here and there*. New York: Oxford University Press.

Maathai, W. (2010). *Replenishing the earth: Spiritual values for healing ourselves and the world*. New York: Doubleday.

Noddings, N. (1992). *The challenge to care in schools: An alternative approach to education*. New York: Teachers College Press.

Orr, D. (2017a). Afterword. In P. Corcoran, J. Weakland, & A. Wals (Eds.), *Envisioning futures for environmental and sustainability education* (pp. 19–29). Wageningen, The Netherlands: Wageningen Academic Publishers.

Orr, D. (2017b). Foreword. In B. Jickling & S. Sterling (Eds.), *Post sustainability and environmental education*. London: Palgrave Macmillan.

Post Carbon Institute. (2015). *Six foundations for building community resilience: A concept paper by Post Carbon Institute*. Retrieved from www.postcarbon.org/

Schumacher, E. (1998). *This I believe and other essays*. Totnes, Devon: Green Books Ltd.

Speth, J. G. (2008). *The bridge at the edge of the world: Capitalism, the environment, and crossing from crisis to sustainability*. New Haven, CT: Yale University Press.

Sterling, S. (2014). At variance with reality: How to re-think our thinking. *Journal of Sustainability Education, 6*.

Sterling, S. (2017). Assuming the future: Repurposing education in a volatile age. In B. Jickling & S. Sterling (Eds.), *Post sustainability and environmental education*. London: Palgrave Macmillan.

Thayer, R. L. (2012). Inhabiting place. In R. De Young & T. Princen (Eds.), *The localization reader: Adapting to the coming downshift*. Cambridge, MA: Massachusetts Institute of Technology.

Tidball, K., Krasny, M., Svendsen, E., Campbell, L., & Helphand, K. (2010). Stewardship, learning, and memory in disaster resilience. *Environmental Education Research, 16*(5–6), 591–609.

Tucker, M. (2008). Learning to see the stars: The earth charter as a compass for the new century. In P. Corcoran & A. Wohlpart (Eds.), *A voice for earth: American writers respond to the earth charter* (pp. 40–53). Athens, GA: University of Georgia Press.

United Nations. (2015). *Transforming our world: The 2030 agenda for sustainable development.* New York: United Nations.

Wals, A., & Blewitt, J. (2010). Third-wave sustainability in higher education: Some (inter) national trends and developments. In P. Jones, D. Selby, & S. Sterling (Eds.), *Sustainability education: Perspectives and practice across higher education.* New York: Earthscan.

Wals, A., Weakland, J., & Corcoran, P. (2017). Introduction. In P. Corcoran, J. Weakland, & A. Wals (Eds.), *Envisioning futures for environmental and sustainability education* (pp. 19–29). Wageningen, The Netherlands: Wageningen Academic Publishers.

PART I

Comprehensive sustainability education perspectives

1

THE CHALLENGE AHEAD

Prioritizing sustainability education

Stephen Scoffham

Sustainability is a relatively new term which first appeared in English diction-
aries in the 1970s. It is derived from the Latin verb 'sustinere' which means to
'maintain', 'hold', or 'endure'. On the one hand, sustainability focuses on the idea
that humanity has to live within its means and that there are limits to economic
growth. On the other hand, sustainability has a social dimension that is encapsu-
lated in the notion of human health and well-being. Developing a sustainability
mindset is about recognizing that people and nature are connected to each other
and their surroundings in multiple ways through complex, overlapping networks. Disrupting these networks can cause damage to people and the biosphere
and threaten the life support systems on which we all depend. Sustainability is
thus about living in harmony with nature and each other in ways that respect
natural limits. It involves developing a blueprint or narrative for the future which
can respond to changes as they unfold and which will generate the conditions
in which people and life can flourish. This is a highly creative endeavour which
spans many aspects of human experience and engages students and educators on
a spiritual as a well as a cognitive level.

Introduction

When the first astronauts ventured into space in the 1960s, they sent back images
showing the Earth as a blue and white globe floating in a vast expanse of deep
darkness. These extraordinary photographs not only illustrated the fragility and
beauty of the planet we inhabit, they also captured the public imagination. For
the first time in history, people were able to visualize the Earth in its entirety.
The extraordinary sequence of events that enabled life to form and develop over
four thousand million years was thrown into sharp relief. No other planet known
to astronomers had benefited from the same particular combination of factors. It

became abundantly clear that in many respects the Earth is a unique and closed system – the only home which humanity is ever likely to have – and that we need to treat it with respect (Figure 1.1).

The new understanding of the Earth that resulted from the moon missions fuelled the growth of the modern environmental movement. A number of publications voiced concerns about contemporary developments, and their implications for the future added further momentum. Three key texts stand out. Rachel Carson drew attention to the insidious effects of pesticides and the threats to biodiversity in *Silent Spring* (1962), Paul Ehrlich highlighted the problem of population growth in *The Population Time Bomb* (1968), and the Club of Rome commissioned *The Limits to Growth* (Meadows et al., 1972) to explore the finite nature of natural resources. With the benefit of hindsight, these early warnings of looming environmental crisis, although criticized on scientific grounds, have an almost prophetic ring. When set alongside Alvin Tofler's *Future Shock* (1970), the challenges of living and adapting to a world of constant change became all too apparent.

One of the scientists who worked at NASA during the 1960s was James Lovelock, who developed the notion that the Earth is a self-regulating system. The radical idea that life creates the conditions for its own existence (Gaia theory) provoked fierce opposition when it was first proposed but was increasingly

FIGURE 1.1 The notion of planetary awareness was fuelled by images of Earth from space

Source: NASA

acknowledged in the 1970s as Lynn Margulis investigated the mechanisms linking organic and inorganic matter. Along with Darwin's theory of evolution,
Gaia theory has heralded a key change in how we think about life on Earth. Cru-
cially, it provides a way to understand how complex interactions, emergent properties, and chaotic events can combine to maintain a delicate and ever-changing
balance which operates on a global scale.

Sustainability education

Sustainability education has evolved along with this growth of global consciousness. It began in the 1960s and 1970s by focusing almost exclusively on ecology
and the natural world. In schools, lessons on nature study began to appear on
the timetable, while universities developed courses on environmental science.
As ideas about sustainability matured, the focus gradually shifted and broad-
ened. Educational initiatives emanating from the 'development education' and
'world studies' movements during the 1980s and 1990s began to draw attention
to socio-economic issues. It was argued that human activity, rather than natural
processes, were the root cause of the environmental crisis. This meant that factors such as global inequalities, population growth, and the impact of industry
and technology were key considerations in any in-depth analysis of contemporary problems. In the current century there has been an increasing tendency
to include the term 'global' in school and university courses and to stress the
importance of action as well as analysis. This has now found expression in the
school strike movement (Thunberg, 2019), which has called for students around
the world to take action on climate change and for politicians to tell the truth
about the state of the environment.

   One of the features of sustainability education is that while it does not com-
mand a discrete body of knowledge, it actually touches on just about everything.
This presents considerable challenges for teachers, particularly those working
at higher levels with significant subject specialism. Parkin (2010) acknowledges
this problem and suggests a pragmatic solution. 'Sustainability', she proclaims,
'is about having *sufficient* knowledge and understanding to make a *good enough*
choice or decision' (2010, p. 10, her italics). This practical wisdom goes straight
to the heart of what it means to be sustainability literate. What matters most is
not so much how much you know, but how you use the knowledge and understanding that you have at your disposal. It is about developing a mindset.

   Sterling (2001), too, takes a broadly philosophical approach to sustainability
education, which he sees as the process of maintaining a healthy system that
draws on qualities such as creativity, self-reliance, self-realization, wholeness,
and resilience. In a subsequent piece on ecological intelligence, Sterling extols
the importance of a new, more participative worldview. "If we want the chance
of a sustainable future," he declares, "we need to think relationally" (2009, p. 77).
Sterling argues that the practices which tend to dominate mainstream education
are likely to meet with only limited success in addressing current challenges

because they operate within existing mechanistic paradigms. Instead, we need to develop transformative approaches, which step outside current frameworks and established modes of thought. Such learning, he contends, needs to be critical, appreciative, and ethical. It will favor synthesis rather than analysis, integration rather than atomisation, and pluralism rather than dualism.

A further question is how pupils will choose to use and apply their knowledge and understanding of sustainability when they have completed their education and grown into adulthood. Will they use their new abilities to seek a more harmonious and equitable relationship with their surroundings, both human and natural, or use them in the pursuit of hyper-consumption and individualism? It can be argued that at the current time school and university education around the world is largely couched in terms of neo-liberal values, which aim to prepare students to play their part in the global economy. This leads David Orr to observe that without critical reflection about fundamental principles, sustainability education may simply lead graduates to be more effective vandals of the Earth (1994, p. 26). Sustainability in itself is morally neutral – it can be likened to a lens through which we see the world. However, the way that we interpret the information which it reveals and the actions that we take as a result will depend on our beliefs and value systems. The moral basis for education is not always so immediately apparent in other disciplines and areas of learning. Sustainability, being an emerging domain, tends to expose hidden beliefs and bring underlying assumptions to the fore.

Getting to grips with sustainability

For various reasons, sustainability education has been very slow to gain widespread traction in higher education. One explanation is that sustainability is itself an elusive and contradictory concept with many different definitions. Sustainability implies continuity but can also be seen as an aspiration or ideal. If sustainability is about conservation, we need to articulate what it is that needs to be conserved. If it is an ideal, then what form does it take? To make matters more complicated, sustainability is often harnessed to other terms to create multiple concepts which change its meaning, such as 'sustainable living' or 'sustainable development'. In educational circles, the term Education for Sustainable Development (ESD) is widely used but the implied tensions between stability and change are overlooked. A number of other terms, such as Education for Sustainable Futures (ESF) and Environment and Sustainability Education (ESE), provide alternative formulations but are also problematic and not so generally recognized. Finding the right language to express a new concept is crucial if it is to take root.

One way to make better sense of sustainability is think in terms of three key dimensions – social, environmental, and economic. These dimensions are sometimes shown diagrammatically as the columns on a temple but they are also portrayed as an overlapping Venn diagram (Figure 1.2). The idea that sustainability can be applied to different contexts, including human welfare, unlocks new levels

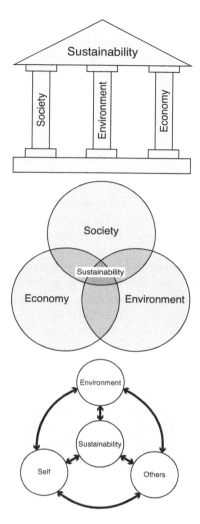

FIGURE 1.2   These diagrams show how sustainability can be represented in different ways

Source: Author

of meaning. However, it would be misleading to think that the three dimensions are given equal weight. In a globalized world committed to neo-liberal ideologies, economics dominates both government policy and business decisions. There are also problems in reducing sustainability to just three dimensions, as power, politics, culture, religion, and values also need to be taken into account. One form of words which takes a more holistic approach expresses sustainability in terms of local and global connections and defines it as a process of reconnecting with (a) the environment, (b) other people, and (c) ourselves. This definition has the advantage of emphasizing relationships – both inter-relationships between humans and relationships between humans and other forms of life. Another strength is that it draws attention to self-understanding and self-awareness. This is important as personal growth and development are fundamental to sustainability education (Capra & Luisi, 2014).

All these definitions recognize that sustainability addresses a range of complex, interrelated problems which are constantly changing. Rather than thinking of them as linear processes with a beginning, a middle, and an end, it may be more helpful to see them in terms of links and connections. Representing sustainability problems in this way suggests they have 'wicked' rather than 'tame' characteristics (Bottery, 2016). One of the features of 'wicked' problems is that they are difficult to define. They are unstable, involve unexpected links, and often contain internally conflicting goals. The very process of acting upon them changes their dynamics. It follows that there are a number of different ways in which they can be understood.

Given that sustainability impacts on the way that society is organized, it is also inevitable that it has a political dimension. The problem is that sustainability can easily become interpreted as a partisan issue. For example, the extent to which governments are willing to intervene in business varies among administrations. A concern for social welfare and global equity tends to be associated with left-wing political movements. Right-wing agendas often place greater emphasis on deregulation, wealth creation, and personal responsibility. Furthermore, labelling policies and practices as 'green' can suggest that they emanate from pressure groups which have their own specific, and perhaps unbalanced, agendas. The idea that sustainability is *just one more* issue that can be treated like a political football marginalizes questions of planetary care and well-being which are of over-riding importance to all humankind. Instead of shying away from teaching about sustainability because it is too controversial, schools, colleges, and universities need to engage with it wholeheartedly in order to better equip learners for the changes that lie ahead.

Constructing a better future

The global economy increased sevenfold in the period between 1950 and 2010 and it goes on growing. This is putting the natural environment under enormous strain and creating an urgent need to understand how natural systems are responding. Over the last few decades, a team of leading scientists has focused on collecting baseline evidence on safe boundaries for nine critical processes which together regulate the planet (Stockholm Resilience Centre, 2018). There is some very sobering news. Current levels of activity have *already* exceeded safe limits in four key areas – species loss, climate change, ocean acidification, and soil pollution (nitrogen and phosphorus loading). Meanwhile, four other areas are under significant pressure. The only good news is that international action on ozone depletion has reversed earlier trends.

Ensuring that people have healthy food, clean water, and fresh air is essential if humanity is to thrive. The relentless pursuit of economic growth is not only putting a huge strain on Earth's natural resources, it has also had the effect of concentrating wealth in the hands of a few, leaving many others struggling for their everyday needs (Wilkinson and Pickett, 2009). This raises profound moral questions. The data on global inequality, for example, makes stark reading. Worldwide, one person in nine does not have enough to eat, one in eleven has no source of safe drinking water, and one in three still no access to a toilet (100 People Foundation, 2019). Meanwhile, air pollution has become a major public health issue in many cities around the world, causing thousands of premature deaths every year, while particles of plastic are now known to have polluted habitats around the globe.

Modern interpretations of sustainability see social deprivation and ecological overshoot as two facets of the same coin – the search for new ways of living that align human and natural systems. Kate Raworth (2017) uses the metaphor of a ring doughnut to illustrate this idea (Figure 1.3). The outer ring of the doughnut

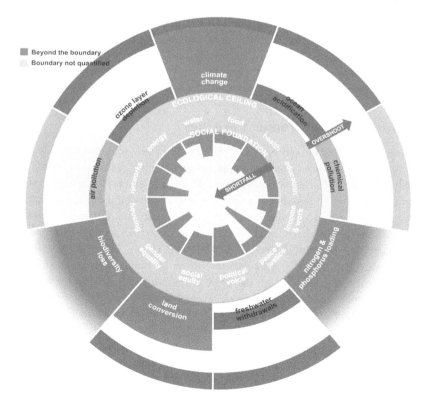

FIGURE 1.3 Sustainability is about aligning human and natural systems to create "safe and just place for humanity" represented in this diagram by the light green area inside the doughnut ring

Source: Kate Raworth: 2017

represents the ecological ceiling beyond which natural systems start to become dangerously destabilized. The inner ring of the doughnut represents the social foundations of well-being which, if breached, result in social deprivation and human misery. Sustainability is about finding ways of staying between these two rings, in what Raworth describes as a "safe and just place for humanity" (2017, p. 44). She sees this as an endeavor that should replace the pursuit of GDP as a key policy objective for the twenty-first century.

The quest to maximize human welfare while respecting ecological limits also provides the foundation for the United Nations Millennium Development Goals (SDGs) of 2015. In all there are 17 goals focusing on issues varying from income poverty and gender equality to food security and climate change. Any program which involves nearly two hundred nations is bound to involve considerable compromises and the SDGs are no exception. One major problem is that they fail to reconcile the contradiction between economic growth and environmental limits, thereby perpetuating the tensions that reside in the notion of 'sustainable development' itself. A second issue is that they fail to recognize unequal global power relations and international trade imbalances. However, the goals provide a rallying point and they have the potential to galvanize action by individuals, businesses and government institutions at local, national and global levels. The 2015 Paris Climate Agreement has similar potential. It is a voluntary agreement which is open to criticism but provides a valuable framework for action.

Responding to environmental issues

Learning about sustainability and environmental issues involves emotional as well as cognitive processes. This has implications not only for education but also for public discourse. In the past, environmental campaigners rather naively assumed that if only people knew the facts, they would respond and engage appropriately. This simply hasn't happened. To take just one example, despite overwhelming scientific evidence that climate change is resulting in higher temperatures in many parts of the world, around 50% of Americans, including the President, still don't think it will pose a serious threat in their lifetime, according to a Gallup poll (Brenan & Saad, 2018). George Marshall (2014) argues that the reason for such widespread public distrust of scientific evidence lies in the way that we think. The pressure from our peers and wider social groups has a crucial influence on our opinions. We are heavily influenced by 'trusted messengers' such as charismatic public figures and politicians. Furthermore, we are prone to what psychologists term 'confirmation bias' and tend to favor arguments which support our existing beliefs. In the past, these strategies proved very effective in promoting the survival of groups in a hostile world. However, such modes of thought do not serve us well when it comes to dealing with future global sustainability problems – problems that are largely abstract and removed in both distance and time from everyday concerns, particularly for those living in industrialized countries who are distanced from nature by their material wealth.

Human beings are remarkably good at living with contradictions and ignoring the things they don't want to see. Environmental problems are particularly prone to be side-lined because they have potentially devastating consequences which are difficult to address. Naomi Klein reviews some of the strategies people use in order to deny climate change. "We look for a split second and then we look away," she says. "Or we look but turn it into a joke." Some of the other maneuvers she notes include saying we are "too busy to care", becoming "hyper-rational", deciding that we need to "focus on ourselves", or telling ourselves "comforting stories about human ingenuity" (2014, p. 3).

Understanding how ecosystems respond to change reveals another issue. The diversity of life and range of feedback loops that characterize healthy systems give them considerable resilience. This means they can absorb stresses such as pollution or biodiversity loss up to a certain level without any apparent impact. However, they eventually reach a point where they can no longer absorb the stress and abruptly readjust. To take an analogy, just as the props in a tunnel can appear to carry more and more weight but eventually snap under pressure, so ecological systems are prone to sudden and dramatic collapse under excessive strain. Even then, such processes may not register in terms of human time frames. Maxton and Randers (2016) propose using a twenty-year period to assess meaningful loss and environmental degradation. The problem is that people adapt to incremental change so the baseline is constantly shifting.

There is the additional point that learning about sustainability and environmental problems is liable to make people feel bad about themselves. Fatalists argue that it is already too late to make any meaningful changes in our lives and that what happens next on a planetary level is out of our control. There is a certain satisfaction in apocalyptic visions and gloom-and-doom scenarios which evoke the shadow of impending catastrophe. Disaster movies have been particularly effective in tapping into this strain of thought, which is one of way of confronting our fear. However, on an emotional level, it is difficult not to be concerned about the way humanity is degrading and polluting the environment on which it depends for survival. And realizing that those of us who live in industrialized countries are complicit in exploiting poor and vulnerable people in other parts of the world through global trade and unequal power relations only exacerbates our sense of guilt and anger.

Anxiety may also lie behind other responses to sustainability. Psychodynamic theory draws on ideas developed by Melanie Klien and Donald Winnicott to explore how we internalize the feeling of total helplessness which we experience in the first weeks of life. It invokes mechanisms such as 'splitting', 'projection', and 'infantile omnipotence' to explain how babies become socialized through a prolonged period of nurturing. However, in situations of acute anxiety, even apparently mature and balanced adults may revert to the strategies that they used at their birth. Sander and Conway (2013) suggest that environmental problems can provoke such anxieties because we know deep down that they threaten our survival. Furthermore, Sander and Conway suggest that adopting extreme positions on environmental issues, either for or against, shows parallels with infantile omnipotence and the delusion that we can manipulate and triumph over the forces which threaten to overwhelm us. It follows that sceptics who seek to deny or dismiss environmental problems may well be invoking the control strategies they used as infants.

Myths and misconceptions

Any in-depth discussion about sustainability and environmental issues eventually begins to reveal the underlying assumptions and beliefs that serve to guide our thoughts. These are not always consciously acknowledged, but they have a pervasive influence and are often deeply held. Three ideas which are often cited in support of a business as usual approach are considered below. As will be seen, they each contain an element of truth but they are also fundamentally flawed.

(a) Technology will save us

Technology and innovation undeniably have a role to play in addressing environmental problems. In recent years, there has been a shift towards using materials and devices more efficiently and reducing some of the more obvious forms of pollution. There are promising developments in forging new business models which focus on the entire life cycle of products rather than just the manufacturing process. Artificial intelligence and smart technologies seem likely to bring huge changes in the future. However, waiting for new discoveries that will reverse long-term global environmental trends may well turn out to be a fruitless endeavour. Experience shows that while technological innovations have produced huge benefits in the past, they have rarely led to an overall reduction in the consumption of resources. On the contrary, they serve to stimulate production and enable people to exploit the environment more efficiently. This relationship, which flies in the face of common sense, is known to economists as the Jevons paradox. It can be explained, as Timberlake (2009) points out, by the way most modern technologies are closely tied to commercial gain rather than human benefit. An even more telling point is that we already have the knowledge and technologies to address environmental problems so there is no need to wait for a miracle solution. What we lack is the conviction and the political will to put them into practice and scale them up.

(b) We must prioritize economic growth

Modern capitalist economies are propelled by economic growth. Development has lifted large numbers of people around the world out of poverty, but the benefits have always been unevenly distributed, as the experience of industrialization in Western Europe and North America in the nineteenth century attests. Today, global inequalities have become increasingly stark and the pressures on the natural environment have reached a breaking point. Capitalism may be the dominant global economic system, but it is hard to see how it can continue to provide a viable model much longer. For example, if the world economy were to go on growing at its present rate, it would be more than twenty percent bigger by the end of the century than it is today (Jackson, 2017). Given that we live on a finite planet, the arithmetic is devastating. Finding out whether modern economies are structurally dependent on growth for their stability is a key question for economists. But it is also clear that "the grand narrative of progress and change" (Massey, 2006) which underpins Western modernity and global capitalism needs to be reassessed as well. The economist Tim Jackson offers a blunt assessment. "The myth of progress has failed us," he declares (p. 21), and he points out how it has failed half the world's population who currently live in poverty, a significant proportion of whom are struggling to survive. What we need, he suggests, is a new and much broader understanding of prosperity.

(c) Human beings are naturally self-seeking

It is often contended that human beings are naturally competitive and greedy and that self-preservation is their overriding priority. This suggests that rather than looking after the environment, people are naturally disposed to exploit it to their advantage. These claims are subject to debate and are being reassessed by new understandings in ecology, neurology, anthropology, economics and other disciplines. However, there is no particular need to dispute them. The point is that they only represent a partial truth. Human beings have many qualities. Altruism, cooperation and empathy for others take their place alongside personal enjoyment and survival needs and may be equally or even more important. Social psychologist Shallom Schwartz concludes from research in different countries and cultures (2012) that there are a number of personal values that people hold in common and he suggests these can be arranged along two main axes. Openness to change (independence and novelty) is juxtaposed with conservation (security and tradition); self-enhancement (status and personal success) is juxtaposed with self-transcendence (empathy and concern for others). Recognizing that people hold an array of personal values is important in understanding their behavior. However, to think that we respond to situations simply in terms of self-enhancement is both limiting and simplistic. Furthermore, there is a danger that it could be self-fulling as our beliefs about human nature can actually play a role in shaping human nature itself.

Moving forward

Constructing a better future is a daunting task that will stretch human creativity, commitment, and vision to the limit. Forging a sustainability mindset has the potential, though, to provide the 'lens' through which to interpret and address contemporary environmental problems. As Sterling (2019) argues, a more relational, ecological, and participative consciousness has the potential to bring about transformative change. Ultimately, it is our beliefs and ideas about what matters that drive our behavior; in turn, these ideas shape the response from government and business. Finding narratives which recognize twenty-first century imperatives is a collective endeavor that will involve many voices and perspectives and need constant revision. Some people are likely to warm to narratives based in values or religion. Others will favor historical or scientific approaches. Ecological perspectives are likely to be especially important. However, these different accounts share a common foundation and purpose. We are all, as Stibbe puts it, involved in "rewriting and re-speaking the world" (2015, p. 193). One of the places where this process can be most effectively facilitated is in educational institutions such as schools, colleges, and universities.

There is now overwhelming evidence that humanity is living beyond its means, consuming more resources, and generating more pollution than the Earth can absorb. Recent reports make it clear that there is an urgent need for action on a range of environmental and ecological issues (IPCC, 2018; WWF, 2018). These problems threaten to trigger irreversible changes, which will affect the welfare of millions of people and bring catastrophic change to the natural environment. Exploring ways to live equitably and sustainably on a finite planet is quite simply the fundamental challenge of our times. Newspapers and media channels now carry reports of environmental foreshocks on an almost daily basis, indicating that, as Rockstrom and Klum put it, nature has already started "submitting her invoices" (2015, p. 11). The trouble is that society as whole has only just begun to recognize this and has failed to appreciate what is at stake at anything other than a superficial level.

It is all too easy to be over-dramatic when writing and thinking about the environment, sustainability, and the state of the planet. For most of us, the patterns and routines of everyday life continue uninterrupted from one week to the next, and the warnings that we receive about environmental crisis are difficult to reconcile with our lived experience. Yet they nevertheless need to be taken seriously – very seriously indeed. The idea which stands at the heart of sustainability is remarkably simple. Ultimately, we have to live within our means or face the consequences of ecological collapse. Even if environmental problems turn out to be less serious than currently anticipated, we know that we are already committed to certain irreversible impacts, particularly with respect to climate change and biodiversity loss. Dave Hicks, a specialist in futures education, believes that, whatever the scenario, we should expect the world to change "dramatically and permanently during the twenty first century" (2014, p. 7). And he concludes that we should prepare for troubled times as periods of change are often associated with economic disruption and social unrest.

There can be little doubt that sustainability in all its different manifestations is the defining issue of the age. The quest for new narratives and ways of thinking about the world touches every aspect of human endeavor from science and economics to literature and religion. It will require new forms of governance and political organization and a major realignment of public and private institutions. Taking account of social and psychological factors will be important, especially during any transitional period. The early stages of ecological collapse are a wake-up call which has already been sounded. As David Orr so eloquently puts it, "time is running out on the experiment of civilization" (2017, p. viii).

Despite the challenges, finding ways to live within planetary means can also be seen as a great opportunity. Human beings have a long history of creative and imaginative thinking. The range and variety of proposals which have been put forward in recent years also give ground for hope. Collectively, they could constitute what James Speth describes as the "bridge at the edge of the world" (2008, p. 13) that will save humanity from falling into the abyss that lies ahead. What part will schools, colleges, and universities play in helping people make the decisions that will lead them to take the path towards this bridge? The subsequent chapters in this book explore some of the possibilities and show how to engage students with local and global environmental problems in novel and exciting ways. There are examples from communities and cultures from several continents as well as an analysis of the knowledge and wisdom of traditional indigenous cultures. We hope that these case studies will play a part in helping to reorientate education towards sustainability awareness. This is a wake-up call which is desperately needed.

References

100 People Foundation. (2019). Retrieved from www.100people.org/statistics_detailed_statistics.php

Bottery, M. (2016). *Educational leadership for a more sustainable world*. London: Bloomsbury.

Brenan, M., & Saad, L. (2018). *Global warming concern stable despite some partisan shifts*. Retrieved from https://news.gallup.com/poll/231530/global-warming-concern-steady-despite-partisan-shifts.aspx

Capra, F., & Luisi, L. (2014). *The systems view of life*. Cambridge: Cambridge University Press.

Carson, R. (1962), (2000). *Silent Spring*. London: Penguin.

Ehrlich, P. (1968). *The Population Bomb*. Cutchogue, New York: Buccaneer Books.

Hicks, D. (2014). *Educating for hope in troubled times*. London: Institute of Education.

IPCC. (2018). *Global warming of 1.5°C: Summary for policy makers*. Retrieved from https://report.ipcc.ch/sr15/pdf/sr15_spm_final.pdf

Jackson, T. (2017). *Prosperity without growth* (2nd ed.). London: Routledge.

Klein, N. (2014). *This changes everything*. London: Penguin.

Marshall, G. (2014). *Don't even think about it: Why our brains are wired to ignore climate change*. London: Bloomsbury.

Massey, D. (2006). The geographical mind. In D. Balderstone (Ed.), *Secondary geography handbook*. Sheffield: Geographical Association.

Maxton, G., & Randers, J. (2016). *Reinventing prosperity*. Vancouver: Greystone.

Meadows, D. H., J. Randers and W. W. Behrens. (1972). *The Limits to Growth*. New York: New American Library.

Orr, D. (1994). *Earth in mind, on education and the human prospect*. Washington, DC: Island Press.

Orr, D. (2017). Foreword. In B. Jickling & S. Sterling (Ed.), *Post-sustainability and environmental education: Remaking education for the future*. Cham, Switzerland: Palgrave.

Parkin, S. (2010). *The positive deviant: Sustainability leadership in a perverse world.* London: Routledge.

Raworth, K. (2017). *Doughnut economics: Seven ways to think like a twenty-first century economist.* London: Random House.

Rockstrom, J., & Klum, M. (2015). *Big world, small planet.* Stockholm, Sweden: Max Strom Publishing.

Sander, J., & Conway, P. (2013). *Psychological approaches with sustainability and global learning: Think global thinkpiece.* London: Development Education Association.

Schwartz, S. (2012). An overview of the Schwartz theory of basic values. *Online Readings in Psychology and Culture, 2*(1).

Speth, J. (2008). *The bridge at the edge of the world.* New Haven, CT: Yale University Press.

Sterling, S. (2001). *Sustainable education: Revisioning learning and change.* Dartington: Green Books.

Sterling, S. (2009). Ecological intelligence. In A. Stibbe (Ed.), *The handbook of sustainability literacy.* Totness, Devon: Green Books.

Sterling, S. (2019). Planetary primacy and the necessity of positive dis-Illusion. *Sustainability, 12*(2), 60–66.

Stibbe, A. (2015). *Ecolinguistics.* London: Routledge.

Stockholm Resilience Centre. (2018). *Planetary boundaries research.* Retrieved from www.stockholmresilience.org/research/planetary-boundaries.html

Thunberg, G. (2019). *No one is too small to make a difference.* London: Penguin.

Timberlake, L. (2009). *The urgency of no.* London: Hard Rain Project.

Tofler, A. (1970), (1984). *Future Shock.* London: Penguin.

United Nations. (2015). Transforming our world: The 2039 agenda for sustainable development. Retrieved from https://sustainabledevelopment.un.org/post2015/transformingourworld/publication

WWF. (2018) *Living planet report.* Retrieved from www.worldwildlife.org/publications/living-planet-report-2018

Wilkinson, R., & Pickett, K. (2009). *The spirit level: Why equality is better for everyone.* London: Penguin.

2

THIS IS ZERO HOUR

Students confront educators

Zanagee Artis, Arielle Martinez Cohen, Ivy Jaguzny, and Kendall Kieras

We are members of Zero Hour, an international youth-led movement for climate action initiated in 2017. We organized The Youth Climate March that took place on July 21, 2018, in 25 cities around the world, including Atlanta; Butere, Kenya; Denver; Las Vegas; London; Los Angeles; New York; Seattle; and Washington, D.C. Zero Hour has fueled the youth climate strike movement and supports the ongoing Juliana v. U.S. lawsuit where youth are challenging the U.S government on grounds that it has violated our rights to clean air. Zero Hour continues to fight for climate justice, working to elevate the voices of frontline youth who are excluded from the climate conversation. Zero Hour is working towards awareness on the roots of climate change in our schools and communities. Recently, we highlighted the many different forms of action being taken in the US and around the world through the event, This is Zero Hour: The Youth Climate Summit, hosted in Miami, Florida, from July 12–14, 2019, where we trained hundreds of youth activists to be leaders in their communities. However, some of our own learning experiences have not always been ideal. We faced obstacles to becoming activists because youth-empowering movements like ours were not available to us growing up. Here are some of our stories.

Arielle Martinez Cohen

I'm 17 years old and from Los Angeles, California. I'm the Director of Partner-ships at Zero Hour and an organizer for the Youth Climate Strikes in LA. I'm also a singer/songwriter and use my music to help inspire change. My song, "Two Minutes to Midnight," is the official song of the Zero Hour movement. I will be starting as a freshman at Brown University in the fall of 2019, and am excited to continue my education in environmental science and music. I have been an activist for many years now, but I wasn't always passionate about saving the environment. I owe my activism to my education on climate change early in life.

I remember sitting in my 5th grade class and hearing my passionate teacher tell us about the horrible effects of palm oil farming and production on the habitats of orangutans. He made the lesson interactive by showing us videos on the subject, and by having us research and find products that include the ingredient. I remember going home and finding every product that had palm oil in it. I told my parents all about what I learned and convinced them to start buying different products. This is how education has made a difference in my life. It has led me to take more action in my community and to learn more about other issues that are plaguing our society. It has fueled − with renewable energy, that is − my passion for problem-solving and making a difference in the world. It has contributed to my empathy for every living creature on the planet.

I just graduated from high school. The things I learned in that 5th grade classroom have stayed with me. They will continue to shape me as I grow. In my senior year, I took a class on environmental science and sustainability. But this time, my teacher was not so passionate about the subject. When I sat in class and listened to her lectures, I got excited because I was already interested in the subject. However, as I looked around the room, I could tell my classmates did not feel the same way. Our teacher would drone on about charts and diagrams for an hour as we sat in our seats staring at the screen. With her teaching method, it was almost impossible for my peers and me to connect climate change to our everyday lives. My heart sank to my stomach as I realized that I was sitting in a classroom of amazing, capable young students, and yet, because of our teacher, many of them will not go on to take action for environmental justice. We need to see the impact of climate change on our lives if our generation is going to be effective in solving this crisis. While she is not doing any direct harm, this teacher will leave a legacy of inaction to her students. With enough inaction, the Earth will continue on its path to becoming unlivable. Conversely, a good teacher, supported by good curriculum, has the power to literally change the world.

Ivy Jaguzny

I'm 17 years old, from Vashon Island, Washington, and a member of the Zero Hour Press Team. Apathy is what sparked me towards my fierce determination to act on climate change. I grew up on a small island, 13 miles long and 7 miles wide, with no stoplights and one major grocery store. Living in a rural area was beautiful, but isolating. There was this sense that the only issues in existence were the ones on our little island. The irony is, the effects of climate change were staring us in the face. The island is a key spawning ground for salmon and for their main prey: forage fish. Anyone that lives in the Pacific Northwest knows that salmon are an important part of our identity, and sacred to the indigenous Salish peoples. The salmon have been dying for a variety of reasons, but mainly because forage fish spawning grounds are shrinking due to rising sea levels. I remember how obvious that was to me because sometimes at high tides the water would come over the bulkhead and flood our basement. I would wake up to find jellyfish all over the lawn. By the time I was six, I had to try to comprehend why the men I saw on TV weren't taking action. By the time I got to my freshman year of high school, I had to comprehend why no one else in the room wanted to talk about climate change. I became frustrated by the apathy I experienced every day. Here was this catastrophic issue, a crisis that affects all people, only no one treated it like one. I took the lead at my school's environmental club, which had only garnered a few members, and felt deeply unsatisfied by the lack of participation and resources. I felt my teachers did not know how to help us. When I moved to Seattle, I was slapped in the face by the reality of inequity, politics, and inaction. The bubble I had lived in my whole life popped, and it was painful. I realized climate action wasn't a teenage phase; it was a necessity. For the sake of our lives, I had no choice but to make climate action a mission in my life. This mission, on account of my education, is something I am obligated and proud to pursue on behalf of my generation.

However, my generation carries the responsibility of action, and yet we are attempting to fix the world's problems with our hands tied behind our backs. Our education is cheating us of our potential to make change. My friends take the environmental science class at our school under the pretext that it is the class for people who "do not like science." We laugh at that class because we all know it is a filler for graduation requirements. As someone with a passion for climate science, I was ready to grow the clean energy conversation with new ideas and the contributions of more women. Unfortunately, I found that the science teachers are notoriously the worst at our school and the curriculum is outdated. In my physics class we had a unit on energy, only we spent less than a class period focused on clean energy. In that class I felt shut down. My teacher has a reputation for denying the theory of evolution, and he made it obvious to me that he was impressed by my performance simply because I exceeded his low expectations of women. Yet I was forced to settle with him as my physics teacher because my school district lacks the funding to make significant staffing changes. This lack of resources surprises me because our school is accommodating, progressive, and rigorous, and yet virtually no attention is given to classes that cover the biggest issues of our time. Most importantly, I had the realization that many youth at my school are vastly more aware of environmental issues than any of our educators. Our schools are desperately trying to catch up.

Kendall Kieras

I am a 16-year-old high school junior from Seattle, Washington. I was inspired to take action for the climate as a result of experiencing the wildfires in my backyard. The month of the wildfires occurred during a period I felt was a crossroads in my life. I had just returned from a month-long writing camp, and the transition back put me in a state of extreme depression. Eventually, I started walking to the local library every day. My walks, which should have been accented by blue sky and sunshine, instead were full of red sunlight and ash particles covering the ground. The outside world matched what I was feeling on the inside, as even the sunshine meant to comfort me turned to ash. This was my first experience with climate change.

I learned that my ability to live a life largely free from the effects of climate change was born from a place of privilege. Although my first experience with climate change was at 14, many people are born into lives already devastated by climate change. Young people in Standing Rock have given their lives for clean water, Puerto Ricans have seen their homes destroyed, homeless LGBT youth freeze in the winter weather. I've never faced any of these things, and for that, I am not only lucky, but systematically privileged.

Still today, learning about the climate has never been a part of my formal education. I'm at school seven hours a day. But my education about the climate and the activism work I do is completely separate from my school day. I believe that needs to change. Saving the world shouldn't be an extracurricular activity.

Zanagee Artis

I am one of the co-founders of Zero Hour. As Logistics Director, I led the team that organized the permitting, staging, march route, and volunteer network for the Youth Climate March on July 21, 2018. At 19 years old, I am beginning my second year at Brown University in the fall of 2019. Aside from a single unit on ecology in IB (International Baccalaureate) Biology in high school (during the second semester of my senior year) and the baseline knowledge that I learned about wildlife and environmental pollution as a homeschooler, I have been forced to independently seek out information on the environment through watching documentaries and doing independent research. I'm passionate about learning about all of the ways in which people are impacted by climate change because I see it as a very human issue. However, my initial interest in the environment came when I was a young kid who just enjoyed learning about sea creatures. When I was younger, I was certain that I would become a marine biologist. Having lived on the coast of Connecticut for over half of my life, water has always been something very important to me, and hearing about oil spills and plastic pollution as a kid was very concerning. In fact, the first non-profit that I ever asked my parents to donate to was Save the Manatee because I was afraid that I'd never get the chance to see one if pollution and the destruction of their habitats continued. Yet as I grew older, and my interest in marine biology shifted to politics, I began to focus less on reducing trash and protecting animals, and began to learn about what climate change could mean for humans, and what damage it has already caused. It wasn't until around the time that I co-founded Zero Hour in the summer of 2017 that I really began to see and understand that climate change would not just impact what I thought of as the environment – what I saw then as the trees and animals – but also humanity itself.

My parents made the decision to ensure that my siblings and I would grow up to be open-minded and globally thinking people, which I believe was a major factor in me becoming interested in politics and grassroots climate activist work. Despite the positives of my education at home until reaching 7th grade, the need to search for information independently has remained consistent throughout the rest of my experience in education.

Brown University is very unique among colleges because of its Open Curriculum, which allows students to begin studying what they know they want to, which in my case is political science and environmental studies, or explore different areas of study unfamiliar to them, without first having to complete general education requirements. This has benefited me especially because it has allowed me to pursue my interests in politics, the environment, and languages (Spanish and Russian), but it also means that to gain a deeper understanding of environmental justice and climate science, students need to self-select that path. Environmental studies is not a field that is actively pushed for students to study, especially low-income students and people of color, because it is not seen as a lucrative field, or something worth devoting time and money towards. Additionally, I believe that the fact that marginalized people, especially Black, Indigenous, and Latinx people, have historically been discriminated against with regard to using spaces connected with nature in the United States, which also contributes to a lack of engagement and interest in the subject by students of these communities. This is despite the fact that people of color are among those most at risk from the impacts of the climate crisis because of, for example, the increased likelihood that fossil fuel infrastructure already exists or will be built in communities of color. As a biracial person of color myself, my experience has been that environmental studies is an area of academia dominated by white students, predominantly women. In addition to the classroom, the rallies and protests that I've attended have also been predominantly white, and I am one of the few people of color in the Rhode Island chapter of the Sunrise Movement.

Highlighting and centering the voices of marginalized and frontline youth who have been historically left out of the mainstream climate movement was a major motivation for founding Zero Hour, and it is also an important step towards achieving what we call climate justice. The climate movement of today cannot simply be about recycling, planting more trees, and living a more sustainable lifestyle of privilege. The climate movement must be centered around us as humans and how we, as well as the environment as a whole, are being impacted by a systematic reliance on petroleum products and corruption among leaders of government and industry in the U.S. and globally, which will inevitably limit the viability of life on the planet unless systemic change occurs. Within Zero Hour, climate justice and the goal of a just transition towards sustainable energy means that everyone, especially those people most impacted by climate change and pollution, must be included in reshaping how we function. If we are to have a just transition away from damaging approaches, such as fossil fuels and industrial animal agriculture, to alternatives such as sustainable energy and community-based farming, we cannot leave the power plant workers and family farmers out of that conversation, or we risk recreating a system in which power is abused by the corporate executives with the most influence over the functioning of our current industrial and political systems. If we truly want climate justice, then we must include the perspectives of the indigenous people whose ancestral lands and traditional ways of life have been gutted by oil pipelines and overfishing, and we must include the perspectives of young people of color living in cities with water too polluted to drink and air so contaminated that it increases their rates of asthma. Historically, the mainstream climate movement has always centered the voices of the most privileged people in this country, many of whom have not been directly impacted by pollution or climate-change-fueled natural disasters. Zero Hour is beginning to change that by centering the voices of youth whose voices have historically been silenced.

Despite the fact that the need to choose to study the environment means that the vast majority of students are not exposed to crucial education about the state of the environment and how we've reached this point, I have found that, even in my first year of college, pursuing an education in environmental studies has been extremely rewarding. In my first year I had the opportunity to take three courses in the environmental studies department and learned about the environmental history of the Arctic and the many indigenous peoples that reside there, how to synthesize spatial data using the ArcGIS software to visually map the impacts of climate change, and about the complex relationships that humans have held with the environment over time, from water scarcity today to the negative impacts of the romanticization of nature in the United States by conservationists including John Muir, founder of the national parks and the Sierra Club, and William Cronon. These knowledge-enriching courses taught me so much about the environment and how we as people have interacted with it over time, yet they also reveal how environmental history, climate justice, and climate policy were previously missing in my education and are still missing for so many students in high school and in higher education. Under my leadership, the Zero Hour advocacy team created and launched our national education campaign, called *Getting to the Roots of Climate Change*, which seeks to begin filling this gap in climate education for high school students. The presentation explains that the root causes of the climate crisis are institutionalized systems of oppression, primarily racism, colonialism, capitalism, and patriarchy, and addresses how we can best combat these systems to address the climate crisis. The presentation has continued to be delivered by Zero Hour Ambassadors in schools around the country.

Environmental education is something that everyone should be exposed to throughout their lives because, regardless of the career path someone chooses, whether it be in fashion, business, the military, journalism, or any other field, every person alive lives in the environment and every professional field is connected to it and impacts it in some way. As a result of the interconnections between most industries and the environment, I believe that every field of study in higher education should incorporate environmental education into its respective curriculum. Educating the next generation must go beyond simply explaining how climate change is caused by the release of greenhouse gases into the atmosphere. Institutions of higher education should be working towards expanding course offerings to include intersectional classes that address subjects like the impacts of pollution on health care for students studying public health, or the future of sustainable infrastructure and energy for students studying engineering or urban development. Only when we engage young people beyond the basic science of what is causing climate change, and focus on issues at the intersection of the environment and their personal lives and future career paths, can we get people involved in the movement who would not have thought about the fight against climate change as an issue that is urgent and will affect them.

Zero hour student leaders' joint statement

We are Generation Z and we want to live. We want clean water, clean air, and an Earth that is habitable for us and generations to come. We not only want to sustain the Earth; we want to regenerate it. We have no choice but to regenerate it. We want you, the reader, to think about the world our generation faces. If we continue the destructive relationship with the Earth as it exists today – if we continue to rely on fossil fuels, on mass production, on plastics, on corporate agriculture – our futures will not be stories of success, they will be battles for survival. Each day will become a struggle for food, for water, and for air. The way we see it, we are at a crossroads. We can decide to look away or we can decide to fix our broken economy, our destructive infrastructure, and our patterns of exploitation. We can create a world where energy is efficient and thriving, where people pushed into the fringes of society finally get a share of the world's wealth, and where we are a more equitable, peaceful world as a whole. But we will not reach that better world if we do not understand the fundamental relationship between society and the environment.

Our lack of understanding is seemingly the result of the growing divide between the Earth and each new generation, as industries take over, inequities polarize, and education becomes the lowest item on policymakers' lists. To them, the education of our generation is not a priority, let alone saving the planet. The institutions that are supposed to promote understanding and connection tend to do the exact opposite. Our education system is diminishing our ability to see the world as a whole. It is pushing pressing issues to the periphery of our minds, and instilling apathy, the very apathy that makes it possible for people to continue blindly while we are on the brink of global disaster. As the people who experience the public education system six or more hours a day, five days a week, we are sick of the mind-dulling, poorly conceived, inadequate environmental curricula of our schools.

This book is a part of an international movement to radically change the way we think about sustainability and how sustainability is taught in our schools. Let us be clear: sustainability is not recycling, it is not a box you check to prove how progressive you are, and it is not an isolated issue meant to be addressed by the "environmental science" course no one wants to take. Sustainability is a lifestyle, sustainability is a global economy, and sustainability is the constant effort of the individual, the community, and the world to reach a regenerative society. The first step towards a regenerative society is not just giving the next generation the tools to survive, but the tools to redefine what sustainability means for them. When people say "we are the future," it's not just because we grew up around the iPhone. We are the future because we define what society becomes as we build it. We can only progress as a truly regenerative society when we allow the youth to understand and to lead us there.

As students, we want to be included in the conversation surrounding our education. We're passionate about learning, and so are our classmates. Most people would want to learn about how they can ensure their survival against the most pressing issue of our time, climate change. We want to talk about solutions, not just problems. We want lessons that are engaging. We want to learn from a teacher who is passionate, who will push us to challenge ourselves and take action in our communities – someone who may even give us the platform to create the next breakthrough solution to climate change. So, with that, we leave you with some demands for our education on sustainability.

Our demands

- Incorporate current climate data into the curriculum of all science classes.
- When addressing climate change, cover more than reducing greenhouse gasses and mitigation. Climate adaptation should be the main focus of the curriculum.
- In environmental science classes, examine environmental philosophy and value systems that counter the anthropocentric norm.
- When studying climate change and pollution, examine solutions so that students are aware of progress that is already occurring.
- Focus on both the environmental and social impacts of climate change, including environmental racism/classism and a just transition.
- Include the environmental movement as a social justice movement in the context of history.
- Civics classes should cover grassroots group organizing and the environmental movement.
- Computer science classes should cover mapping technology and how it is used to study spatial and environmental patterns.
- Connect the curriculum in the classroom to all aspects of the community students live in; there should be an intersection of multiple fields.
- All experiential learning should include direct involvement with relevant community action.

- Environmental science should include involvement with stewardship, sustainable food sources, clean energy, economics, and advocacy, and should address the divide between public and private sectors.
- The goal of the curriculum is to give students the tools to advocate for change in their communities.

With these demands, we intend to build an education system that is a framework for incorporating sustainability into every class, field, and aspect of life. Youth inherit our society, but students will build the society we become. With these demands, we help students build careers that address our most pressing issues. With these demands, we can help create a regenerative society: one that will last our generation and many generations to come.

3

OPPORTUNITIES FOR RE-ENCHANTMENT

Exploring the spirit of place

Stephen Scoffham

Introduction

Sustainability focuses attention on our relationship with the environment and the places which make it up. Whether it is understood as local or global, place contributes to our sense of identity and the attachment that we feel for it helps to anchor us psychologically. Some of the complexities of place relationships and the implications for higher education are considered in this chapter. The overarching theme is that people are not separate from the environments that they inhabit but integral to them. Moreover, it is argued that the feelings that people have for place provide the foundations for their environmental consciousness. Put simply, we value the things that we love. It follows that if we treasure the Earth, then we will do our best to treat it carefully. In the absence of any emotional involvement, there is no particular reason to look after the world around us. In these circumstances sustainability becomes reduced to little more than utility and self-interest.

Ideas about place

When they engage with sustainability, higher education students bring with them many different ideas about 'place' which inform their thinking. On one level, they may think of place as the physical environment that is found in a particular locality. This includes the mountains, hills, valleys, streams, and rivers which make up the landscape as well as the plants and creatures that live in it. Such an environment is often thought of as having enduring qualities and is regarded as fixed in time and somehow immune from the forces of change. Place is also sometimes understood in terms of the built environment. There are settlements of different sizes all over the globe and they vary greatly in character. Some are sedate and orderly; others are chaotic and exciting. It is easy to see that the streets, buildings and spaces which make up a settlement have been made by people. This makes the human dimension of place immediately apparent.

Both these characterizations – place as the natural or built environment – focus on visible qualities. However, places can also be seen as meeting points where people's lives intersect at a particular moment in time. We are probably all aware how, when returning to a school that we once attended or a house where we used to live, it no longer seems the same. The physical reality may not have changed but we feel differently about it because the people we shared it with have moved on. The idea that place is a meeting point, that it is a sociological rather than a physical entity, is explored by Dorren Massey (2005). Massey argues that rather than seeing places as enclosed and possessing hard boundaries, they may also be seen as nodes for a network of connections which reach out into the world. Some fascinating repercussions stem from this contention. In a digital age in which we connect to other people through electronic communication, place takes on an almost abstract quality. For example, meetings which once used to happen in rooms can now be organized through virtual conferences, which means they are no longer tethered to a specific geographical location.

Place, then, is a hybrid concept which can be interpreted in many ways. It is constantly changing, involves physical and human dimensions and is fragmented rather than homogeneous. What people feel about places is important in understanding them. In his classic study of place and space, Yi Fu Tuan (1977) makes the point that when people believe the world is changing too rapidly they tend to evoke the image of an idealized and stable past. The home and homeland then come to be represented as places which are safe, secure and timeless. But, as Massey and Jess (1995) point out, it is highly dubious to romanticize places as settled, coherent and unchanging. Also relevant are questions about power relations, as place boundaries are socially constructed. Exploring such issues touches on highly emotive issues and evokes complex, often ambivalent, feelings.

People and nature

The reason for considering these different interpretations of place is that how students relate to the world around them is central to understanding the concept of sustainability. Throughout evolutionary history, people have been intimately linked with their surroundings. They have always depended on the natural environment for water, food and shelter, responding to it in different ways according to their culture, beliefs and level of technological expertise. In the modern world, where three quarters of the population is set to live in cities by 2050, it is easy to lose sight of the fact that we still rely on the soil and its bounty for our everyday survival. Clean air, pure water and an adequate supply of nutritious food are the essentials of life. This is acknowledged in both the Earth Charter and the SDGs (see for example SDG 2 'Zero Hunger' and SDG 6 'Clean Water and Sanitation').

Not only is our relationship with nature crucial to meeting our physical needs, it is also fundamental to our spiritual health and mental well-being. From a psychological point of view, although individuals differ greatly, our identity is vested (to some extent at least) in our surroundings. A sense of place attachment also contributes to feelings of security and well-being. Young children especially tend to treasure the settings in their neighborhood where they experience significant events, the memory of which gradually builds up to create layers of meaning (Vujakovic, Owens, & Scoffham, 2018). Adults, too, remember their childhood environment with affection but extend their notion of place as they travel more widely and come to adopt more comprehensive and less egotistical viewpoints.

For many people, the natural world is a source of pleasure and they enjoy the experience of being in different environments. Whether climbing mountains, walking in the countryside, canoeing down rivers, or simply sitting on the beach, people like being outside. The natural world is also a source of creativity for musicians, poets, artists, architects, designers, and others who draw inspiration from their surroundings. The idea that some places are particularly conducive to learning is affirmed by Mihaly Csikszentmihalyi (1997), who notes that places of beauty such as majestic peaks or thundering seas are a particularly powerful stimulus. Stephen Kellert, too, extols the value of nature, arguing that it gives meaning to our lives because it inspires our sense of wonder, curiosity, and imagination. He describes nature as a "magic well," and rather grandly proclaims it is "the source of our genius as a species which determines who we are and who we can become" (2012, p. xii).

The benefits that we derive from engaging with place and the natural world were well known to the Ancients and were described thousands of years ago by Aristotle and other Greek philosophers. The modern notion of 'biophilia,' developed by Erich Fromm and E.O. Wilson, also provides a way of encapsulating this relationship. The term itself literally means 'love of life' and emphasizes the attraction between humans and other organisms. By stressing positive attraction (philia) as opposed to aversion (phobia), biophilia suggests that there is a psychological mechanism that draws people to be interested in nature and other forms of life. But an equally fundamental point is that people, rather than being separated from nature, are actually part of it. This may seem a rather uncontentious observation but it actually has very far-reaching implications, as will emerge shortly. For the time being, it is sufficient to note that if people become cut off from the natural world for prolonged periods, there is a real danger they will suffer some form of psychological damage. This is an argument which has been expressed by many commentators and which is supported by numerous reports on children's health (see for example Louv, 2008; Layard & Dunn, 2009; RSPB, 2010). It may also be one of the factors which accounts for the growth of psychological disorders that is affecting increasing numbers of university students in industrialized countries.

People and nature apart

The relation between people and nature has varied at different times in the past. One of the most significant landmarks was the Scientific Revolution, which occurred in the sixteenth and seventeenth centuries in Europe. This heralded the beginning of the modern era and represented a major shift in thinking about the world. Copernicus, Galileo, Bacon, Descartes, Newton and the other think- ers of the age developed their theories by focusing on phenomena which could be measured and quantified through careful observation. By representing the material world in terms of exact mathematical laws, they were able to make predictions which could be tested and verified. The resulting breakthroughs in physics, chemistry, astronomy, mathematics and other areas of learning brought huge rewards and are responsible for many of benefits we enjoy today. However, like all advances, they came at a cost (Capra and Luisi, 2015).

The scientific revolution involved a complete change of thinking. It posi- tioned people as outsiders who noted and recorded events as they occurred. The organic view of the world, which had been prevalent in the Middle Ages, was replaced by a mechanistic model. A key metaphor was the idea that the universe, once set in motion by God, operated like a mechanical clock, ticking precisely according to the laws of physics. Such thinking set people apart from nature and had the effect of alienating them from it. Revolutionary breaks of this kind have been described by Thomas Kuhn (1962) as 'paradigm shifts' and they involve changes not only in shared concepts and techniques, but also the in the values which underpin society and the way it is organized.

The idea that humans are separate from nature lies at the heart of modern capitalism, and there is a growing realization that this could have potentially disastrous consequences. Such thinking regards the environment as a resource to be exploited and denies its intrinsic value. The benefits that accrue from natu- ral processes, such as soil regeneration or the sequestration of carbon dioxide by plants (ecosystem services), are not quantified or recognized. Instead they are regarded as externalities with no particular economic value. Equally, there is no obvious way to calculate the damage that results from different forms of pol- lution, even though plastic has been found to be harming life in every major marine ecosystem, causing untold damage (WWF, 2018).

The fundamental problem is that modern capitalism is geared towards growth. Many commentators have pointed out that the word 'economics,' if traced back to its linguistic root, means 'household management.' In the past, when industry was localized and small in scale, the environment could eas- ily accommodate its impact. However, since the 1950s, economic activity has increased tenfold and it goes on increasing (Jackson, 2017). It is now becoming clear that the idea of progress and economic development which is so deeply embedded in modern thinking is incompatible with planetary limits. This sug- gests the need for a new vision of prosperity, which includes human and plane- tary well-being. The present notion, which measures prosperity simply in terms of material wealth, is so deeply compromised it can now only be regarded as 'household *mis-management*'.

It is fascinating to consider whether the physical manifestations of alienation which are evident today match the development and structure of the human brain. In a ground-breaking work, Iain McGilchrist (2012) points out that the cerebral hemispheres, although they are both involved in just about everything we do, have different insights, values and priorities. Most significantly, the right hemisphere sees itself as connected to the world, whereas the left hemisphere stands aloof from it. McGilchrist suggests that many features of contemporary society exhibit left-brain tendencies, which are then reflected back to the brain as in a hall of mirrors. He identifies a "mixture of unwarranted optimism mixed with paranoia and feelings of emptiness" (2012, p. 6), along with denial and a desire for certainty, as left-brain qualities. The qualities that are associated with the right hemisphere, such as a sense of wholeness, spirituality and the ability to tolerate ambiguity, which are particularly important for a sustainability mindset, appear to have been outflanked in the industrialized West.

Traditional cultures

Traditional hunter-gather cultures tend to give much greater prominence to what might be loosely termed right-brain modes of thought. They are imbued with a deep realization of the unity of all forms of life and attribute great significance to the natural and physical world, which they see as the embodiment of the divine. To take just one example, the Australian Aborigines believe that the land and all the plants and creatures within it, including themselves, were created by their ancestors and animal spirits at the beginning of time. They call this time the dream time, which they see as a beginning which never ends, as it is a continuum that links past, present and future. The ancestral spirits made some places sacred. Performing ritual ceremonies and songs near these sites pleases the spirits and keeps them alive.

Around the world, many ancient cultures have similar beliefs in the spirit world. Animism and a deep sense that some places are sacred is part of the traditional wisdom of people as varied as the Indian Adivasis, the Maoris of New Zealand and the First Nations of North America. This idea was expressed particularly clearly by Luther Standing Bear, Chief of the Lakota, who reflected on traditional Sioux wisdom as follows:

> Kinship with all creatures of the earth, sky, and water was a real and active principle. . . . The wolf, duck, eagle, hawk, spider, bear, and other creatures had marvellous powers and each one was helpful to us. . . . The world was a library and its books were the stones, leaves, grass, brooks, and the birds and animals that shared, alike with us, the storms and blessings of earth. We learned to do what only the student of nature ever learns and that is to feel beauty.
>
> *(Luther Standing Bear, 1933, 2006, pp. 193–194)*

The idea of kinship with the natural and physical world resonates with modern sustainability thinking. It expresses the notion that people and the environment are connected at a fundamental level in a way that transcends materialism and resists quantification. Traditional North American culture even recognizes that the dislocation between a person and their surroundings can be so traumatic that it can trigger what is termed a 'soul wound'. It might be argued that by extension, a society which exploits natural resources and which regards the Earth in almost entirely utilitarian terms may itself be suffering from collective 'soul wounds' or alienation. There is a natural balance in the world which has become disrupted by 'progress' and needs to be reestablished. Restoring harmonious relations between the mind, body and spirit is integral to sustainability education and part of a healing process and re-enchantment with nature, as Chara Armon argues in chapter four of this book.

It is easy to become over-enthusiastic about the significance of traditional wisdom and indigenous cultures. The people of the past certainly exploited their environment and used it for their advantage. In Britain, for example, Neolithic people had a major impact on woodland cover, and although the population at that time was extremely sparse and tools were very basic, they succeeded in reducing it by around fifty percent by 2000 BC. There is also the danger of cherry picking examples as there are many traditional practices, ranging from female genital mutilation to honor crimes, which many people today regard as utterly abhorrent. However, it is not suggested here that we should seek to return to the past, even if this were possible. What is at stake is whether the beliefs which were prevalent in many ancient societies have any relevance today. Should we be seeking to learn from the experience of those who lived many centuries ago, or is it better to simply ignore their example because times have changed and people have moved on?

Spiritual and religious perspectives

Religion is one of the ways in which ideas from the past have been handed down through the generations. The idea that some places and things are sacred is a common thread. Seyyed Nasr (2003) points out that the Quran tells us how everything in the universe sings out God's praises simply by virtue of its existence. Buddhist thinking includes the notion of dharma or correct way of living, one aspect of which is being gentle and loving to nature. Christians believe that God is revealed in the wonders and beauty of nature. Similarly, the Upanishads see the entire existence as imbued with the sacred. The idea that we should care for the world and treasure it as a gift permeates religious texts around the world.

But religion also recognizes the importance of transcendental experiences – experiences which go beyond the material to reveal levels of meaning that are not normally accessible through cognition. These experiences are characterized by mystery rather than certainty, and they are difficult to articulate even though they somehow seem to be deeply significant. What defines such experiences is that they evoke a deep sense of awe and wonder together with a feeling of deep humility. And they are often ascribed to a particular place or event (Figure 3.1).

Being aware of the mystery of life can also lead to a sense of oneness and belonging with the universe as a whole. For example, in his autobiography *Memories, Dreams, Reflections*, Carl Jung reflects on his life on the shore of Lake Zurich in Switzerland in the following words:

> At times, I feel as if I am spread out over the landscape and inside things, and am myself in every living tree, in the splashing of the waves, in the clouds and the animals that come and go, in the procession of the seasons . . . Thoughts rise to the surface which reach back into the centuries, and accordingly anticipate a remote future.
>
> *(1974, p. 252–253)*

Un missionnaire du moyen âge raconte qu'il avait trouvé le point
où le ciel et la Terre se touchent...

FIGURE 3.1 A nineteenth century engraving showing a pilgrim with a staff crawling under the edge of a starry sky to peer into a mysterious world beyond

(*Source*: Wikimedia Commons Available at: https://commons.wikimedia.org/wiki/File:Flammarion Woodcut.jpg)

Not only does this passage suggest an extraordinary sense of unity and harmony with the natural world, it also captures a deep sense of timelessness. The fact that it was written by the founder of analytical psychology makes it particularly significant.

The idea that there are a group of non-rational emotions associated with the holy or sacred is explored by Rudolf Otto in his classic work *The Idea of the Holy* (1923). Otto develops the notion of the 'numinous' to capture the sense of human nothingness in the face of an all-powerful being – in Latin 'numen' means 'to bow the head.' Otto argues that the feeling of awe that results from the numinous is the starting point for religious development. Awe is a term which has changed its meaning in recent times. Rather than associating it with wonder, Otto interprets awe as religious dread, as something which is literally 'awful' (i.e. full of awe). Being aware of the majesty and wrath of God emphasizes our own insignificance and stimulates a profound sense of humility. But it can also be interpreted another way. An awareness of nothingness can lead us to a sense of transcendence.

Otto explains that the numinous cannot, strictly speaking, be taught, but can only be evoked or awakened in the mind "just as everything else that comes 'of the spirit' must also be awakened" (1923, p. 7). But it can also be aroused from feelings that are analogous. Otto notes how religious art sometimes blends "appalling frightfulness" with "exalted holiness," thereby giving expression to what is both fearful and exalting. Architecture is a particularly powerful example as it was one of the first ways in which the sublime appears to have been realized. But the arts, poetry, and music also have the capacity to address the numinous. William Blake's poem, 'The Tygr,' is just one example, evoking as it does the idea of the immortal power that framed the tiger's "fearful symmetry." (Figure 3.2).

We can probably all identify ineffable experiences in our own lives – experiences which we cannot articulate but which somehow seem to be deeply meaningful. And the idea that there is some deeper purpose to what we are doing is

FIGURE 3.2 'The Tyger' in Blake's 'Songs of Innocence and Experience' (1794) was one of the poems which inspired the English romantic movement

(*Source*: Wikimedia Commons. Available at: https://commons.wikimedia.org/wiki/File:The_Tyger_LC_1826.jpg)

something that resonates across cultures. These experiences lead some people to religion, but they can also attract people to work for all manner of causes they believe to be just and right.

With respect to sustainability education, focusing on the spiritual aspects of life can be a double-edged sword. It imbues enthusiasts with a sense of passion and purpose but it can also give them the uncompromising zeal of the converted. The danger here is that earth care, rather than being seen as a rational choice which is essential to the future prosperity and well-being of humanity, becomes an ideological position that is viewed as a non-negotiable revelation. Those who take a contrary view can be equally adamant and fixed in their views. It is important, therefore, that educators recognize the power of the preconceptions or 'frames of reference' (Mezirow, 2009) which students bring to their learning and that they find ways to negotiate this crucial but ambiguous terrain.

The search for new narratives

Learning about global problems can be overwhelming. The issues are so big and their impact so extensive that many people feel that there is nothing individually that they can do to address them. Furthermore, we are all trapped in the social and economic systems of our times. This means that even if we succeed in changing one part of our lives, we are likely to undermine our endeavors in other things that we do. The problem is that surface-level actions, such as turning off the lights or recycling paper, while laudable in themselves, are manifestly insufficient to address global problems. What could make a real difference, though, is to re-appraise the values and beliefs which guide our actions. In turn, this suggests a shift in thinking about our relationship with the environment and our sense of meaning and belonging.

In his detailed and extensive study of cultural history and humanity's search for meaning, Jeremy Lent argues that we have to manage the 'operating systems' that control our civilization and he probes the root metaphors which lie at the heart our world view (2017, p. 28). He argues that stories and narratives have the power not only to encapsulate but also to reformulate our relationship with the environment and the values we hold towards it. These stories take many different forms and are often hidden from view and not consciously acknowledged, ranging from myths and metaphors to historical accounts of the rise and fall of nations. They occur, as Stibbe (2015) points out, in such apparently innocent texts as news reports, instruction manuals and conversations with friends. The same applies on a communal level where the deep assumptions which underpin society are expressed in art, music, literature and religion, or applied in economics, engineering and medicine. Whether we recognize it or not, we all subscribe to over-arching narratives which help us find meaning in our lives. "Stories", as Monbiot puts it, "are the means by which we navigate the world" (2017, p. 1).

What has become clear in recent years is that the stories of progress, human centrality, and separation from nature, which have been at the heart of Western thought for hundreds of years, are no longer appropriate to current needs. Paul Kingsnorth and Dougald Hine, the joint authors of the *Dark Mountain Manifesto*, explain how the ecological crisis that now confronts us is rooted in outdated narratives:

> We have been led to this point by the stories we have told ourselves – above all the story of civilization. . . . It is the story of human centrality, of a species destined to be lord of all it surveys, unconstrained by the limits that apply to other, lesser creatures. What makes this story so dangerous is that, for the most part, we have forgotten that it is a story. . . . So we find ourselves. . . . trapped inside a runaway narrative, headed for the worst kind of encounter with reality
>
> *(2009, pp. 17–20)*

Kingsnorth and Hine highlight the need for new stories and they set out an agenda for writing and art which is grounded in place and time. Many others also recognize the power of narrative to support or bring about change. Korten (2006) argues that we need stories which reframe the way we define human nature, purpose and possibilities. Gardner (2006) sets out the case for compelling stories which are emotionally resonant and evoke positive experiences. Moltmann (2012) declares that people need to find new ways of understanding themselves. Meanwhile, Stibbe argues that people need to reinvent themselves and construct more environmentally beneficial stories about who they are (see chapter 16 of this volume).

Formulating new narratives is bound to be a slow process because there are many different interlocking elements. One of the features of a world view or paradigm is that it has considerable internal stability. This means it is not enough just to dislodge one element: change, when it comes, requires a comprehensive readjustment of ideas and is liable to be experienced as an abrupt break rather than as a progressive shift. Writing some twenty years ago, Berry (1998) noted that the reason we are in trouble is that we haven't yet formulated a new account of the world and our place within it. A more recent observer, Eisenstein (2013), sees signs of progress and observes although the new story is not yet formed, each of us is aware of some of its threads. As he puts it, "here and there we see patterns, designs, emerging parts of the fabric." And he concludes that there is something rather precious – almost sacred – about abiding in the "space between stories" (p. 14).

The importance of language in shaping our thoughts is well attested. Even place names matter. In a fascinating study of lost vocabulary, Robert Mac-Farlane (2016) argues that if a landscape goes undescribed it becomes to some extent unseen and, therefore, vulnerable to exploitation. Conversely, once a place or animal has been named, it finds a place in our hearts. MacFarlane is wary of the tyranny of naming things; instead, he explores the power of imagination to illuminate the mutual relations among place, language and spirit. He argues that "language is fundamental to the possibility of re-wonderment, for language does not just register experience, it produces it" (p. 25). At the same time, he acknowledges that there are some landscape experiences that are so total that they resist articulation. "Nature does not name itself" and "granite does not self-identify as igneous," he observes. "Sometimes, on the top of a mountain I just say, 'Wow.'" (p. 10)

The idea of re-enchantment has potential both to reposition and to reinvigorate the sustainability agenda. It focuses attention on ways of thinking which have been recognized throughout human history and are perhaps most strongly represented in religious belief. It is striking how indigenous people and others who live close to the soil have a deep understanding of the mutual dependence of all forms of life and a spiritual sense of belonging to place. The associated notion of 'oneness with nature' affirms the intrinsic and irreducible meaning of life. When the American conservationist Aldo Leopold declared that "the last word in ignorance is the man who says of animal or plant, 'What good is it?'" he went straight to the heart of the matter. MacFarlane puts the same thought in a different way when he calls for "a glossary of enchantment for the whole earth" that will allow "nature to talk back and us to listen" (2016, p. 32). Nurturing a sense of wonder runs alongside developing an ethic of Earth care.

Conclusion

In today's academic world it is very difficult to explore the affective and spiritual dimension of education. The emphasis on measurable targets and outcomes has focused attention on quantifiable performance rather than depth of experience. The fragmentation of the curriculum into disciplines limits the options for making links and connections between different courses and faculties. Furthermore, a concern for financial survival has elevated recruitment, retention, employability and other business agendas at the expense of deep engagement with meaning and learning. Despite these trends, there are some encouraging signs. The idea of eco-literacy is gaining traction. The United Nations SDGs have set out an agreed-upon framework which is being adopted by educational institutions. The value of experiential learning, practical activity and collaborative learning environments is widely acknowledged. The school strikes for climate change (see chapter two of this book) and extinction rebellion (Extinction Rebellion, 2019) also offer grounds for hope.

It has been argued in this chapter that people need to reconnect with place. There is nothing backward-looking in acknowledging the wisdom of traditional cultures which respect the unity of life and acknowledge the importance of balance and harmony. Bringing the spiritual dimension back into our understanding of sustainability deepens our understanding. It acknowledges feelings and honors experiences that cannot be put into words. It recognizes that the sum is more than its parts. And it invites us to reconsider the assumptions and beliefs – the deeply held narratives – that underpin our actions. The Earth Charter (2000) framed this idea in the following way:

> We stand at a critical moment in Earth's history, a time when humanity must choose its future. As the world becomes increasingly interdependent and fragile, the future at once holds great peril and great promise. . . . Let ours be a time remembered for the awakening of a new reverence for life, the firm resolve to achieve sustainability, the quickening of the struggle for justice and peace, and the joyful celebration of life.

These words are as true now as when they were written. Responding to the promise of the future while recognizing the risks that lie ahead is the urgent task of education today.

References

Berry, T. (1998). *Evening thoughts*. San Francisco, CA: Sierra Club.

Capra, F., & Luisi, L. (2015). *The systems view of life*. Cambridge: Cambridge University Press.

Csikszentmihalyi, M. (1997). *Creativity: Flow and the psychology of discovery and invention*. London: HarperPerennial.

Earth Charter. (2000). Retrieved from http://earthcharter.org/discover/the-earth-charter/

Eisenstein, C. (2013). *The more beautiful world our hearts know is possible*. Berkley, CA: North Atlantic Books.

Extinction Rebellion. (2019). *This is not a drill: An extinction rebellion handbook*. London: Penguin.

Gardner, H. (2006). *Changing minds: The art and science of changing our own and other people's minds*. Boston, MA: Harvard Business School (see Speth 2008, p. 212).

Jackson, T. (2017). *Prosperity without growth* (2nd ed.). London: Routledge.

Jung, C. (1974). *Memories, dreams, reflections*. London: Fontana.

Kellert, S. (2012). *Birthright: People and nature in the modern world*. New Haven, CT: Yale University Press.

Kingsnorth, P. & Hine, D. (2009). *Uncivilisation: The dark mountain manifesto*. Retrieved from https://dark-mountain.net/about/manifesto/

Korten, D. (2006). *The great turning: From empire to earth community*. San Francisco, CA: Berrett-Koehler.

Kuhn, T. (1962). *The structure of scientific revolutions*. Chicago, IL: University of Chicago Press.

Layard, R., & Dunn, J. (2009). *A good childhood, Searching for values in a competitive age*. London: Penguin.

Lent, J. (2017). *The patterning instinct*. New York: Prometheus Books.

Louv, R. (2008). *Last child in the woods*. Chapel Hill, NC: Algonquin.

Luther Standing Bear. (1933, 2006). *Land of the spotted eagle*. Lincoln and London: University of Nebraska Press.

Macfarlane, R. (2016). *Landmarks*. London: Penguin.

Massey, D. (2005). *For space*. London: Sage.

Massey, D., & Jess, P. (1995). *A place in the world*. Oxford: Oxford University Press.

McGilchrist, I. (2012). *The master and his emissary*. New Haven, CT and London: Yale University Press.

Mezirow, J. (2009). Transformative learning theory. In J. Mezirow & E. W. Taylor (Eds.), *Transformative learning in practice: Insights from community, workplace, and higher education* (pp. 18–32). San Francisco, CA: Jossey Bass.

Moltmann, J. (2012). *The ethics of hope*. Minneapolis, MN: Fortress Press.

Monbiot, G. (2017). *Out the wreckage*. London: Verso.

Nasr, S. (2003). The spiritual and religious dimensions of the environmental crisis. In B. McDonald (Ed.), *Seeing god everywhere*. Bloomington, IN: World Wisdom.

Otto, R. (1923). *The idea of the holy*. London: Oxford University Press.

RSPB. (2010). *Every child outdoors*. Retrieved from ww2.rspb.org.uk/Images/everychild-outdoors_tcm9-259689.pdf

Stibbe, A. (2015). *Ecolinguistics: Language, ecology and the stories we live by*. London: Routledge.

Tuan, Y. F. (1977). *Space and place: The perception of experience*. London: Arnold.

Vujakovic, P., Owens, P., & Scoffham, S. (2018). Meaningful Maps: What can we learn about "sense of place" from maps produced by children? *Society of Cartographers Bulletin*, *51*, 10–19.

WWF. (2018). *Living planet report*. Retrieved from www.worldwildlife.org/pages/living-planet-report-2018

PART II
Theory to practice

4

AN EDUCATION THAT HEALS

Purposes and practices guided by the Great Work

Chara Armon

Historian and religion scholar Thomas Berry situated his assessment of environmental crises in the deep-time history of Earth's geological eras of existence, including the Mesozoic, the Cenozoic, and the hoped-for Ecozoic, or era of mutually beneficial human-Earth co-existence. Berry noted that humanity in the modern era is "changing not simply the human world, [but also] the chemistry of the planet, even the geological structure and functioning of the planet" (1999, p. 74). Addressing higher education's response, Berry wrote in 1999, "The universities must decide whether they will continue training persons for temporary survival in the declining Cenozoic Era or whether they will begin educating students for the emerging Ecozoic . . . it is the time for universities to rethink themselves and what they are doing" (1999, p. 85).

As higher education institutions endeavor to inform students about the environmental crisis via increasingly comprehensive forms of sustainability education, questions proliferate regarding optimal approaches to teaching in this time. Here I discuss an approach arising from Thomas Berry's idea of the Great Work of transforming the human-Earth relationship into one that is as beneficial for Earth as for humanity. My core question asks how a Great Work orientation can guide course design in ways that respond to the global environmental crisis and its effects on the human and other species, with the aim of creating a comprehensive sustainability education that serves a healing function for the natural world, humanity, and the human-nature relationship. Hereafter, I use "environmental crisis" to denote the interplay of problems involving climate change, ecosystem imbalance, species decline, and pollution; related structural problems such as poverty and injustice and their development from social, governance, and economic systems; and the associated effects on animal, plant, and human survival and well-being.

In the conversation about how to address our environmental crisis, a core role for the humanities typically has been overlooked. During recent decades of heightened environmental awareness, most attention has been paid to scientific, technological, economic, and political responses to environmental problems, with virtue-seeking perspectives from the humanities sidelined due to assumptions that they hold less practical relevance. The problem is that it is through humanities disciplines that humans, over millennia, have assembled our tools for asking and attempting to answer the "why" questions about human existence – why are we here, how should we treat one another and the Earth, what is a good life? Students typically encounter "sustainability" as simply an environmental science and economics problem and a concern of the modern world only in the latter twentieth century, which is an inaccurate conceptualization. In fact, environmental problems, such as air and water pollution, existed well before the twentieth century and human environmental impacts, such as extensive deforestation, occurred as early as the ancient and medieval eras (Ponting, 2007). Modern beliefs promoting objectification of the Earth date back at least to ancient Greek and early Christian thought, while human interaction with the natural world, whether benign or damaging, is as old as humanity itself. David Orr has asserted that ecological disorder develops from disorder in human thought (2005). In order to evaluate this claim, students need to know how we have thought in human and Western history, and humanities disciplines are important repositories of these ways of thought. The developing field of environmental humanities addresses the humanities' crucial role in supporting our understanding of how our environmental crisis developed over millennia of thought and practice, and how the humanities tradition can support our selection of responses (Petersen-Boring, 2010, 2014; Filho & Consorte-McCrae, 2018; Sörlin, 2012; Ferkany & Whyte, 2012). As Petersen-Boring states, "Our answers to the challenges of sustainability cannot be primarily data-driven, technological, or resolved from within current perceptions or paradigms. . . . [W]e must re-examine values, draw on cultural wisdom, and re-energize spiritual and philosophical traditions" (Petersen-Boring, 2014, pp. xiv, 50).

The Great Work

In his 1999 book, *The Great Work*, and his body of writing from the 1970s to his death in 2009, Thomas Berry pondered our identity as a human species and our relationships to planet Earth, its other-than-human inhabitants, and one another as humans. Berry defined a "Great Work" as a large-scale movement that provides "shape and meaning to life by relating the human venture to the larger destinies of the universe" (1999, p. 1). Past Great Works, in Berry's assessment, include the ancient Greek establishment of the humanist tradition and India's and China's developments of vital spiritual and philosophical traditions embedded in complex civilizations. The Great Work of the twenty-first century, Berry believed, "is to carry out the transition from a period of human devastation of the Earth to a period when humans would be present to the planet in a mutually beneficial manner" (1999, pp. x, 3, 7, 55).

The Great Work is a framework that helps to make sense of sustainability in the contexts of past, present, and potential future human culture. Asserting that we need a "New Story" about human life and its purpose to guide our Great Work of restoring the Earth and our relationship to it, Berry offered a conceptual framework that can help teachers and students deeply understand sustainability. Berry envisioned the New Story "as a comprehensive basis for nurturing reciprocity between humans and for fostering reverence between humans and the Earth" (Tucker, 2014, p. 11). As a framework for assessing sustainability from a broad human and Earth-centered viewpoint, the Great Work and its New Story help us to move far beyond overly simple solutions (e.g., Reduce, Reuse, Recycle or "sustainable development"), and into the complex, necessary territory of re-defining and reestablishing the human-Earth relationship and the well-being of both humanity and the planet. The Great Work and New Story are, in the terminology of transformative education theorist Edmund O'Sullivan, forms of "transformative criticism" (O'Sullivan, 2004, p. 164).

One way to understand Berry is as a systems thinker within both humanities and science frameworks. Not only humanities-based, the Great Work is a science-literate systems approach grounded in disciplines such as geology, biology, cosmology, and ecology. Thinking on the large human and Earth scale, Berry advocated for systemic and substantive reconsideration of our human ways of thought and practice, from economics, education, and government to spirituality and religion, and from gender and race relations to technology and law. Some critics have faulted the lack of specificity in Berry's broad-brushstroke approach, including those who have identified a need for more detailed focus on the injustices faced by people of color, women, and people in poverty. Although Berry did acknowledge these injustices and their dire need for attention, his wide worldviews focus indeed does not account for all particulars; he assumed that the millions of people who may implement the Great Work will attend to the millions of aspects of creating a mutually beneficial human-Earth relationship that includes careful tending of all aspects of human well-being. Berry began to discuss, and scholars such as Andreas Hernandez and Heather Eaton have pointed out, that core to the Great Work are the inclusion and participation of people who suffer exclusion, impoverishment, and injustice, in compatibility with views expressed in documents such as The Earth Charter and Sustainable Development Goals (Berry 2015, p. 36–37; Hernandez, 2018, pp. 150, 167, et passim; H. Eaton, 2014, p. xiii). Berry, Matthew Hall (Hall 2011), Marc Bekoff (Bekoff 2014), Robin Wall Kimmerer (Kimmerer 2013), Stephan Harding (Harding 2013), and many others also have acknowledged that similarly crucial to the Great Work are the inclusion and participation of species other than the human, ecosystems and their functions, and indeed, all aspects of the living Earth.

To contextualize Berry's ideas, it is worthwhile to note important predecessors. Previous expressions of Great Work thinking appear in the thought of writers such as Basil the Great in the fourth century, Francis of Assisi in the thirteenth century, and Liberty Hyde Bailey in the nineteenth. Similarly, as Berry knew as a scholar of religion, most or all world religions, in at least some of their scriptures and accounts of right living, articulate the existence of important connectedness or unity within the life system rather than a hierarchy dominated by humans (for detailed discussion, see Harvard University Press's Religions of the World and Ecology series). Late 20th century and early 21st century environmental thinkers who, like Berry, consider humanistic and scientific ideas in tandem include scientist-activists Vandana Shiva and Wangari Maathai; writer and farmer Wendell Berry; ecologist Stephan Harding; political scientist David Orr; and economist David Korten. Similarly to both Berry and Korten, Arran Stibbe, Stephen Scoffham, and Tom Hudspeth in this volume point to the need for a "new story" to depict our understanding of human life and its inter-relationships with the Earth. Thus, a course with a "Great Work orientation" may most fruitfully present it not simply as Berry's ideas which students should adopt, but as a set of ideas articulated over time by a variety of like-minded thinkers in the humanities and sciences.

Berry urged his readers to grow beyond the modern tendency to "think of the universe as a collection of objects rather than a communion of subjects" (1999, p. 16; 2015, p. 45–46; 2006, p. 18). What students, faculty, and society can gain, thus, from an education oriented toward the Great Work is an education that heals: an education that heals by cultivating understanding of humanity's Old Story and its harms that led us to our current ecological crisis; awareness of the New Story being crafted as we discern reasons and methods for sustainability and regeneration; opportunities to discern personal contributions to the unfolding New Story; and insights into how individuals and communities can select actions that benefit both human well-being and Earth's well-being. Designing courses based on Berry's articulation of ethics that promote "the well-being of the comprehensive life community and the attainment of human well-being within that community" may create an education that heals (1999, p. 105; 2006, p. 21).

The Great Work as transformative education

How does Berry's articulation of the Great Work fit with environmentally oriented educational approaches of the past forty years? As we embark on what some are terming "third wave" approaches to sustainability in higher education in the twenty-first century, some universities are attempting "to re-orient teaching, learning, research and university-community relationships in such a way that sustainability becomes an emergent property of [their] core activities," rather than a siloed activity occurring only in discrete departments, programs, and campus greening endeavors (Wals & Blewitt, 2010, p. 56). Third-wave sustainability in higher education usually involves "the creation of space for transformative learning: learning that helps people transcend the 'given,' the 'ordinary' and the often 'routine ways of doing' to create a new dynamic and alternative ways of seeing and doing" (Wals & Blewitt, 2010, p. 66). Berry's Great Work approach fits within this third wave of sustainability education endeavors, and specifically within the fold of transformative education, or TE. Like Berry's thought, TE portrays humans as embedded in nature, rather than in control of it (Selby & Kagawa, 2015; Berry, 1999). Also in harmony with Great Work approaches, TE emphasizes paradigm change rather than small shifts, and often includes engagement in restoration endeavors (Selby & Kagawa, 2015; Sterling, 2004). As Joan Armon discusses in our Introduction to this volume, we use the term "comprehensive sustainability education" to indicate a form of TE that is systemic in its focus and relational and participatory in its forms of engagement.

Selby represents TE in a way very compatible with Berry's thought when he asserts that "any unlearning of unsustainability needs to involve a challenge to prevailing myths and assumptions about ourselves and our place in the world" (Selby, 2015, p. 32). Berry anticipated Selby's and Kagawa's recommendations that "Learning should interrogate root drivers of the crisis of unsustainability" and "Learning needs to be predicated upon an intrinsic valuing of nature and the importance of deep immersion in nature" (Selby & Kagawa, 2015, pp. 277–280). Writing from the perspective of TE, Selby suggests that "In rethinking education's potential contribution to rolling back unsustainability, we need to shift the view of the human-nature relationship from the doministic, instrumental and exploitative to one of seeing ourselves embedded in a natural world of intrinsic value" (Selby, 2015, p. 36). As Simon Wilson suggests in this volume, referencing not only the intellectual but the emotional aspects of sustainability education, "sustainability education should actually be a praxis of love." This is an education that is founded in relational awareness and can be an education that heals.

Transforming undergraduate sustainability education

Berry took a strong, if preliminary, interest in Great Work-oriented curriculum and made numerous statements about the role of universities in the Great Work, noting that the goal of such an education is not simply knowledge, but moving from "a human-centered to an Earth-centered norm of reality" (Berry, 1999, p. 58). As he stated, "the universities have the contact with the younger generation needed to reorient the human community toward a greater awareness that the human exists, survives, and becomes whole only within the single great community of the planet Earth" (Berry, 1999, p. 80). In practical terms, how can a curriculum and teaching approaches orient undergraduates toward viewing "the universe as . . . a communion of subjects" rather than "a collection of objects" (Berry, 1999, p. 16)? Specifically, within the context of a given course, what educational approaches enhance caring attentiveness to the life community and all its members rather than their objectification on utilitarian grounds? A Great Work orientation may involve infusing sustainability and Great Work concepts throughout a course or program of study, or adding them to a course as a unit. Notably, the youth who in 2018 and 2019 have been protesting worldwide against climate inaction, including via school walkouts, are calling for sustainability education to be infused throughout curricula rather than taught in isolated courses, as Artis, Cohen, Jaguzny, and Kieras discuss in this volume.

Three goals can guide teaching and learning that are oriented toward the Great Work and aim to create an education that heals:

- *Goal 1: Assess the Old Story and Develop New Stories.* This education assesses the Old Story and allows students to see the New Story that is developing. It fosters Resilience and Regeneration by building students' awareness that human culture is co-created continually via our choices, and therefore regenerative actions are within our grasp.
- *Goal 2: Focus on Care and Flourishing in the Context of Learning about Sustainability and Regeneration.* This education focuses not only on human well-being but on the well-being of the life community as the "basic ethical norm." It therefore promotes acquisition of practical knowledge about methods of sustainability and regeneration. It thus cultivates an Ethic of Care deeply grounded in both past and present human culture, and prepares students to Advocate for Life's Flourishing.
- *Goal 3: Facilitate Active Learning in Sustainability and Regeneration.* This education provides experiences in which students observe sustainability innovations, gain skill in implementing regenerative practices, and identify opportunities for their own potential contributions. Students thus gain experience in Fostering Resilience and Regeneration and Advocating for Life's Flourishing.

Given the scope of the Great Work, a Great Work orientation can fit anywhere in the curriculum, including in the sciences, but certainly in the humanities in courses such as literature, philosophy, ethics, history, and religion, as well as in the social sciences curriculum. The breadth of Berry's ideas also makes the Great Work a suitable guiding concept for law or business courses.

Goal 1: assess the old story and develop new stories

Students do not gain deep learning about sustainability by studying it from only a contemporary perspective; the cultural causes of our problems, and our toolbox of solutions, lie as much in our past as in our present. Studying multiple sustainability-relevant perspectives from diverse cultures, time periods, disciplines, and genres allows students to encounter sustainability as an enduring human problem and construct their own assessment of Great Work approaches. As students encounter the ecological thought and practice (or lack thereof) of several cultures, time periods, and/or genres of text, they become aware that our current environmental crisis has millennia-old roots and appreciate why the sustainability transition requires reinvention of human values and cultural norms, not only adjustments. For example, such learning may reveal how Western views of human domination of nature developed and spread globally, and how spirit-mind-body hierarchies common in Western thought asserted that just as the human body is inferior to the human mind and spirit, the natural world is inferior to human beings. In readings that problematize approaches of controlling land, resources, women, and indigenous peoples, students discover cultural choices that led to the development of our current environmental and human problems, such as the Scientific Revolution's tendency to view nature as a realm to be controlled, and even as a feminine entity destined to be dominated by male intellectuals.

Simultaneously, in culturally foundational texts students may discover statements about humans' role as the divinely benign caretakers of the natural world, or about nature as an expression of transcendent wisdom. As students see that the practice of thinking about the human-nature relationship is as old as the human written record, and that both controlling and cooperative human attitudes toward nature existed in the human past, they are able to see the possibility of developing new stories that favor mutual flourishing for people and the Earth. They are then able to consider their own values in regard to the human-nature relationship and move toward discerning a personal ecosophy, as Arran Stibbe discusses in this volume.

Goal 2: focus on care and flourishing in the context of learning about sustainability and regeneration

My students have been drawn to Paul Hawken's statement, "If you look at the science about what is happening on earth and aren't pessimistic, you don't understand data. But if you meet the people who are working to restore this earth and the lives of the poor, and you aren't optimistic, you haven't got a pulse" (Hawken, 2009). Students often begin their undergraduate studies having felt powerless, anxious, or even depressed in response to their high school environmental science curricula (Eaton, Davies, Williams, & MacGregor, 2017, p. 3). I find my students eager for information that allows them to feel something other than ashamed of their civilization and hopeless about the future, and I believe they receive a poor sustainability education indeed if all they learn about are climate metrics and international arguments over emissions (cf. Petersen-Boring, 2010). What Berry called The Great Work and others refer to as The Third (or Fourth) Industrial Revolution, The Great Transition, or The Great Turning, is occurring now through the efforts of millions of people working in community development, agriculture, science, education, activism, and other fields; yet undergraduates often need guidance in discovering how to become informed about these hope-inspiring movements. In his Foreword to Petersen-Boring's *Teaching Sustainability*, Orr calls this "a curriculum of applied hope" for a "life-centered education" (2014, xi). Comparably, Joan Armon mentions Freire's "hope education" in our Introduction.

The Great Work makes sense most easily when students learn about transformative ideas and actions already in existence. Students may discover these through learning about the environmental and social principles and actions of the Transition Towns movement; permaculture or regenerative agriculture; ecological economics and the innovations occurring in sustainable business; an ethical statement such as *The Earth Charter* and its implementation in K–12 and higher education; a political/economic development document such as the *Sustainable Development Goals*; a scientific article discussing ecological regeneration; or a news article reporting on solar energy implementation in communities experiencing poverty. This learning alerts students to the possibility that human culture perhaps may flourish as we increasingly make choices that are beneficial to the Earth rather than devastating. A first-year student commented that when I assigned her class to explore the U.S. and U.K. websites of the Transition Network, she took the time to read further online and discover what is occurring with Transition in her home city of Philadelphia. Impressed by the local focus, she wrote that she found it notable that Transition encourages people to be "more aware of the changes that are happening in our current societies, and engage with the world's problems on a more local scale." Transition, she commented, "[a]llows the shift from anthropocentrism to ecocentrism to really make progress." She ended by noting that she wished our university would establish a Transition initiative on campus.

Goal 3: facilitate active learning in sustainability and regeneration

Experiential learning is a crucial way of linking students' education to their interest in real-world implementation and their own future contributions. While Goal 2 emphasizes teaching students *about* current endeavors in sustainability and regeneration, Goal 3 allows them to begin participating. Students can engage in contemplative experiences in nature to learn what it is to have a subject-subject encounter with an ecosystem, plant, animal, soil, or body of water, supported by readings from authors such as Kimmerer, Hall, Harding, or Simon Wilson, who writes in this volume of "loving engagement." Guest speakers and experiential fieldtrips expand students' awareness of what is being created in the New Story and can include skill-building experiences. In my humanities course on sustainable and justice-oriented agriculture, students engage in ten hours of fieldwork on local farms, ranging from mid-sized suburban organic farms to small suburban or urban gardens producing food for their surrounding neighborhood, which often is facing food scarcity. When students have opportunities to hear farmers articulate the relational way in which they perceive their farm's interactions with land, ecosystems, other-than-human species, and human customers, then see composting practices, weed a vegetable patch, and interact with community residents who obtain produce at the garden because of their neighborhood's lack of a grocery store, they begin to own their knowledge while testing it physically. They both observe and practice how a New Story is being created that positions humans more as members of the life community than dominators of nature or one another. A senior nearing graduation wrote in response to this fieldwork, representing many similar comments over the years: "this assignment . . . is actually what drove me to take your class. Field work and tangible experience is so beneficial to everyone involved and the lessons that I learned from my time with [leaders at a food distribution and cooking instruction site] have proven to be invaluable. I wish more classes did things like this."

Concluding thoughts

This chapter suggests ways to shift higher education toward being a key part of the implementation of what Thomas Berry conceptualized as The Great Work. I advocate presenting the Great Work more as a diverse, global, and human quest than one based in a single worldview. Humanities and social science courses that demonstrate how ecological values have been present to some degree in most human ethical perspectives over time allow students to see that there is much more to ecological awareness than current environmentalism. Courses that offer students multiple opportunities to encounter Great-Work-oriented thinking across disciplines, time periods, and cultures facilitate the breadth necessary for the ethical and cultural re-visioning our environmental crisis demands. The aim is to provide opportunities to consider that the ecological and cultural restoration necessary on planet Earth may be within our reach. This education teaches about the human role in the context of a unique planet that is our life-support system, and gives students practical tools for being present in a manner that benefits both humans and the Earth community, for an inter-dependent mutual flourishing.

Reading, writing, and discussion within the humanities, and indeed in any discipline, should give students opportunities to discern what they value and believe, while experiential learning should allow them to discover possibilities for implementation of their values and beliefs. It is necessary that higher education now be reconfigured so that every institution provides an exquisite level of both intellectual learning and the acquisition of practical regenerative skills such that each student envisions her or his desired contribution to a regenerative human society situated harmlessly within the larger life community. This approach has the potential to constitute an education that heals.

Course Planning

This assignment sequence aims, first, to help students understand the environmental crisis in both its current and historical contexts; and second, to invite them to begin envisioning solutions and their own potential contributions. Before students write the paper(s), ideally they have had at least two active learning experiences, usually involving a field trip and independent time in nature, and often involving participation in a project that builds regenerative knowledge and skills. Experiential learning allows students to be solutions-oriented and alert to how an ethic of care may function in practice.

TABLE 4.1 Readings, Experiences, and Writing Assignments Adaptable for Undergraduate or Graduate Humanities Seminars

Sample Authors/Texts	Some Concepts for Discussion	Sample Assignments and Experiences
Creation stories: *Genesis*, *Qu'ran*, Native American and African creation stories. Berry's *Great Work*	How have we imagined the human role on Earth over millennia?	Fieldtrip to an arboretum or organic farm How is the Great Work a lens for examining the human–nature relationship in Hebrew, Christian, Islamic, and indigenous creation stories?
Plato's *Timaeus*, Robin Wall Kimmerer's *Braiding Sweetgrass*, and Wangari Maathai's *Replenishing the Earth*	Plato's hierarchy of soul-mind-body marginalizes the physical. As scientists and indigenous women, Kimmerer and Maathai argue for valuing the physical world.	Relying on Genesis 1–2, indigenous creation stories, and *Timaeus*, discuss the texts' accounts of what conditions are important for life to flourish.
Gospel of Mark, Augustine's *Confessions*, *Life of Cuthbert*, *Life of Francis*, the medieval Islamic text, *The Case of the Animals versus Man*, Albert Schweitzer's "Reverence for Life"	What is the relationship of a human being to the natural world in medieval thought and modern ethics?	Develop an essay comparing *Genesis*, *Timaeus*, or Augustine's writings to the Cuthbert and Francis texts, or comparing concepts in the *Life of Cuthbert* and *Life of Francis*, such as how each saint perceives hierarchy or egalitarianism in the human-nature relationship.
The Earth Charter and *Sustainable Development Goals*	What are current international responses to environmental crisis?	*Oral exam questions:* *Question 1:* Using 2 ancient readings and 1 modern reading, respond to the idea of the Great Work (disagreeing, agreeing, or assessing). *Question 2:* Maathai writes about over-consumption and materialism. Similar concerns appear in *Timaeus*, the *Qu'ran*, and the *Gospel of Mark*. Referring to ancient and modern readings, explain how culturally important texts may guide considerations of material consumption.

Sample Authors/Texts	Some Concepts for Discussion	Sample Assignments and Experiences
Shakespeare's *The Tempest* and Aimé Césaire's 20th c. Afro-Carribbean retelling, *A Tempest*	What relationships have existed among colonists, colonized peoples, and land?	How does Shakespeare present the natural world in *The Tempest*? How do Césaire's revisions of the play respond?
Francis Bacon, excerpts of *The Great Instauration* and *Novum Organum*	Bacon advocates an empirical science that improves human life through domination of nature.	Classroom discussions explore benefits and harms of scientific innovation, and how harms might be prevented via deeper ethical conceptualization of science's purposes oriented toward mutual well-being for people and the natural world.
John Locke, excerpts of *Second Treatise of Government;* Michael Northcott, *Place, Ecology, and the Sacred.*	Locke theorizes humans' natural right to own land and depicts land that is not cultivated as 'wasted,' thus helping craft modern views of land development.	Discussions explore past and current land-use dilemmas and their regard for land as object or land as subject.
Marc Bekoff's *Rewilding Our Hearts* and Stephen Harding's *Animate Earth*	Scientists Bekoff and Harding advocate ethical, compassionate, intuitive interactions with nature.	Write an essay that places Bacon's Scientific Revolution values in dialogue with Marc Bekoff's science-based, ethically focused assertions about the need for compassion toward the natural world.
R.W. Emerson, "Nature;" H.D. Thoreau, "Walking;" Walt Whitman, "Song of the Rolling Earth;" Matthew Hall, *Plants as Persons*; essays by the Dalai Lama and Thich Nhat Hanh.	Explorations of transcendent human encounters with the natural world and new scientific assessments of interrelationship and intelligence in nature.	Fieldtrip to an arboretum, park, or hiking trail; possible assignment of quiet reflection time in nature and reflective writing.

TABLE 4.2 Course Content Guide for an Undergraduate or Graduate Humanities Course

Conceptual Framework Dimensions	Lesson, Activity, or Project	Learning Informed by the SDGs (Goals 1.1 to 17.19) and The Earth Charter (Principles I.1 to IV.16)
Ethic of Care **Resilience &** **Regeneration** **Advocacy** **for Life's** **Flourishing**	*Experiential learning*: One or more fieldtrips as a class, and/or fieldwork sessions in groups. Locations may include rural or urban farms, "green" construction projects, sustainable community projects, ecosystem regeneration endeavors, "green" industrial facilities, etc. Ideally, students encounter projects that attend to racial, economic, and cultural diversity; justice needs; and democratic principles. Students observe and practice an Ethic of Care, and observe and often gain practical skills in Resilience and Regeneration. They receive mentoring from professionals, volunteers, and activists who model Advocacy for Life's Flourishing.	1.5 By 2030, build the resilience of the poor and those in vulnerable situations and reduce their exposure and vulnerability to climate-related extreme events and other economic, social, and environmental shocks and disasters. 4.7 By 2030, ensure that all learners acquire the knowledge and skills needed to promote sustainable development, including . . . through education for sustainable development and sustainable lifestyles, human rights, gender equality, . . . global citizenship, and appreciation of cultural diversity and of culture's contribution to sustainable development. See also Goals 15 and 16. I.2: Care for the community of life with understanding, compassion, and love. I.3: Build democratic societies that are just, participatory, sustainable, and peaceful. II.7: Adopt patterns of production, consumption, and reproduction that safeguard Earth's regenerative capacities, human rights, and community well-being. IV.14: Integrate into formal education and life-long learning the knowledge, values, and skills needed for a sustainable way of life.

Conceptual Framework Dimensions	Lesson, Activity, or Project	Learning Informed by the SDGs (Goals 1.1 to 17.19) and The Earth Charter (Principles I.1 to IV.16)
Ethic of Care	*Experiential learning:* "Determine six times when you will devote 20–30 minutes to spending time outdoors, either in a single location or different locations. You may choose a location such as your own yard, a 'damaged/ threatened' location such as an abandoned lot, or a place you find beautiful. For each of the six sessions, write two pages of typed reflections. During each session, consider your surroundings, which include the land you are sitting or standing on, plants, air, living creatures perceptible to your senses (and those you cannot perceive), weather, etc. Reflect on the interactions occurring between you and these multi-faceted surroundings. Add references to at least two of our readings in your discussion of each of your six observations, using our readings to help you see deeper into your experience, or using your experience to critique our readings." Experiences such as these can foster an Ethic of Care and interest in Advocacy for Life's Flourishing.	I.1: Respect Earth and life in all its diversity. IV.15: Treat all living beings with respect and consideration.

(Continued)

TABLE 4.2 (Continued)

Conceptual Framework Dimensions	Lesson, Activity, or Project	Learning Informed by the SDGs (Goals 1.1 to 17.19) and The Earth Charter (Principles I.1 to IV.16)

Ethic of Care
 Resilience &
    Regeneration
 Advocacy
    for Life's
    Flourishing
	Written assignments:
	 "Select an ecological crisis of interest to you (or a humanitarian or economic crisis with ecological roots), then assess its causes and optimal solutions. Your sources should include at least three of our course readings, plus at least two additional scientific or cultural documents that give you solid information on the details of the crisis. Craft a paper that explores a current situation in a scholarly way through the lens of our readings."
	 I often include a requirement that students envision a regenerated world. Thus, the essay/paper assignment may include these directions:
	 "In your final paper, envision specific aspects of a more just and reciprocal relationship among humans and other life forms and ecosystems. How might humanity and the natural world co-exist in a more thriving interdependence? This assignment is a chance to think again about aspects of our course readings that have inspired you the most and test them out by imagining a practical application."
		13.3 Improve education, awareness-raising, and human and institutional capacity on climate change mitigation, adaptation, impact reduction, and early warning
		 I.1: Respect Earth and life in all its diversity; I.2: Care for the community of life with understanding, compassion, and love.
		 II.5: Protect and restore the integrity of Earth's ecological systems; II.7: Adopt patterns of production, consumption, and reproduction that safeguard Earth's regenerative capacities, human rights, and community well-being.
		 IV.14: Integrate into formal education and life-long learning the knowledge, values, and skills needed for a sustainable way of life; IV.14b: Promote the contribution of the arts and humanities . . . in sustainability education.

Source: Chara Armon, Ph.D.

The written assignments require students, first, to become informed about an environmental problem of interest to them; second, to consider it via a philosophical, ethical, spiritual, religious, or historical lens they select; and third, to synthesize humanities-based approaches that are virtue-seeking or aspirational with data-oriented scientific approaches to create a fuller assessment of a problem's multi-faceted aspects, as well as to consider how it can be solved with attention to the multiple needs of people, animals, plants, and ecosystems. Types of historical and current texts students may read in support of this assignment sequence appear in Table 4.1.

References

Bekoff, M. (2014). *Rewilding our hearts: Building pathways of compassion and co-existence.* Novato, CA: New World Library.

Berry, T. (1999). *The great work: Our way into the future.* New York: Bell Tower.

Berry, T. (2006). *Evening thoughts: Reflecting on earth as sacred community.* San Francisco, CA: Sierra Club Books.

Berry, T. (2015). *The dream of the earth.* Berkeley, CA: Counterpoint.

Eaton, H. (Ed.). (2014). *The intellectual journey of Thomas Berry: Imagining the earth community.* Lanham, MD: Lexington Books.

Eaton, M., Davies, K., Williams, S., & MacGregor, J. (2017). Why sustainability education needs pedagogies of reflection and contemplation. In M. Eaton, H. J. Hughes, & J. MacGregor (Eds.), *Contemplative approaches to sustainability in higher education.* New York: Routledge.

Ferkany, M., & Whyte, K. P. (2012). The importance of participatory virtues in the future of environmental education. *Journal of Agricultural and Environmental Ethics, 25,* 419–434. https://doi.org/10.1007/s10806-011-9312-8.

Filho, W. L., & Consorte-McCrae, A. (Eds.). (2018). *Sustainability and the humanities.* Cham, Switzerland: Springer.

Hall, M. (2011). *Plants as persons: A philosophical botany.* Albany, NY: SUNY Press.

Harding, S. (2013). *Animate earth: Science, intuition, and gaia.* Cambridge: Green Books.

Hawken, P. (2009). *University of Portland commencement speech,* May 3, 2009.

Hernandez, A. (2018). Another worldview is possible: Grassroots social movements and the "great work". *Journal of the Study of Religion, Nature, and Culture, 12*(2), 147–171. Retrieved from https://journals.equinoxpub.com/index.php/JSRNC

Kimmerer, R. W. (2013). *Braiding sweetgrass: Indigenous wisdom, scientific knowledge, and the teachings of plants.* Minneapolis, MN: Milkweed Editions.

Orr, D. W. (2014). Foreword. In W. Petersen-Boring & W. Forbes (Eds.), *Teaching sustainability: Perspectives from the humanities and social sciences.* Nacogdoches, TX: Stephen F. Austin University Press.

Orr, D. W. (2005). Foreword. In M. K. Stone & Z. Barlow (Eds.), *Ecological literacy.* San Francisco, CA: Sierra Club Books.

O'Sullivan, E. (2004). Sustainability and transformative educational vision. In *Higher education and the challenge of sustainability.* Dordrecht: Kluwer Academic Publishers.

Petersen-Boring, W. (2010). Sustainability and the Western civilization curriculum: Reflections on cross-pollinating the humanities and environmental history. *Environmental History, 15*(2), 288–304. Retrieved from https://search-proquest-com.ezp1.villanova.edu/docview/750494692/fulltextPDF/4C76D22952E8412CPQ/1?accountid=14853

Petersen-Boring, W., & Forbes, W. (Eds.). (2014). *Teaching sustainability: Perspectives from the humanities and social sciences.* Nacogdoches, TX: Stephen F. Austin University Press.

Ponting, C. (2007). *A new green history of the world: The environment and the collapse of great civilizations.* New York: Penguin Books.

Selby, D. (2015). Thoughts from a darkened corner: Transformative learning for the gathering storm. In D. Selby & F. Kagawa (Eds.), *Sustainability frontiers: Critical and transformative voices from the borderlands of sustainability education.* Berlin: Barbara Budrich Publishers.

Selby, D., & Kagawa, F. (2015). Drawing threads together: A critical and transformative agenda for sustainability education. In D. Selby & F. Kagawa (Eds.), *Sustainability frontiers: Critical and transformative voices from the borderlands of sustainability education.* Berlin: Barbara Budrich Publishers.

Sörlin, S. (2012). Environmental humanities: Why should biologists interested in the environment take the humanities seriously? *BioScience Magazine, 62*(9), 789. https://doi.org/10.1525/bio.2012.62.9.2. Retrieved from www.jstor.org/stable/10.1525/bio.2012.62.9.2

Sterling, S. R. (2004). Higher education, sustainability, and the role of systemic learning. In P. Corcoran & A. Wals (Eds.), *Higher education and the challenge of sustainability.* Dordrecht: Kluwer Academic Publishers.

Tucker, M. E. (2014). Thomas Berry and the new story: An introduction to the work of Thomas Berry. In H. Eaton (Ed.), *The intellectual journey of Thomas Berry: Imagining the earth community.* Lanham, MD: Lexington Books.

Wals, A., & Blewitt, J. (2010). Third-wave sustainability in higher education: Some (inter) national trends and developments. In P. Jones, D. Selby, & S. Sterling (Eds.), *Sustainability education: Perspectives and practice across higher education.* New York: Earthscan.

5

'WAYS OF BEING FREE'

Finding 'pulses of freedom' in the border zone between higher and public education for sustainable development

Heila Lotz-Sisitka

Introduction

Education for Sustainable Development (ESD) in Higher Education has long been a subject of discussion (e.g. Sterling, 2010; Togo & Lotz-Sisitka, 2013; Baarth, Michelsen, Rieckmann, & Thomas, 2016), with an increasing number of arguments being put forward for transformative, and even transgressive (i.e. transgressing the taken for granted) learning in these contexts (Lotz-Sisitka, Wals, Kronlid, & McGarry, 2015). There is, however, as yet little theoretical or practical work that focuses on the border zone or *the interface between Higher Education and Public Education*, due perhaps to an overemphasis on internal change in Higher Education settings. Public Education brings sustainable development (SD) into everyday life focus (Von Poeck et al., 2012), as it is here that complex, 'wicked' problems (Rittel & Webber, 1973) are experienced. Such problems defy easy resolution. In this chapter I address this gap in the ESD literature by drawing on three cases of public education praxis in the border zone between Higher Education and Public Education: 1) using mobile learning tools to transform markets for small holder farmers; 2) building social learning networks that cross boundaries between colleges, farmers, and universities; and 3) using arts-based creative practice methods for public action. I start with these case stories, exploring them theoretically in order to illuminate new possibilities for ESD praxis in the sections that follow.

Cases of ESD that expand the imagination and transform praxis in the border zone between higher education and public education

The southern African cases that I share below emerge from work I am doing with a number of graduate researchers, educators, and community members in developing generative research designs and transgressive, transformative learning approaches for ESD (Lotz-Sisitka et al., 2015; Macintyre et al., 2018) in the border zone between university and community. The cases, amongst others, show how graduate researchers, educators, and community members (also referred to as 'publics' in this chapter) can collaborate via co-engaged research praxis to expand the imagination and transform praxis via learning processes emergent in open systems (www.transgressivelearning.org).

The motive to focus on southern African cases is not just geographical, but is also deeply contextual. Southern Africa has been identified as a region with high levels of vulnerability to climate change impacts (IPCC 2104). In this context, the sustainability debate is intertwined with ethics-led social-ecological justice efforts to address historical underdevelopment and poverty in ways that take sustainability into account (Ferguson, 2006). Carruthers (2006) explains environment and sustainability thinking in southern Africa as being deeply rooted in critiques of African dispossession, capitalist industrialization, the disruption of indigenous lifestyles, and African strategies of resistance to colonial and apartheid oppression. Ensuring viable sustainable livelihoods for communities and finding 'pulses of freedom' in the context of the contemporary institutional dynamics of the Sustainable Development Goals cannot be detached from this history.

In thinking about how to approach sustainable development and the SDGs in southern Africa, it may be easy to fall into the trap of defining them as 'needs' or 'living standards' that all should embrace and implement. However, Amartya Sen (2009) reminds us not to interpret the SDGs as 'needs' or as 'goals' removed from people – or as nature-based imperatives that separate humans from nature. He proposes that while we can recognize that people do have needs, ". . . *they also have values and, in particular, cherish their ability to reason, appraise, choose, participate and act*" (p. 250, my emphasis). He argues for an interpretation of sustainable development that expands the substantive freedoms and capabilities of people in ways that recognize the potential of humans as 'agents' whose "freedom to decide what we can value can extend far beyond our own interests and needs" (ibid). The point that he makes is important, as it centers the *process of expanding values and actions for sustainability* as *an agentive, freedom-oriented process*, not an imposed implementation process; see Dan McKanan's chapter in this volume for additional discussions of the crucial interrelationships of personal agency and sustainability. A process of sustainable development is impossible without giving attention to the emergence of valued beings and doings, imagination, and expansive learning processes that emerge in border zones, which I also refer to as 'pulses of freedom' after Bhaskar (2008), discussed further below.

Ben Okri, a renowned African poet and novelist, proposes that being free is intimately linked to our capacity for imagination. He argues that we all have imagination. The problem, he says "is with those who are frightened of the rather limitless validity of the imagination, frightened of people who continually extend the boundaries of the possible, people who ceaselessly redream the world and reinvent existence . . ." (1997, p. 2). What Okri does here in his inimitable way is propose a 'manifesto' for contemporary ESD, for surely it is the task of ESD educators to mobilize the imagination, to help us 'redream the world' and 'reinvent existence'. Mobilizing the imagination also needs philosophical and pedagogical guidance in exploring a diversity of open-ended possibilities, especially as we approach this task in Higher Education out of centuries of colonial intrusions and structuring. As Ben Okri says:

> *"The poet turns the earth into mother, the sky becomes a shelter, the sun an inscrutable god, and the pragmatists are irritated. They want the world to come with only one name, one form"*

(Okri, 1997, p. 2)

The three case studies briefly described below are each a case of expanding the imagination and engaging transformative praxis in ways proposed by Sen and Okri. As each case is extensive, and has been described in detail elsewhere, I concentrate mainly on illuminating some dimensions of the emerging pedagogical praxis in this border zone.

• **Case 1: Using mobile learning tools to transform markets for small holder farmers**
   (Durr, 2019; Durr & Lotz-Sisitka, 2019).

The first case study is of the Food for Us project in the Eastern Cape, South Africa (Ward, Jenkin, Durr, Swanepoel, & Lotz-Sisitka, 2019; www.foodforus. co.za), where ESD researchers sought to use the development of a mobile application for cell phones (hereafter referred to as an application) to transform markets for smallholder farmers, thus offering a mediating tool that could assist farmers to find alternative markets for their unsold and otherwise wasted produce. This project addresses a wider contradiction in that roughly 26% of South African households are food insecure (von Bormann et al., 2017), while 2.7 million tons of good food are lost a year to on-farm food waste (Oelofse, 2015). Important to this initiative as a Higher Education–Public Education border zone project was the emphasis on transformative social learning which enabled farmers and buyers on a landscape of practice to *learn* to use the application. This occurred through their participation in conceptualizing and using the application through two trial periods in which the technological affordances of the application were improved. While attention was being given to the technological affordances, equal attention was given to supporting the learning of members of the different social learning networks (farmers, buyers, and intermediary organizations) who were aiming to use the application. This involved supporting farmers in a series of informal training interactions; organizing social learning #matchmaking events among farmers, intermediary organizations, and buyers; and in-field practices aimed at supporting youth to learn the technological affordances of the application in order to support intergenerational learning in their communities.

Various kinds of value (Wenger, Trayner, & de Laat, 2011) were created for those participating in the project. These included immediate forms of value, such as improved knowledge and skills to use the mobile application and identify potential buyers for on-farm surplus produce; applied forms of value, which included using the social learning network for expanding transactions; and realized value, which included intergenerational learning. We found reframing value to be particularly interesting (Durr, 2019). Wenger et al. (2011) explain reframing value as the transformation capital that emerges where participants start to reimagine success based on previous cycles of value that emerge from a social learning process. Here we observed trial users starting to reframe how they imagined using technology as an effective mediating tool for furthering their agricultural or consumer businesses. Through improving their skills (potential value), applying their skills in the use of the application (applied value), and becoming more confident in mobile technology use (realized value), the users started to reimagine what mobile technology could do for them to address social, ecological, and economic dimensions of SD *at the same time* (Durr, 2019; Durr & Lotz-Sisitka, 2019). This case shows the way in which the valued beings and doings of people are interconnected with the formation of imagination and reframed value, which allow for both seeing and being differently. For ESD graduate scholars in higher education, and educators working with communities, this case indicates the need to give attention to how communities learn to use new technologies in ways that take cognizance of people's valued beings and doings.

- **Case 2: Building learning networks that cross boundaries between colleges, farmers, and universities**
  (Pesanayi, 2019; Lotz-Sisitka et al., 2016; Lotz-Sisitka &
  Pesanayi, 2019, cf. Pesanayi, this edition)

In the second case reported here, ESD researchers sought to work closely with farmers in a spatially bounded agricultural learning network around a key matter of concern to farmers, namely water for food production. The farmers in focus were small-scale farmers and household food producers in a rural area in the Eastern Cape, South Africa, who were given back their land in the post-apartheid period after 1994, but were not given adequate access to water, as expressed in the statements below from local farmers.

Farmer 1: "In my village I do have enough water, but we have to pay for it. The problem we are having is that to get a water license we have to pay, also for water pumps and diesel which is expensive. I would like to have visible water harvesting practices in my garden".
Farmer 2: "We suffer from water cut offs".
Farmer 3: "We have low rainfall and currently we don't know the methods of cultivating with rain water . . . I want to learn more about rainwater harvesting techniques to more effectively harvest water".

To address this problem, a local learning network was formed which involved multiple actors: Higher Education graduate scholars and lecturers, farmers, the local economic development office, government extension services, and a local farmers' association. They gathered initially to deliberate their water for food problem, but discussion was not enough. Graduate scholars and academics working in the network co-designed a range of mediation processes with other learning network members over a period of four years. The network structure provided the border zone for this co-engaged interaction. The mediation processes included a training of trainers' course on rainwater harvesting and conservation practices, change laboratories involving development of productive demonstration sites by multi-actors, hosting of regular social learning network meetings, ongoing use of social media, including WhatsApp and community radio, and college curriculum development (Pesanayi, 2019; Lotz-Sisitka & Pesanayi, 2019). Over time, the learning network expanded to include a wider diversity and range of actors in the local agricultural learning system, showing an increase in participation from government departments, smaller enterprises, and cooperatives and smaller development organizations. This showed the local agricultural learning system to be richly textured, with potential for expanding co-learning among the learning network members. From the initial knowledge of only three rainwater harvesting practices in 2014, the learning network is now working with over ten different rainwater harvesting practices, which community members are demonstrating to each other. Students in the local college, previously disconnected from the farmers, are now regularly working with farmers on development of productive demonstration sites that integrate water harvesting knowledge with knowledge of seed-saving and agro-ecology principles and practices. The students respond to farmers' requests for on-site support for special field-based actions (e.g. planting, digging furrows, mulching, etc.) and with their lecturers' support, they are able to use these experiences for practical learning. This case provides evidence of emerging valued beings and doings, reframed value around people's matters of concern, and the widening of imagination driving new ways of seeing and being. This is resulting in greater food security and a wider range of options for farmers as they seek to address their core matter of concern, which is to feed their families and expand their production systems in sustainable ways, thus addressing social, economic, and ecological dimensions of sustainability *at the same time*. It is also offering students real-world practical engagements in community.

- **Case study 3: Using suitably strange arts–based creative practices for public pedagogy action**

(McGarry, 2013, 2016, 2019)

The third case study involves graduate researchers working with various members of the public on developing their reflexivity around climate change and other wicked problems in times of 'ecological apartheid' (McGarry, 2013). The learning processes that have been emerging in the border zone between Higher Education and Public Education in this case are based on a concept of 'immersive empathy' (McGarry, 2013, 2016) in which artists and scientists engage empathetically with members of the public creatively around their matters of concern. At one end of the spectrum, is an extensive engagement with members of the public using a social sculpture[1] approach called 'earth forum', developed collaboratively with Sacks and other co-researchers (McGarry, 2013) in 17 South African towns across the country on a 'climate listening train' (McGarry, 2016). The social sculpture creative practices on the Listening Train (ibid) were inspired by Joseph Beuys (2004), whose work similarly engaged publics around complex issues in need of transformation. In the case of the Listening Train, publics were engaged over 44 days in a variety of spaces and sites around the country *en route* to the Climate Change Conference of the Parties (COP 17) hosted in Durban in 2012, evoking activism and reflexivity (see McGarry, 2016, 2013).

At the other end of the spectrum in scale, but equivalent in impact, is a small-scale, local, week-long social sculpture activity hosted at Rhodes University where the unusual or 'suitably strange' (McGarry, 2019; see also www.uncan nyjustness.org) practice of an e-waste funeral was developed to engage university students, staff members, and members of the wider community in addressing the issue of e-waste on campus and in the wider community. Researcher Dylan McGarry describes this pedagogical practice as follows:

> *The scene is macabrely familiar a gathering of black-clad mourners, hats and sunglasses to hide the tears, a circle of chairs, flowers, an altar and the dead resting quietly before the mourners, the eulogy begins:*
>
>> *"This is a funeral, a funeral for the electronic extensions of our humanity. We are here today to stay with the troubling reality of the mass-grave-mountain of discarded electronic technology that grows here on campus, and around the world. Those laptops, those PCs, those Casio calculators that stayed up late with us before every deadline, our confidants and coaches for so many years of our lives . . . The hair dryers that dried us, the fans that cooled us and the kilometers of extension cords that connected us to this global electrical rhizome. Today we honor their role in shaping our society and our culture"*
>
> *The recent "E-waste funeral" encouraged students, staff and visitors to 'redream the world' through becoming 'pallbearers' to dead e-waste on and around the Rhodes University campus for a week. Each day they shouldered the burden of other people's waste, carrying old computers and keyboards to meetings and lectures, a process of absenting the absence of waste that is so taken for granted. At the funeral reflexive enquires in their personal experiences as consumers and waste producers were revealed. Pallbearers were confronted by their engagement with the bodies they carried, and critically examined their relational entanglement into the complexity of waste in Africa, and in their personal lives*
>
> (McGarry, pers. comm, 2019).

Reflecting a similar commitment to supporting people's engagement with complex, wicked sustainability issues via emergent public learning in the border zone between Higher Education and Public Education as the other two case studies, but using a different style of public engagement, these practices also supported people to articulate their most intimate, valued beings and doings in ways that cultivated imagination for change. McGarry describes the outcomes of the initiative as follows: "A relational connection that vastly expanded the normative subject/object dualisms within the funeral party emerged. From here, discussions around consumption of technology, hacking, and reclaiming agency of technology that controls us, and recognizing the intimate relationality we have with technology emerged in the different eulogies" (pers. comm, 2019). This led to the university finding alternative, safe recycling options for its massive e-waste pile up, previously just stored in a big warehouse. As stated by McGarry, "The e-waste funeral was not merely an environmental awareness campaign, nor was it a publicity stunt, but rather a deep social learning process that was aimed at facilitating an embodied arts-based approach to learning in complex contexts around complex nexus problems" (ibid). McGarry reflects, "The funeral was the most recent incarnation of a decade of public pedagogy action through creative praxis in South Africa and beyond" (ibid, see also www.uncannyjustness.org).[2]

ESD, expanding the imagination and finding ways of 'being free'

In this section I consider the theoretical foundations of these and other case examples of pedagogical praxis that are emerging in our research program in the border zone between Higher Education and Public Education. I argue that to interpret the interface between wicked problems and Higher Education, there is need for well-founded theoretical perspectives for forms of transformative social learning in ESD that both expand the imagination and develop transformative praxis in border zone areas and open systems. This argument emerges from the examples outlined above (and others developed in our research program over more than twenty years), but also from a recent review of critical theory's influence in Higher Education for Sustainable Development (Lotz-Sisitka, 2016a), in which I noted that despite three generations of critical theory, we are still left with inadequate methodological and conceptual tools to expand human agency for change in our educational work.

To develop a theoretical framework for ESD praxis in the border zone between Higher Education and Public Education, I have drawn on work in the field of literature (Ben Okri), and development theory (Amartya Sen) – see above. The work is also inspired by cultural psychology (Yrjö Engeström) and emancipatory philosophy (Roy Bhaskar) – see below – which helps develop an argument for expansive, open-process pedagogies that allow for the emergence of dialectical 'pulses of freedom' in open systems at the interface of Higher and Public ESD.

Deepening insight into what was going on in the case studies, Bhaskar's (2008) dialectical critical realist philosophy revises positivism and hermeneutics to offer a non-anthropocentric theory of emergence in open systems in which he articulates situated, dialectical 'pulses of freedom' to be at the heart of emancipation and change. He describes *learning* as the nexus of this dialectical process, and 'pulses of freedom' as those moments where people are able to claim their agency for change in ways that are valued by them personally, but also more widely by society. Bhaskar's argument is that via learning, and by implication via public pedagogies and ESD research engagements, we can actively 'absent absences' (Lotz-Sisitka, 2016b) in open, creative learning processes involving depth enquiries (e.g. farmers and buyers analyzing their market and food surplus problems; or farmers analyzing their water for food problems; or publics analyzing their e-waste problems); immanent critiques (in which publics and researchers critically probe the problems in more depth); and the redreaming and reinventing of existence at multiple levels and in diverse ways (i.e. by finding ways out of the problematic situations via co-learning), including ways that allow for border crossing between Higher and Public Education, as the three case studies all show to be possible. In a similar way, Yrjö Engeström's (2016) extensive body of work out of cultural psychology and learning theory offers the concept of expansive learning, or learning 'what is not yet there'.

As shown by the three case studies, such processes are not fantasy, or fantastical, but occur in the 'tensed socio-temporal spaces' of lives lived where collective transformative agency pathways can be opened up by co-learning, engaged deliberations, experience, and openness to events and the co-creation of new forms of human activity where subject-object dualisms merge in relational connection. My case studies and analysis of them are comparable to Dan McKanan's work, described in this volume, of bringing graduate students, farmers, and residents of Camphill communities into dialogue regarding shared and different experiences of work and sustainability. The relational connection that I have explored in this chapter is the ESD connection which exists between Higher Education and Public Education (Burdick, Sandlin, & O'Malley, 2014). Building such a relational connection requires crossing boundaries (Akkerman & Bakker, 2011) between formal learning and informal learning settings. Many arguments from ESD research communities have been put forward for transformative learning in Higher Education in response to sustainability challenges (e.g. Baarth et al., 2016; Lotz-Sisitka et al., 2015). Public Education has been identified as an emerging arena for environmental education/ESD praxis, for it is a space where wicked problems are engaged, and where the complexity of enabling and achieving sustainability can potentially be realized via multi-actor engagements (Von Poeck et al., 2012) and via boundary-crossing learning processes (Sol & Wals, 2015). Higher Education, as shown in the case studies, can be intimately engaged in such boundary-crossing learning processes, and through this, transform both its own pedagogical praxis, and that of public education.

Conclusion: finding and enabling the 'pulses of freedom' to transform our world(s)

Based on the case studies and the theoretical deliberations above, I propose that Bhaskar's notion of 'pulses of freedom' can be an important process frame for capturing and enhancing ESD theory and praxis. It involves imagination, criticality, dialogue, values deliberation, and co-learning in engaged, situated processes in and with public/community settings, as was outlined in the three case studies and the theoretical argument above. To provide guidance for the use of ESD pedagogies in such border zones, I can recommend the following broad process framework that can be applied variously to lesson planning and/or program design (captured in Figure 5.1 below):

- Take care to identify wicked problems *with people* as these affect their lives lived; this involves careful listening, contextual profiling, and co-engagement with diverse actors in local settings.
- These wicked problems can be helpfully framed as 'matters of concern' (Latour, 2004) that involve not only people's concerns, but also concerns associated with environmental well-being, reflecting the intimate relations that exist between people and plants, water, carbon, and technologies that they create (as shown in the three case studies, amongst others). Identifying absences that can be absented (Bhaskar, 2008; Lotz-Sisitka, 2016b) is also helpful (e.g. the absence of a suitable communication system between producers and consumers in Case 1).
- From here, there is need to co-develop interactive and participatory public pedagogical processes that vary from setting to setting and may involve

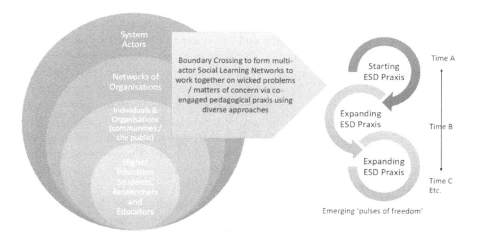

FIGURE 5.1 Expanding the scope of ESD to the border zone of Higher Education and Public Education via Social Learning Networks and Expanding ESD Praxis over time

(but are not limited to) use of mobile technologies (Durr, 2019), productive demonstration sites, training programs applied in context (Pesanayi, 2019), suitably strange creative practices (e.g. e-waste funerals), empathy and imaginative social sculptures (McGarry, 2013, 2016, 2019), and more. Each setting and matter of concern will lend itself to varied pedagogical processes, as shown in the cases. Importantly, these are not pre-scripted, but are rather co-engaged and emergent in context around responses to the matters of concern.

- Give enough time to consider people's valued beings and doings – at the start of the process, but also as the boundary-crossing processes unfold, and try to reflexively review how these change over time. As shown in the case studies, reframed value emerges, and people's valued beings and doings change as they mobilize their commitments, relationships, agency, and capacity to act.

- Be open to expansive learning, to learning 'what is not yet there' as advised by Engeström (2016). This kind of learning is not just individual (i.e. involving cognitive or emotional gains), but it is collective and social, involving co-defining and co-creating new forms of activity together (e.g. finding solutions to e-waste problems or food system problems) (ibid; Sannino et al., 2016). When these are oriented towards shared ethical commitments for the common good, these can also be seen as being transformative or transgressive of the norm (Lotz-Sisitka et al., 2017).

- Finally, consider these changes as 'pulses of freedom' (Bhaskar, 2008) that allow people to ethically and collectively chart new ways of imagining the world, but also of re-enacting the world in ways that are less destructive, more benign, and more sustainable and socially just.

There is increased awareness of the importance of boundary-crossing learning processes and learning in boundary zones between Higher Education and Public Education, but as yet, there is inadequate exploration of how such learning processes mobilize imagination and transformative praxis (Blackmore et al., 2011), and how these give rise to, and emerge from, collective expressions of transformative agency (Sannino et al., 2016), understood here to mean the collective capacity to change activity or practice. Transformation of human activity via processes of expansive learning, as outlined in the case studies above and in the work of Engeström (2016) and Engeström and Sannino (2010), implies change and movement in terms of imagination, properties, and relationships, and is triggered by agentive forces, including volition or will (Engeström & Sannino, 2010; Sannino et al., 2016). Individual agency involves the will and capacity to act upon situations towards a purpose (Sibeon, 1999, referred to in Lewis, 2002), while collective agency involves groups of people who agree to use their collective capacity to act upon situations towards a common purpose (Emirbayer, 1997). Through relational and ethically framed encounters, people can produce new "relational goods" (Donati & Archer, 2015) which are more than the sum of the individual actors' contributions (ibid). Engeström and Sannino (2010) state that transformative agency is the most important outcome of expansive learning, especially in situations of complex change. It is about 'learning what is not yet there' for both university students and scholars, and the public and communities they can engage with (Engeström, 2016).

Linked to the argument of Sen (2009), Roy Bhaskar's (2008) approach to emancipation and agency offers ways of thinking about such forms of transformative agency. He explains that agency is an experiential, embodied process of transformative change, which involves people who have traditionally and historically been subjugated by oppressive power relations, transforming those power relations through new forms of imagination, volition, and activity (praxis), which potentially produce better living conditions or choices. Such transformations, Bhaskar (ibid.) argues, take place as a "tensed spatio-temporalising process"; i.e. in the world with people present, in simple or more complex time-space configurations where various social-ecological conditions, cultural histories, ethical possibilities, and power relations are present, as shown in the case studies above.

It is here that 'pulses of freedom' can emerge, and following Engeström and Sannino's arguments (2010), education and pedagogical praxis have an important role to play *if* generatively oriented in open systems. It is the emergence of such 'pulses of freedom' that I have sought to briefly illuminate in the three case studies, in order to point to potential for ESD praxis and the constituting of transformative learning pedagogies in the border zone between Higher and Public ESD.

Acknowledgements

In this paper I particularly wish to acknowledge the work of Sarah Durr, Tichaona Pesanayi, and Dylan McGarry whose ESD post-graduate and post-doctoral scholarly research work I have referred to in the three case studies. The three cases are among many others that I have supervised and worked along with, and which I could also have surfaced save for space. I also wish therefore to acknowledge the many other scholars whom I have worked with on similar emergent, transformative pedagogical praxis processes over the years at the Environmental Learning Research Centre at Rhodes University and more recently in the NRF/ DST South African National Research Chair in Global Change and Social Learning Systems that I hold, which I also acknowledge. The work here also contributes to the International Science Council's Transformations to Sustainability Research Programme focusing on 'Transgressive Learning in Times of Climate Change', which I led from 2016–2019.

Notes

1 Social sculpture is an expanded conception of sculpture and public art, engaging citizens in participatory social processes facilitated around a single connective aesthetic, i.e. a sculpture, an artifact, or a curated space/installation. The term social sculpture was originally coined by Joseph Beuys (Beuys, 2004). What is Art? In V. Harlan (Ed.) (2004). Joseph Beuys, What is Art?. East Sussex: Clairview Books.)

2 This body of work forms part of a growing practice-based public pedagogy research initiative incubating at the Environmental Learning Research Centre (Rhodes University) called 'The Institute of Uncanny Justness: Re-Imagining Learning, Activism and

Justice Through Suitably Strange Creative Practice' (www.uncannyjustness.org) led by McGarry and an expanding team of researchers.

References

Akkerman, S. F., & Bakker, A. (2011). Boundary crossing and boundary objects. *Review of Educational Research*, *81*(2), 132–169.

Baarth, M., Michelsen, G., Rieckmann, M., & Thomas, I. (2016). *Routledge handbook of higher education research for sustainable development*. London: Routledge.

Beuys, J. (2004). What is art? In V. Harlan (Ed.), *Joseph Beuys, what is art?* East Sussex: Clairview Books.

Bhaskar, R. (2008). *Dialectic: The pulse of freedom*. London: Routledge.

Blackmore, C., Chabay, I., Collins, K., Gutscher, H., Lotz-Sisitka, H. B., McCauley, S. . . . van Eijndhoven, J. (2011). *Knowledge, learning, and societal change: Finding paths to a sustainable future: Science plan for a cross-cutting core project of the International Human Dimensions Programme on Global Environmental Change (IHDP)*. Berne: IHDP. Retrieved 30 August 2017 from www.ihdp.unu.edu/docs/Publications/KLSC/KLSC%20FINAL%20Science%20Plan%2004.09.11.pdf

Burdick, J., Sandlin, J., & O'Malley, M. (2014). *Problematizing public pedagogy*. London: Routledge.

Carruthers, J. (2006, October). Tracking in game trails: Looking afresh at the politics of environmental history in South Africa. *Environmental History*, *11*, 804–829.

Donati, P., & Archer, M. (2015). *The relational subject*. Cambridge: Cambridge University Press.

Durr, S. (2019). *How can the introduction of a farmer-buyer based mobile application enable social learning to stimulate value creation towards a circular economy?* Unpublished Masters in Education Dissertation, Rhodes University Environmental Learning Research Centre, Grahamstown, South Africa.

Durr, S., & Lotz-Sisitka, H. (2019). *Exploring the social learning value enabled by affordances of the Food for Us mobile application: A South African food redistribution app case study*. Paper prepared for the International Mobile Education Conference, Utrecht, March 2019. Environmental Learning Research Centre, Rhodes University, South Africa.

Emirbayer, M. (1997). Manifesto for a relational sociology. *American Journal of Sociology*, *103*(2), 281–317.

Engeström, Y. (2016). *Studies in expansive learning: Learning what is not yet there*. New York: Cambridge University Press.

Engeström, Y., & Sannino, A. (2010). Studies of expansive learning: Foundations, findings and future challenges. *Educational Research Review*, *5*(1), 1–24.

Ferguson, J. (2006). *Global shadows: Africa in the neo-liberal world order*. Durham, NC and London: Duke University Press.

Intergovernmental Panel on Climate Change (IPCC). (2014). *Climate change 2014: Impacts, adaptation, vulnerability*. Cambridge: Cambridge University Press.

Latour, B. (2004). *Politics of nature: How to bring the sciences into democracy*. Cambridge, MA: Harvard University Press.

Lewis, P. A. (2002). Agency, structure and causality in political science: A comment on Sibeon. *Politics*, *22*(1), 17–23.

Lotz-Sisitka, H. B. (2016a). A Review of three generations of critical theory: Towards reconceptualsing critical HESD research. In M. Baarth, G. Michelsen, M. Rieckmann, & I. Thomas (Eds.), *Routledge handbook of higher education research for sustainable development* (pp. 207–222). London: Routledge.

Lotz-Sisitka, H. B. (2016b). Absenting absence: Expanding zones of proximal develop-ment in environmental learning processes. In L. Price & H. B. Lotz-Sisitka (Eds.), *Critical realism, environmental learning and social-ecological change* (pp. 318–339). London: Routledge.

Lotz-Sisitka, H. B., Mukute, M., Chikunda, C., Baloi, A., & Pesanayi, T. (2017). Trans-gressing the norm: Transformative agency in community-based learning for sustain-ability in Southern African contexts. *International Review of Education, 63*(6): 897–914. http://doi.org/10.1007/s11159-017-9689-3

Lotz-Sisitka, H. B., & Pesanayi, T. (2019, February). *Mediation processes to support systems approaches to knowledge flow in water for food social learning networks.* Paper submitted to the Water Research Commission.

Lotz-Sisitka, H. B., Pesanayi, T., Weaver, K., Lupele, C., Sisitka, L., O'Donoghue, R. . . . Phillips, K. (2016). *Water use and food security: Knowledge dissemination and use in agricul-tural colleges and local learning networks for home food gardening and smallholder agriculture. Vol-ume 1: Research and development report.* WRC Research Report No. 2277/1/16. Pretoria: Water Research Commission.

Lotz-Sisitka, H. B., Wals, A. E. J., Kronlid, D., & McGarry, D. (2015). Transforma-tive, transgressive social learning: Rethinking higher education pedagogy in times of systemic global dysfunction. *Current Opinion in Environmental Sustainability, 16*, 73–80.

Macintyre, T., Lotz-Sisitka, H., Wals, A., Vogel, C., & Tassone, V. (2018). Towards transformative social learning on the path to 1.5 degrees. *Current Opinion in Environ-mental Sustainability, 31*, 80–87. https://doi.org/10.1016/j.cosust.2017.12.003

McGarry, D. (2013). *Empathy in times of ecological apartheid. A social sculpture practice-led inquiry into developing pedagogies for ecological citizenship.* Unpublished PhD Thesis, Envi-ronmental Learning Research Centre, Rhodes University, South Africa.

McGarry, D. (2016). The listening train: A collaborative, connective aesthetics approach to transgressive social learning. *Southern African Journal of Environmental Education, 31*(1), 8–21. www.ajol.info/index.php/sajee/article/view/137658/127221

McGarry, D. (2019). *Personal communication narrative on the e-waste funeral.* Rhodes Univer-sity Environmental Learning Research Centre, Rhodes University.

Oelofse, S. (2015). *Food waste in SA – The magnitude, cost and impacts.* Presented at the SAAFoST Lecture. Retrieved from www.saafost.org.za/Events/BRANCH_Northern/2014/Mar27/Food%20waste%20SAAFost%20Lecture.pdf

Okri, B. (1997). *A way of being free.* Nairobi, Kenya: Phoenix Publishers.

Pesanayi, T. (2019). *Boundary crossing expansive learning across agricultural learning systems and networks in southern Africa.* Unpublished PhD Thesis, Environmental Learning Research Centre, Rhodes University, South Africa.

Rittel, H. W., & Webber, M. M. (1973). Dilemmas in a general theory of planning. *Policy Sciences, 4*(2), 155–169.

Sannino, A., Engeström, Y., & Lemos, M. (2016). Formative interventions for expansive learning and transformative agency. *Journal of the Learning Sciences, 25*(4), 599–633.

Sibeon, R. (1999). Agency, Structure, and Social Chance as Cross-Disciplinary Concepts. *Politics, 19*(3), 139–144.

Sen, A. (2009). *The idea of justice.* Cambridge, MA: Bleknap Press of Harvard University Press.

Sol, J., & Wals, A. E. (2015). Strengthening ecological mindfulness through hybrid learning in vital coalitions. *Cultural Studies of Science Education, 10*(1), 203–214.

Sterling, S. (2010). *Sustainability education: Perspectives and practice across higher education.* London: Taylor & Francis.

Togo, M., & Lotz-Sisitka, H. (2013). Exploring a systems approach to mainstreaming sustainability in universities: A case study of Rhodes University in South Africa. *Environmental Education Research Journal, 19*(5), 673–693. ISSN: 1350–4622.

Von Bormann, T., de Vries, L., Jenkin, N., Tian, N., Modau, I., Pillay, P. . . . Notten, P. (2017). *Food loss and waste: Facts and futures: Taking steps towards a more sustainable food future.* Cape Town, South Africa: World Wide Fund for Nature South Africa.

von Poeck, K., & Vandenabeele, J. (2012). Education for sustainable development in the light of public issues. *Environmental Education Research, 18*, 541–552.

Ward, M., Jenkin, N., Durr, S., Swanepoel, S., & Lotz-Sisitka, H. B. (2019). *Reducing food waste, supporting social learning, creating value.* Food for Us report. Retrieved from www.foodforus.co.za

Wenger, E., Trayner, B., & de Laat, M. (2011). Promoting and assessing value creation in communities and networks: A conceptual framework (April). *Ruud de Moor Centrum, 18*. Retrieved from www.open.ou.nl/rslmlt/Wenger_Trayner_DeLaat_Value_creation.pdf

6

SUSTAINABILITY EDUCATION

From farms and intentional communities to the university

Dan McKanan

About once a year, I bring graduate students from Harvard University to visit biodynamic farms, ecovillages, and social therapeutic communities in rural New England or New York. Some of these places are sites of ethnographic field work for me. I have written extensively on the biodynamic movement in agriculture and on the Camphill movement (McKanan, 2007, 2016, 2017, under review). Biodynamic agriculture is one of the first movements in the West to reject chemical fertilizers and pesticides on principle; it also seeks to treat each farm as a living organism and to enlist cosmic forces through alchemical and homeopathic practices. Camphill is a network of one hundred intentional communities where people with and without intellectual disabilities live and work cooperatively. Both biodynamics and Camphill grow out of the teachings of Rudolf Steiner (1861–1925), whose anthroposophical movement also provides the foundation for Waldorf education and other practical initiatives that seek to unite spirit and matter. When students visit the places I study, they enhance my research by sharing observations, questions, and critiques that may disrupt my assumptions and too-hasty conclusions. But my students and I are not the only ones engaged in learning during these site visits. Many of the people we meet are apprentices in training to become biodynamic farmers, young people with disabilities seeking a meaningful life path, or Camphill volunteers pursuing a community-based undergraduate degree. Like my students, these idealistic young people are engaged in sustainability education, but within a very different curricular framework than that offered at Harvard. These encounters challenge all of us to create what I will call a third learning space. This is a place of learning that is equally distinct from Harvard, Camphill, and the biodynamic farm, and that allows participants from all of these sites to build relationships of mutual growth.

For me, sustainability education includes any practice that empowers participants to *think* clearly about the relationships connecting the members of the

Earth community, *feel* themselves fully a part of the interconnected web of life, and *act* in ways that foster biodiversity. Sustainability education thus requires, as Heila Lotz-Sisitka (in this volume) and Amartya Sen (2009) insist, that every person be recognized as an agent who wishes to "reason, appraise, choose, participate, and act." Within this framework, encounters among Harvard students, biodynamic apprentices, and Camphillers provide unique opportunities to address two complex sustainability problems: the social and economic decline of rural communities, and the loss of opportunities for meaningful, life-sustaining work, especially for U.S. Americans born after 1980. These problems are both social and ecological. A declining rural population is less able to choose farming practices that contribute to biodiversity, and an urban population without purposeful work is apt to seek meaning in unsustainable habits of consumption. Working together, the rising generation has an opportunity to revitalize rural communities and reimagine work for themselves and others.

Diverse curricula for sustainability education

Biodynamic farms, Camphill communities, and Harvard Divinity School offer contrasting and potentially complementary models of sustainability education. Apprentices at Hawthorne Valley Farm in Harlemville, New York, are part of an interdependent social organism that seeks to "nurture the land that nurtures us" by maintaining a farm, a Waldorf School, and a panoply of adult education and holistic research programs (Hawthorne Valley Farm, 2016/2017). Whole Farm Apprentices rotate among the farm's different areas, learning about livestock management, dairying, field crops, and vegetable gardening, as well as the spiritual philosophy underlying biodynamics and the economic principles of community supported agriculture (Hawthorne Valley Farm, 2018). They also participate in the North American Biodynamic Apprenticeship Program, which combines classroom and on-farm experiences in a comprehensive, two-year curriculum.

A short drive from Hawthorne Valley, Triform Camphill Community in Hudson, New York, offers a college-like experience for young adults with intellectual disabilities. Triform promises to help its students "discover their unique potential and graduate ready to embark on the next stage of their life's journey with confidence." Their methods for achieving this goal include family-style home life, a rotation of agricultural and artistic work experiences, classroom-based learning, holistic therapies that engage body, soul, and spirit, and a rich cycle of annual festivals (Triform, 2018).

Other Camphill communities work with adults, elders, and children with intellectual disabilities. At almost every Camphill community in North America, the young "coworkers" (that is, those who do not have special support needs) may pursue a bachelor's degree through the immersive curriculum offered by Camphill Academy. The Academy's "path of transformative learning" begins with a "foundation year" that introduces participants to anthroposophy, the spiritual philosophy underlying Camphill and biodynamics. Over the next three years, they specialize in "curative education" (work with children with special support needs) or "social therapy" (work with adults with special support needs). A fifth year of distance learning courses offered by Prescott College, SUNY Empire State College, or Excelsior College allows them to complete the bachelor's degree. Ultimately, the Academy promises its students that it will allow "you to unfold your potential to contribute to the healing of the human being, society and the earth" (Camphill Academy, 2018a, 2018b).

Harvard Divinity School, for its part, identifies as "a nonsectarian school of religious and theological studies" that prepares students for scholarly careers or "leadership in religious, governmental, and a wide range of service organizations." Two- or three-year master's degrees feature small classes oriented to close reading of challenging texts and rigorous questioning of both religious and academic presuppositions, as well as field placements in religious and nonprofit organizations (Harvard Divinity School, 2018).

The differences among these curricular approaches can be fruitful. When students pursuing different sustainability curricula meet one another, they may ask new questions and consider new possibilities for transformation. This is why Camphill Academy fosters dialogue among students at different Camphills, as well as with classmates at the three partner colleges. Likewise, Hawthorne Valley works with neighboring farms to offer its students brief encounters with other modes of farming. There is even more transformative potential in a dialogue that includes the relatively conventional curriculum of Harvard Divinity School, for Harvard students bring the critical skills needed to get to the root of ecological problems, while the more experiential models empower students to imagine themselves as part of the solution. A third learning space that includes all these models may reveal creative solutions to rural decline and the loss of meaningful work.

Two pressing problems

By *rural decline*, I refer to the depopulation and political abandonment experienced by rural communities in the United States and around the world. The share of the United States population living on farms and in farm communities has declined steadily for more than a century. Food prices have fallen as a result, but much soil has been lost and many ecosystems have been degraded. Agricultural methods that maximize biodiversity and minimize energy and chemical inputs are inherently labor intensive, and thus hard to sustain within a capitalist economy that puts profit first. More recently, one political party in the United States has abandoned rural communities in favor of the diverse metropolises that attract talented young people, while the other party peddles nativism and white supremacy under the guise of rural populism. Sustainability students in both settings are implicated in this pattern. Those who study at mainstream universities contribute to the concentration of progressive voices in liberal cities. Biodynamic

TABLE 6.1 Four Sites of Sustainability Education

	Harvard Divinity School	Camphill Youth Guidance Communities	Camphill Academy	Biodynamic Apprenticeships
		Four Sites of Sustainability Education		
Who?	Students of ages 21–70+ from a wide range of religious and academic traditions	Young adults of ages 18 to 30 with special support needs	Mostly young adults ages 18 to 30	Students of all ages
Where?	Cambridge, MA	Camphill Triform in New York, Camphill Soltane in Pennsylvania, and other locations around the world	Camphill communities throughout North America that support children, young adults, adults, and elders with special support needs	Hawthorne Valley Farm and many other locations around the world
What?	Master of Divinity and Master of Theological Arts programs with a rigorous, fairly traditional pedagogy and opportunities for field education	Holistic curriculum with classroom, home, workshop, and therapeutic elements	Community-based Bachelor of Arts curriculum in social therapy or curative education	Farm-based curriculum with a classroom component and site visits to multiple farms
Summary	"Illuminate. Engage. Serve."	"Living – Working – Growing Together"	"Study within the context of community living"	"Get to know biodynamics from the inside out"
For more information. . . .	https://hds.harvard.edu/	http://triform.org/	http://camphill.edu/	www.biodynamics.com/farmer-training

farms and Camphill communities offer an appealing model for the re-population of rural America, but still struggle to frame a vision for this re-population that appeals to young people of all races and classes, instead of catering mostly to professional-class whites who have less to lose if the agrarian vision proves financially unsustainable. By *thinking* together about the rural divide, students in both settings can begin to *feel* their interconnectedness and *act* in ways that help bridge the divide.

By the *loss of work*, I refer to the decline in meaningful and sustainable job opportunities, as automation and artificial intelligence eliminate the need for human labor in one field after another. These changes make it more difficult to attain the Earth Charter's aspiration for "social and economic justice, enabling all to achieve a secure and meaningful livelihood that is ecologically responsible." (I.3.b) Farm communities were among the first casualties of this transformation, as were the developmentally disabled individuals who live in Camphill communities. As a consequence, biodynamic farms and Camphill communities have long sought modes of human creativity and purposefulness that can be sustained outside the framework of a capitalist economy. Mainstream universities, by contrast, are still wedded to the proposition that ever-higher levels of formal education will allow a privileged few to continue deriving their identity and purpose from paid work. This pressing social problem can be addressed most effectively in the context of a sustainability paradigm in which meaningful work fosters biodiversity and honors the interconnectedness of life.

From rural decline to revitalization

Rural decline touches students at Harvard, Hawthorne Valley, and Camphill where they live. The farm apprentices and Camphillers may or may not be originally from rural America, but they live there now. They know farmers who struggle to find a just price for agricultural products in the global market, and who mourn their failure to persuade their own children to continue family traditions of farming. They know neighbors, including nonresidential employees of Camphill and Hawthorne Valley, who have struggled to find work within chronically depressed economies. If they are both young and single, they may be painfully aware of just how few young adults still live in rural America. And if they "go into town" for a movie during election season, they are reminded by ubiquitous lawn signs of the populist and xenophobic politicians favored by many rural residents.

The Harvard students, meanwhile, are immersed in the cultural ferment of a cosmopolitan city with world-class universities, a growing biotechnology industry, quirky urban festivals, and perilously high rents. They may perceive rural America as hostile and dangerous, with good reason. The Harvard Divinity School community is religiously and culturally diverse, with a high percentage of queer and transgender students and several who are undocumented immigrants. All our students have friends who have experienced violence or discrimination because of their religion, race, or gender identity, and they rightly wonder what it is that inspires so many rural voters to support policies who stigmatize people.

An ethic of care for rural and urban communities

Relationship building is the first step toward rural revitalization. Few urban and suburban Americans know anything about the people who grow their food. Rural Americans' images of urban life may be colored by Hollywood images of decadent excess; they may have little feel for the real dangers that have led many immigrants, people of color, and queer and transgender people to concentrate in the cities. But an ethic of care can bridge the rural-urban divide when people hear one another's stories at first hand, and thus learn to feel their interconnectedness.

Each group of students brings important learning tools to the dialogue. For Camphill Academy students, relationship building is already a central part of the curriculum, and many have developed collaborative projects either with one another or with persons with special support needs. At the 2018 Camphill Research Symposium, for example, several Camphill Academy students shared art projects that they had created in partnership with one of the persons they had helped support. Biodynamic apprentices can testify to the unique economic challenges of farm country. Harvard students, for their part, may bring some relevant critical vocabulary to the conversation. Many are devoted to the "queer theory" of Judith Butler and other contemporary philosophers, which explores how hegemonic structures of patriarchy and heteronormativity shape individual subjectivities (Butler, 1990). Within the study of religion, queer theory is often applied to aspects of identity other than sexuality, equipping Harvard students to reflect on the formation of "rural subjectivities," "disabled subjectivities," "farm subjectivities," and the like. Similarly, many of my students have learned from my colleagues Todne Thomas and Cornel West about the religious consequences of neoliberalism, or the ideology that views all human experience through the lens of the marketplace (Day, 2015; Harvey, 2007; Johnson, 2016). This positions them for an interesting conversation with Camphillers who may have been introduced to Rudolf Steiner's "threefold" social theory, according to which a healthy society must distinguish and nurture the cultural, political, and economic spheres (Lamb, 2016; Steiner, 2000).

The gathering of Camphillers, farm apprentices, and Harvard students that I envision may not be a perfect venue for rural-urban dialogue, insofar as some members of each group are only temporary sojourners in their respective contexts. For this reason, it might be valuable to invite individuals who are long-term residents of the surrounding community to join the conversation; these might be neighbors who are employed by Camphill or Hawthorne Valley, or persons with special support needs who have chosen to live at Camphill because of its proximity to their hometowns.

Resilience and regeneration in the rural landscape

Rural communities are already home to small-scale revitalization projects, and students in both groups can build knowledge and skills for resilient and regenerative action by getting to know these projects better. Farmers' markets and community supported agriculture are two of the most visible practices that currently build bridges between rural and urban America, and it is likely that several dialogue participants will already be engaged in these ventures as producers or consumers. In the past, I have occasionally brought students to the farm where I personally have a CSA share. What I have not done is to ask them to reflect in advance on their own experience and values as consumers of food. Do they shop at farmers' markets and CSAs and, if so, how has their relationship to rural America changed? Do they experience these projects as genuine bridges to rural America, or as venues for hipster virtue signaling that exacerbate the divide between urbanites who can afford farmers' markets and rural residents who must shop at Walmart? If they don't frequent farmers' markets, what economic structures – rising rents, exorbitant student loans – limit their ability to make sustainable food choices? With advance preparation, my students can ask deep questions of the apprentices and Camphillers who have experienced CSAs or farmers' markets from the producers' side. Those students in turn may wish to share their own experiences of connection or disconnection with the people who eat the food they produce.

This dialogue has the potential to enhance the practice of farmers' markets and CSAs directly. If concrete ideas for change emerge from the conversation, some participants may be able to enact those changes immediately, or bring them to the attention of farmers who can do so.

Advocating for rural flourishing

The dialogue among students can also be a starting point for advocacy on government policies that exacerbate the urban/rural divide. The two groups of participants are likely represented by different Congresspeople and state legislators. Presumably the urban legislators rarely hear from constituents about rural concerns, and vice versa. If participants reflect in advance on the policies and upcoming legislative votes that impact their communities, they can ask their new friends to bring these concerns to the attention of legislators who otherwise might not hear of them. Camphill and biodynamic participants might talk about the Farm Bill, a piece of legislation that is of paramount importance in rural communities but rarely discussed in the cities. My students might talk about the animal rights initiatives that are often on the ballot in Cambridge and surrounding communities. The point would not be for the students to seek a uniform opinion. Rather, the goal would be to foster a diversity of views that are richly informed by the perspectives of others. People are more likely to take action, such as calling a legislator, when they attach faces to issues.

From loss of work to its reimagining

My discussion of rural revitalization has assumed that dialogue participants bring diverse, mutually informative perspectives because of their different geographical locations. When it comes to the loss of work, on the other hand, all these students and apprentices have much in common. All are preparing for challenging and meaningful forms of work that may not exist in the future. Harvard Divinity School students are very diverse in their vocational aspirations, but the two largest clusters hope to achieve careers in ministry or in college teaching. The would-be ministers are keenly aware that religious participation is in rapid decline in the United States, making it difficult for many congregations to afford full-time ministers. Some hope to pursue "entrepreneurial" ministries, perhaps catering to religiously unaffiliated young adults, but as yet there are few examples of such ministries with the fundraising prowess needed to support their leaders. The future professors among my students face even grimmer prospects. The share of college students majoring in the humanities has declined precipitously since the financial crisis of 2008; the share majoring in religion has dropped 43% from its peak early in the century (Schmidt, 2018). Even before this drop, job openings for professors were scarce. Disrupted by new online educational platforms, and public skepticism about the value of higher education, many schools balance their budgets by dividing their faculties between a tenured elite and an adjuncting proletariat. Many of my students can anticipate being part of the latter if they achieve any academic position at all. Biodynamic apprentices, for their part, typically lack the economic resources needed to buy land and start farming, even on a small scale. Camphill Academy students are fortunate in that they have the option to avoid the dangers of the job market by becoming income-sharing coworkers within vibrant intentional communities – but they also know that many Camphill communities have abandoned their communal practices under pressure from government regulators, who are pressured in turn by national policies of austerity. The developmentally disabled students at Triform, finally, are at an especially fraught juncture in their vocational path. United States disability policy has generally been more successful at promoting social inclusion for K-12 students than for adults. Though some Triformers will find meaningful work within "adult" Camphill communities, others will discover that there are no vacancies or that Camphill is not quite that right fit for them. These students may then struggle to find settings where they are truly free to share their unique gifts with the world.

An ethic of caring for good work

Given these daunting realities, the first step in fostering an ethic of care in relation to work is thus for dialogue participants to name and reflect on their shared predicament. For most, the predicament is generationally specific. Millennial Americans have much worse prospects than previous generations of attaining a lifestyle comparable to that of their parents. While eighty percent of baby boomers out-earned their parents (after correction for inflation), only half of millennials enjoy incomes equal to those of their parents at similar ages. They also face unprecedented levels of student debt and housing costs that are rising at twice the rate of inflation (Leatherby, 2017). And their technologically mediated lifestyles exacerbate the alienation from nature that is a hallmark of modernity. Most millennial-generation students are well aware of the structural challenges they face, but when they face individual setbacks they may still interpret them as personal failings. Harvard Divinity School students, in particular, suffer alarmingly high rates of depression despite their apparent academic success. My hope is that an open dialogue will allow students to practice the solidarity they need not only to find work, but to choose work that is good for the planet. I also hope that engagement with the agrarian practices of Camphill and biodynamic farms will expand their imagination of what work might look like.

Models of resilient and regenerative work

Camphill communities and biodynamic farms offer appealing models of how work can be organized so that everyone is free to offer their unique gifts and everyone's needs are met. Traditionally, Camphill communities practice income sharing: residential coworkers do not receive salaries for the agricultural, administrative, and care work they perform, but they and their families are provided with comfortable housing, abundant and healthy food, and middle-class opportunities for travel and education. In recent years, many Camphills have moved away from strict income sharing, in part because it creates real obstacles for those Camphillers whose vocation calls them away after many years in community. But Rudolf Steiner's fundamental social law, which holds that in a healthy society people will work for the benefit of others while being sustained by the work of those others, remains a benchmark and aspiration for the movement. The same cooperative idealism led biodynamic farmers to develop and promote community supported agriculture, a system in which a community of consumers shares the costs and risks of each season of farm production. Hawthorne Valley Farm maintains an especially large CSA program, reaching all the way to New York City, and it is embedded in a larger nonprofit that provides an appealing organizational model for idealists seeking good work. The Hawthorne Valley Association is a single nonprofit that sponsors a farm, a Waldorf school, a grocery store, and many research and educational projects. This model protects its farmers from the vagaries of the market, ensuring that the land will continue to be farmed sustainably in the future.

The organizational model of Harvard Divinity School is less idealistic than those of Camphill or Hawthorne Valley, but as part of a university that is nearly four centuries old it certainly has a track record of sustainability! More to the point, every organizational model has both strengths and weaknesses, and when students at Harvard, Hawthorne Valley, and Camphill share their experiences, they can begin to envision new possibilities for the future. What's more, it is not enough for millennial students to know how cooperative organizations work. They must also reflect honestly on the reasons why so few millennials are availing themselves of existing opportunities to find work outside the neoliberal mainstream. This is often a puzzle for young Camphillers and biodynamic farmers: why do so few other members of their generation pursue the paths that they personally find so enriching? Honest dialogue with the Harvard students may offer some clues, and thus possible solutions that will make these alternatives more accessible.

Advocating for good work

Idealistic workplaces like Camphill and Hawthorne Valley can sometimes function as isolated bubbles, providing good work to a few without addressing the structural challenges that make it difficult for the majority to pursue meaningful vocations. For this reason, my envisioned dialogue will also explore the large policies that shape work opportunities. Many Camphillers and biodynamic farmers, for example, are deeply interested in the idea of a "universal basic income" – a government program that guarantees every citizen enough income to sustain life, allowing everyone to choose a vocation that is personally meaningful. And longtime Camphiller Ha Vinh Tho is one of the architects of Bhutan's "gross national happiness" initiative, which seeks to craft national policies that foster integral well-being rather than narrowly defined economic growth. Since many Harvard Divinity School students have connections to the Buddhist philosophies that also inform gross national happiness, a Camphill-Harvard dialogue could deepen everyone's understanding of the vision.

Conclusion

In this essay, I have emphasized the human dimensions of sustainability: how we can sustain rural communities as life-affirming places for humans to live and work, and how we can sustain meaningful work opportunities for U.S. Americans born after 1980. I have stressed these questions because I believe they create unique opportunities for Harvard students, farm apprentices, and Camphillers to learn from one another. Elsewhere in this volume, Heila Lotz-Sisitka has offered vivid case studies of what can happen when farmers build relationships with students and university researchers whose expertise is in information technology or rainwater collection systems or – significantly – the arts. Similarly, I suggest that students in the humanities may be able to contribute as much as engineers and policy experts.

At the same time, students are most likely to think, feel, and act on behalf of human interconnectedness if they are also participating in a sustainability education that helps them think, feel, and act in connection to plants, animals, and ecosystems. If we do not "recognize that all beings are interdependent and every form of life has value regardless of its worth to human beings," in the words of the Earth Charter, the human future will be impoverished and endangered.

For this reason, the shared practice of sustainability education that I envision is embedded within my students' encounter with all the ways that biodynamic farms and Camphill communities sustain the diversity and vitality of nonhuman life. At Hawthorne Valley, my students learn how the dairy farmers honor the "cowness" of their cows by allowing them to keep their horns, by grazing them on abundant pastures, and by following weaning practices that minimize the pain of separation. They may also learn strategies for maintaining the biodiversity of agricultural spaces from Hawthorne Valley's Farmscape Ecology Program, or how to "think like a plant" at a workshop offered by the nearby Nature Institute. Similarly, our time at Camphill includes time spent in the healing herb garden, the dairy barn, or at Turtle Tree Seeds, a producer of open-pollinated, biodynamic seeds.

Biodynamic farms and Camphill communities offer compelling models of how humans can honor the intrinsic value of all beings, not only in wilderness areas that are protected from human activity but also in the agricultural spaces on which we rely for our sustenance. This is good work, and work that requires far more willing workers than are currently available. Those workers are likely to emerge as soon as we create curricular spaces where they can meet one another.

Course Planning

Field trips are a powerful tool for fostering dialogue among students pursuing diverse sustainability curricula. I have frequently led students on multi-day field trips to Camphill Village USA, Triform Camphill Community, Camphill Heartbeet, Hawthorne Valley Association, Abode of the Message (a Sufi community whose farmers were trained at Hawthorne Valley), Sirius Community (an ecovillage rooted in New Age spirituality), and other farms and intentional communities. In arranging these visits, I rely on longstanding connections to leaders, though I have also received warm welcomes from communities with whom I lacked a pre-existing relationship. I usually ask students to make a modest contribution ($10 for a meal, $50 for overnight accommodation) to the communities that host us. Depending on whether students own cars, we carpool or obtain a rental van. All of the sites are within 200 miles of Harvard. When I taught in rural Minnesota, I arranged visits to such communities as Camphill Village Minnesota and Starland Hutterite Colony in Minnesota, and Community Homestead and Anathoth Farm in Wisconsin. Instructors at most colleges should be able to locate accessible partners for similar trips; I recommend consulting with the Fellowship for Intentional Community (which publishes a directory of intentional communities), the Biodynamic Association of North America, the Camphill Association of North America, and the North American region of the Global Ecovillage Network.

TABLE 6.2 Sustainability Education Grounded in the Sustainable Development Goals and The Earth Charter

Conceptual Framework Dimensions	Lesson, Activity, or Project	Learning Informed by the SDGs (Goals 1.1 to 17.19) and The Earth Charter (Principles I.1 to IV.16)
Ethic of Care – Values – Attitudes – Behaviors	**Preparatory Questions on Rural Revitalization** What is your personal relationship to the geographical region (rural or urban) where you currently live? Have you always lived there? Do you consider yourself part of the local culture and community? What are the strengths and challenges of your region? What do you most want outsiders to know about your region?	**Goal 2.3** By 2030, double the agricultural productivity and incomes of small-scale food producers, in particular women, indigenous peoples, family farmers, pastoralists, and fishers, including through secure and equal access to land, other productive resources and inputs, knowledge, financial services, markets, and opportunities for value addition and non-farm employment.
Resilience & Regeneration – Knowledge – Skills	********************** In what projects are you currently participating that build economic or cultural bridges between rural and urban America (e.g. farmers' markets, community supported agriculture)? In what projects is your larger organization participating? What are some of the best practices you have observed?	**Goal 8.3** Promote development-oriented policies that support productive activities, decent job creation, entrepreneurship, creativity and innovation, and encourage the formalization and growth of micro-, small-, and medium-sized enterprises, including through access to financial services.
Advocacy for Life's Flourishing – Action – Critique – Reflection	********************** What are the most urgent political issues in your community? What policies now under consideration would have the greatest positive impact on your community?	
Ethic of Care -Values -Attitudes -Behaviors	What do you want legislators in other regions to know about your region and its challenges? What new projects would you like to build? What have you learned, through your curriculum, that would help other people trying to build bridges between rural and urban communities?	

Conceptual Framework Dimensions	Lesson, Activity, or Project	Learning Informed by the SDGs (Goals 1.1 to 17.19) and The Earth Charter (Principles I.1 to IV.16)
Resilience & Regeneration – Knowledge – Skills	**Preparatory Questions on Meaningful Work** What is the work you personally feel called to? What is "the place where your deep gladness and the world's deep hunger meet" (Frederick Buechner)? What obstacles stand in your path as you pursue your vocation? What support do you hope to receive from others with similar challenges? What support are you prepared to give?	**Goal 11.a** Support positive economic, social, and environmental links between urban, peri-urban, and rural areas by strengthening national and regional development planning.
Advocacy for Life's Flourishing – Action – Critique – Reflection	★★★★★★★★★★★★★★★★★ How is work currently organized in your setting? What practices in your setting might be helpful in other organizations? What changes would you enact in your setting if you knew how? How has your curriculum helped you reimagine work?	**Goal 2.a** Increase investment, including through enhanced international cooperation, in rural infrastructure, agricultural research and extension services, technology development, and plant and livestock gene banks in order to enhance agricultural productive capacity in developing countries, in particular least developed countries.
Ethic of Care	★★★★★★★★★★★★★★★★★ What local and national policies shape work life for your generation? What new policies are needed? What steps are you willing to take to enact those policies?	**Goal 4.7** By 2030, ensure that all learners acquire the knowledge and skills needed to promote sustainable development, including, among others, through education for sustainable development and sustainable lifestyles, human rights, gender equality, promotion of a culture of peace and non-violence, global citizenship, and appreciation of cultural diversity and of culture's contribution to sustainable development.

(Continued)

TABLE 6.2 (Continued)

Conceptual Framework Dimensions	Lesson, Activity, or Project	Learning Informed by the SDGs (Goals 1.1 to 17.19) and The Earth Charter (Principles I.1 to IV.16)
Resilience & Regeneration	**Dialogue Questions on Rural Revitalization** Please share, individually, your personal relationships to the regions in which you live. Please share, as groups, the strengths and challenges of your regions. Please share, as groups, what you most want outsiders to know about your regions.	Goal 4.4 By 2030, substantially increase the number of youth and adults who have relevant skills, including technical and vocational skills, for employment, decent jobs, and entrepreneurship.
Advocacy for Life's Flourishing	★★★★★★★★★★★★★★★★★ As groups, please describe one or two projects of rural-urban bridge building that are happening in your settings. As groups, please share some of the tools that your curricula provide you for fostering rural-urban bridge building.	Goal 8.5 By 2030, achieve full and productive employment and decent work for all women and men, including for young people and persons with disabilities, and equal pay for work of equal value.
Ethic of Care	★★★★★★★★★★★★★★★★★ As groups, please take turns sharing an issue or proposed policy that is important in your region. As groups, please share what you most want legislators in other regions to know about your region.	I.1.b. Affirm faith in the inherent dignity of all human beings and in the intellectual, artistic, and spiritual potential of humanity.
Resilience & Regeneration	**Dialogue Questions on Reimaging Work** As individuals, please share your personal vocations and some of the obstacles you face in achieving them. As individuals, please describe some of the ways you would like to be supported, and some of the ways you are prepared to support others.	II.7.f. Adopt lifestyles that emphasize the quality of life and material sufficiency in a finite world.

Conceptual Framework Dimensions	Lesson, Activity, or Project	Learning Informed by the SDGs (Goals 1.1 to 17.19) and The Earth Charter (Principles I.1 to IV.16)
Advocacy for Life's Flourishing	★★★★★★★★★★★★★★★★★★ As groups, please share some of the ways work is organized in your setting, and what people in other settings might learn from your example. As groups, please share some of the ways your curricula are preparing you to reimagine your own life's work.	**III.9.b.** Empower every human being with the education and resources to secure a sustainable livelihood, and provide social security and safety nets for those who are unable to support themselves.
Ethic of Care	★★★★★★★★★★★★★★★★★★ As a single large group, please brainstorm local and national policies, to be enacted either by governments or other organizations, that would improve work prospects for persons born since 1980.	**II.8.b.** Recognize and preserve the traditional knowledge and spiritual wisdom in all cultures that contribute to environmental protection and human well-being.
Resilience & Regeneration	**Reflective Questions on Rural Revitalization** What were the most surprising things you learned about the other region? What insights will you share with classmates, friends, and neighbors who did not participate in this dialogue?	**IV.13.a.** Uphold the right of everyone to receive clear and timely information on environmental matters and all development plans and activities which are likely to affect them or in which they have an interest.
Advocacy for Life's Flourishing	★★★★★★★★★★★★★★★★★★ What most excited or inspired you about the bridge-building projects that you discussed? How might you bring these projects to your region, or expand them if they are already present? What tools did your dialogue partners gain from their curriculum that you wish were part of your curriculum? How might you organize to make changes?	**IV.13.b.** Support local, regional, and global civil society, and promote the meaningful participation of all interested individuals and organizations in decision making

(Continued)

TABLE 6.2 (Continued)

Conceptual Framework Dimensions	Lesson, Activity, or Project	Learning Informed by the SDGs (Goals 1.1 to 17.19) and The Earth Charter (Principles I.1 to IV.16)
Ethic of Care	★★★★★★★★★★★★★★★★★ What issues are you newly committed to bringing to the attention of your legislators? How might you work together to do this?	**IV.14.** Integrate into formal education and life-long learning the knowledge, values, and skills needed for a sustainable way of life.
Resilience & Regeneration	**Reflective Questions on Reimagining Work** What were the most surprising things you learned from the vocational stories of the other dialogue participants? What are you personally committed to doing to foster good work for people of your generation?	**I.2.b.** Affirm that with increased freedom, knowledge, and power comes increased responsibility to promote the common good.
Advocacy for Life's Flourishing	★★★★★★★★★★★★★★★★★ What did you find exciting or inspiring about the ways work is organized in the other setting? What practices would you like to bring to the organizations where you might work in the future? What tools did your dialogue partners gain from their curriculum that you wish were part of your curriculum? How might you organize to make changes? ★★★★★★★★★★★★★★★★★ What local or national policy changes are you prepared to work for, to ensure that people born after 1980 have abundant opportunities for good work?	**I.3.b.** Promote social and economic justice, enabling all to achieve a secure and meaningful livelihood that is ecologically responsible.

Source: Course Content Guide: A Collaborative Conversation for Sustainability Students, Professor McKanan

Typically, each site visit includes a tour (at Camphill, usually led by Camphillers with intellectual disabilities); meals in community houses; the opportunity to join in physical work that benefits the community, preferably alongside community members; and a conversation between my students and community members. This course content guide envisions how the "conversation" component might be enhanced by making it a formal part of the curriculum not only for my students, but also that of biodynamic apprentices, Camphill Academy students, and/or young adults with special needs studying at Triform or other Camphill training colleges. I hope to foster a third space of learning through three dialogues. In the first, students prepare separately in their distinct settings; in the second, they gather jointly during the field trip; in the third, they reflect separately on the fruits of the dialogue.

I have structured the proposed dialogue around the themes of rural revitalization and work that is meaningful and sustainable. Other instructors might adapt the structure to focus on other themes, as appropriate to their courses.

References

Butler, J. (1990). *Gender trouble: Feminism and the subversion of identity.* New York: Routledge.

Camphill Academy. (2018a). *Study within the context of community living.* Retrieved from http://camphill.edu/

Camphill Academy. (2018b). *Studying social therapy.* Retrieved from http://camphill.edu/programs/social-therapy-program/

Day, K. (2015). *Religious resistance to neoliberalism: Womanist and black feminist perspectives.* New York: Palgrave Macmillan.

Harvard Divinity School. (2018). *About HDS.* Retrieved from https://hds.harvard.edu/about

Harvey, D. (2007). *A brief history of neoliberalism.* New York: Oxford University Press.

Hawthorne Valley Farm. (2016/2017). *Farm learning program handbook & application.* Retrieved from https://farm.hawthornevalley.org/apply-for-an-apprenticeship/

Hawthorne Valley Farm. (2018). *Apply for an apprenticeship.* Retrieved from https://farm.hawthornevalley.org/apply-for-an-apprenticeship/

Johnson, C. C. (2016). *Race, religion, and resilience in the neoliberal age.* New York: Palgrave Macmillan.

Lamb, G. (2016). *Associative economic: Spiritual activity for the common good.* Chatham, NY: Waldorf Publications.

Leatherby, L. (2017, August 29). Five charts show why millennials are worse off than their parents. *Financial Times.* Retrieved from www.ft.com/content/e5246526-8c2c-11e7-a352-e46f43c5825d

McKanan, D. (2007). *Touching the world: Christian communities transforming society.* Collegeville, MN: Liturgical Press.

McKanan, D. (2016). Camphill at seventy-five: Developmental communalism in process. *Communal Societies, 36,* 25–49.

McKanan, D. (2017). *Eco-alchemy: Rudolf Steiner's anthroposophy and the environmental movement.* Berkeley, CA: University of California Press.

McKanan, D. (under review). Camphill and the future: Spirituality and disability in an evolving communal movement.

Schmidt, B. (2018, August 23). The humanities are in crisis. *The Atlantic.* Retrieved from www.theatlantic.com/ideas/archive/2018/08/the-humanities-face-a-crisisof-confidence/567565/

Sen, A. (2009). *The idea of justice.* Cambridge, MA: Belknap Press of Harvard University Press.

Steiner, R. (2000). *Toward social renewal: Renewing the basis of society* (Barton, M., Trans., 4th rev. ed.). London: Rudolf Steiner Press.

Triform Camphill Community. (2018). *Welcome to a very special community.* Retrieved from http://triform.org/

7

LEARNING FROM TRADITIONAL WISDOM IN PAPUA NEW GUINEA

The value of indigenous and traditional ecological knowledge in higher education

Sangion Appiee Tiu and Joan Armon

Introduction

Traditional Ecological Knowledge is crucial to the survival and well-being of Papua New Guinea's Indigenous communities and their natural environments. It is a knowledge system that has withstood the test of time and has been passed from one generation to the next as a guide to reciprocal, relational, and ethical interactions among humans and their natural environments and spirituality. Traditional Ecological Knowledge (TEK) features decision-making informed by knowledge of complex ecological relationships that support the well-being of current and future generations. It is a knowledge system that is dynamic, changing, and locally situated. Furthermore, it often encourages positive actions and just and peaceful resolutions for sustainable resource use intended to ensure that humans and other-than-humans benefit equally from environments held in common by all.

The purpose of this chapter is to describe sustainability principles and practices of TEK that enable Indigenous as well as concerned non-Indigenous people to collaboratively envision and enact a present and future in which all lives flourish. In particular, this chapter articulates why and how to embed TEK in college and university courses so that students graduate with the values, knowledge, and skills that empower them to participate in and advocate for short- and long-term pathways to sustainable living.

The TEK approaches encouraged here ensure sustainable community development of natural resources, which may impact the health of human and other species, as well as cultures and their systems. Tribal communities are often unable to address the loss of local biodiversity and ecosystems solely with the guidance of TEK because the ancient ecological wisdom is not always passed from one generation to the next. Due to influences of Western domination, TEK has been fragmented by economically-motivated globalization, consumerism, and scientific manipulation that demean Indigenous relationships with ecosystems. Individualism has replaced communal living and interdependence with local environments and the lives within them (Namunu, 2001). In urban upbringings, families and communities less commonly teach and practice the values, attitudes, and beliefs associated with TEK. With the decline in Indigenous or tribal education, children, youth, and adults might not learn the power of their TEK heritage to map out traditional resource management practices (Tiu, 2016). Thus, members of Indigenous communities may be unprepared to invoke TEK perspectives and practices that could address ongoing environmental degradation by multinational corporations. As Namunu points out, Indigenous communities require backing from global interest groups to stand against corporate profit-based ideologies "that destroy our environment and our bio-cosmic relationship to the earth" (2001, p. 272).

Lacking sustainability orientations and relationships with local environments or community members, corporate leaders pursue unsustainable resource extraction for short-term profits rather than the protection and regeneration of local environments' long-term health and well-being (MacDonald, 2001). Corporations using unsustainable methods for logging, mining, fishing, petroleum extraction, and cocoa, coffee, palm oil, and coconut harvesting undermine Indigenous communities' equal participation in caring for and accessing natural resources in sustainable ways. As globalization proceeds, however, some Indigenous communities determine a need to pursue economic and technological development but to pursue it without compromising traditional economic, cultural, and environmental well-being (Mason, 2018; Tilbury, 2006). Sustainable development must be accomplished within limits. TEK traditions, values, and practices can determine these limits when they are included in decision-making and implementation.

Two international documents provide guidelines in this era of globalization. The Sustainable Development Goals, for example, include Goal 15, which advocates for protection, restoration, and promotion of sustainably managed lands, reversing degradation, and halting biodiversity loss. The Earth Charter's Principle 12b calls on the global community to "Affirm the right of Indigenous peoples to their spirituality, knowledge, lands and resources and to their related practice of sustainable livelihoods" (2000). Adherence to these documents' goals and principles is critical to protecting Indigenous rights and the vitality of TEK, particularly when governmental and corporate entities pursue unsustainable development of natural resources. Amidst threats from unsustainable development, Indigenous people aware of their TEK heritage continue to perceive themselves as caretakers of the natural world. This caretaking role includes kinship with all living things and is at the core of Indigenous peoples' identity as individuals and as a group (Posey, 2001). Fortunately, in the Indigenous Papua New Guinean context, full and equal participation in the care of and access to natural resources is being revived through Indigenous or tribal education and traditional resource management practices, as described later in this chapter (Tiu, 2016).

Notable roles in traditional ecological knowledge

College and university educators can create opportunities for students, both Indigenous and non-Indigenous, to learn about past and present roles that contribute to reviving and strengthening TEK in Papua New Guinea and potentially in other communities. One starting point can be introducing students to the various roles of individuals, communities, and environments.

Roles associated with Traditional Ecological Knowledge include the roles of individuals, communities, and environments that exist as a living and whole system. Reciprocal interactions between these develop over time and pass from one generation to the next to convey values, beliefs, traditions, and practices that are dynamic, changing, and locally situated.

Role of individuals

In TEK, all individuals have a role to play for the betterment of their community. These roles are distinct and depend on what expertise each individual has to contribute. For instance, one individual may be the protector of the knowledge of herbal medicines, while another may be an expert artisan who has the knowledge of types of trees that can be used for lumber to build canoes, carvings, or shelters. Similarly, a female may have special knowledge of planting yams that produce large yields while a male may have special knowledge of where there is a large supply of tuna fish. Thus, every individual in an Indigenous or tribal community has a role to play in society.

Role of community

The community's role is to ensure that its land and resources are protected and used in a manner that ensures continuity for present as well as future generations. It is also the role of the community to ensure that any available resources are equally accessed and distributed.

The Indigenous community, as articulated by Gregory Cajete, a Tewa Pueblo member in New Mexico, USA, is the primary context for traditional Indigenous education; the individual not only acquires a sense of affective being and identity in a particular place but also of participation in the life of the group to learn responsibility and relationship (2015). Linking community and environment, Namunu emphasizes that "For the Melanesians, the environment cradles life and the community, in turn, vows to protect it." This relates to the "give-and-take" exchange people experience in relationships among humans, the ecosystem, and spirits (2001, p. 264). Significantly, Namunu identifies this concept as a holistic, communal perspective that, over thousands of years, has served as a means of intentional or unintentional control of environmental degradation. In roles as guardians of the environment, Indigenous communities reinforce values of responsibility and strong relationships among environments, humans, and other entities. The intent of these values is to ensure a continuity of resources that minimizes degradation and maximizes sustainable futures.

Role of environments

In the Papua New Guinean context, the environment has more than one role. First and foremost is the role of providing the necessary resources for a community's survival. Tiu, for example, learned this role of the environment in childhood. Children's play involved respecting and caring for their urban environments as they foraged for edible leaves, wild eggs, fruits, and firewood, which involved taking enough for their needs but avoiding damaging plants or taking food that animals might need. These forays into local environments enabled children to learn the traditional names of resources both in their own dialect with children from their own community, as well as those of the children from other PNG provinces with whom they played. In this way, children learned words for and knowledge about environmental resources.

Second, the environment holds the spiritual and ecological values of Indigenous PNG people through which they find their identity. As Namunu points out, "Indigenous people are conscious of the relationship with their environment because it is the place where spirits live – spirits whose presence provide hope for the security, peace, and happiness they share together" (2001, p. 253). Cajete depicts a comparable way that Indigenous peoples in New Mexico express this concept, stating that "we are of this land and this land is us" (2015, p. 50). This sensibility represents an ecologically-oriented relationship embracing all facets of traditional life as intimately connected to the environment, which offers both survival and identity to Indigenous peoples as well as shaping ceremony, language, music, art, dance, and social organization.

As Figure 7.1 shows, the interconnected roles of the individual, community, and environment can and should support urgent, concerted, and collaborative efforts to establish sustainable futures for those yet unborn. Future generations

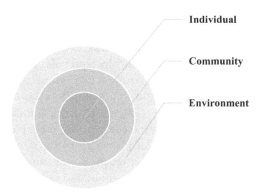

Individual

Community

Environment

FIGURE 7.1 Traditional Ecological Knowledge: Notable Roles

rely on current generations to guard and implement their heritage of Traditional Ecological Knowledge. Future kinship responsibilities held by members of a community mean that each member has an obligation to their kin members to ensure that all have immediate and equal access to resources. Thus, the core TEK values of taking responsible actions, feeling concern for future resource use and availability, and ensuring that resources are thriving and equally accessible to all are consistent with sustainability principles of responsible action and intergenerational equity.

Priorities for sustainability education

Sustainability education is a holistic approach to teaching and learning within the traditions of Indigenous and tribal education. It immerses students in experiences of the human-nature relationship, which develop students' capacities for reciprocal care, relational awareness, and empathy toward self and others, both human and other-than-human, and the natural environment. Sustainability education calls forth students' emotional, physical, mental, and spiritual capacities. Ideally, it inspires students' emotional and spiritual connections to their inner selves and outer surroundings. These connections may foster wise decisions and actions within a give-and-take relationship toward others and the natural environment, with a goal of social, economic, and environmental balance (Namunu, 2001).

Two forms of sustainability education occur simultaneously, as Tiu reports in a study of the role of Indigenous knowledge in biodiversity conservation and in a later study of Indigenous perceptions of TEK and sustainability in Papua New Guinea (2007, 2016). One form is Indigenous education that promotes Indigenous knowledge, practices, and ways of life. Another form is tribal education that focuses on a specific tribe's way of life and actions, which reinforce values, principles, and perspectives. Both forms rely upon holistic approaches to teaching and learning that integrate students' emotional, physical, mental, and spiritual capacities.

Community methods of sustainably oriented, traditional Indigenous and tribal education in Papua New Guinea may vary according to educational purposes, content, location, and participants. Such educational approaches are informal in nature, whereby teaching and learning occur on an ad hoc basis – as and when a need arises. The acquisition, interpretation, and dissemination of knowledge is an ongoing process occurring in different settings depending upon the type of activity. For example, those learning to construct canoes harvest trees sustainably by selecting from different thriving stands of trees to avoid over-harvesting in any one area. Canoe construction takes place near the beach, while learning sustainable methods of planting yams occurs in a garden. Such approaches mean that learning TEK is practical and suited to a specific environment, climate, and setting. Materials, tools, and tasks function in authentic learning environments that encourage holistic experiential participation. Such active participation bolsters learners' competence as they accomplish a task that makes them feel freely happy.

University approaches to immersing students in TEK also depend upon authentic settings. The following example of a current university course in Papua New Guinea outlines the purposes, content, methods, and settings that are appropriate in Papua New Guinea but can be adapted to universities in other places.

A current course at Goroka University in Goroka, Papua New Guinea

In Papua New Guinea, Tiu and her colleagues witness the deteriorating state of the environment along with social, ecological, and cultural relationships. Modernization and development of Papua New Guinea's natural resources contribute to declining awareness of TEK with its relationships to the natural world. In response, Tiu and colleagues created a course for third-year undergraduate students majoring in environmental studies. Students enrolled in this course are from all over Papua New Guinea and include a small number of students from the South Pacific island nations of Solomon Islands and Vanuatu. These students are preparing to work in environmental management and protection, conservation, community development, education, environmental planning, and other areas within natural resource management.

This course for third-year university students, entitled "Community Conservation and Development Tools," was developed by Tiu & Bozie in 2018, and is summarized in Table 7.1. Because it was developed with the community in mind, the course elevates the significant role that community plays in the creation and strengthening of relationships and the need to ensure that this practice continues for the benefit of present and future generations. The course meets the needs of different stakeholder groups that include students, government officials, civil society organizations, and the larger community. People in these groups recognize the urgent need for graduating citizens who possess community engagement skills and knowledge focused on conservation and natural resource management. With over 80% of Papua New Guinea's population living in rural areas, students who enroll in this course can learn to enter rural communities in ways that respect TEK's cultural and traditional interactions and decision-making. One aim of this course is to examine how rural populations enact traditional knowledge and practices in sustainable ways that make it possible to continue accessing resources for daily sustenance. Another aim is for students to identify which aspects of TEK they can integrate into their chosen fields and how they might best accomplish that integration.

Broad conservation and development issues pertinent to Papua New Guinea are included in this course so that students learn to analyze Indigenous and tribal development processes in relation to land and environment. This equips students with skills and knowledge to effectively engage with local communities and to

TABLE 7.1 Course Content Guide

Conceptual Framework Dimensions	*Project for Student Groups*	*Learning Informed by the SDGs (Goals 1.1 to 17.19) and The Earth Charter (Principles I.1 to IV.16)*
Ethic of Care – Values – Attitudes – Behaviors	**Title: Identify Factors that Reinforce human relationship with nature** **Identification of Practices and Systems** Examine changes that have impacted the community and identify factors that encourage reflective actions to reinforce human–nature relationship. Visit a rural or semi-urban Indigenous or tribal community over a period of one or two days that is involved in some aspects of sustainable natural resource management. Questions to consider: Who lives in this community? What kind of sustainable natural resource management activity are they involved in and why? What aspects of local or traditional ecological knowledge are visible? How do humans manipulate the environment? What resource use patterns have occurred in this community involving changes in human behavior? How does this influence your perception about prioritizing sustainability?	*Goal 12.2*: Achieve sustainable management and efficient use of natural resources. *Goal 12.8*: Promote universal understanding of sustainable lifestyles. *Goal 12.8*: Promote universal understanding of sustainable lifestyles.
Resilience & Regeneration – Knowledge – Skills	**Toward a Sustainable Future** With community members, orient yourself to their distinctive ecosystems, histories, cultures, and awareness of the significance of the land and resources within their environmental, social, political, and economic contexts. Identify a practice that applies local or traditional ecological knowledge and its aspects that contribute to prioritizing sustainability. Envision a sustainable future in this setting and how it will be achieved. Determine if communities are shifting to a desirable and sustainable future for all and why/why not.	*Principle 1.1a:* Recognize that all beings are interdependent and every form of life has value regardless of its worth to human beings. *Principle 1.4b:* Transmit to future generations the values, traditions, and institutions that support the long-term flourishing of Earth's human and ecological communities.

Conceptual Framework Dimensions	Project for Student Groups	Learning Informed by the SDGs (Goals 1.1 to 17.19) and The Earth Charter (Principles I.1 to IV.16)
Advocacy for Life's Flourishing – Action – Critique – Reflection	**Advocacy Outcomes** This environment relies on human–nature relations and needs regular maintenance and care. Why, how, and where might you advocate for environmental relationship and care? **Exhibition Outcomes** Present and debrief your findings. **V. Reflection Outcomes for Journal and Discussion** In what ways is the practice you observed environmentally sound or unsound? Are environmental resources sustainably extracted and utilized? In what way(s) do these resources benefit from this system? How would you critique these practices? Do these practices enhance an ethic of care to re-vision a new human–nature relationship that considers sustainability for all living beings and respects their rights to exist?	*Principle 1.4b:* Transmit to future generations the values, traditions, and institutions that support the long-term flourishing of Earth's human and ecological communities.

Source: Traditional Ecological Knowledge: Nature Conservation and Sustainability Education

facilitate self-determination and ways of managing land and resources that are their natural heritage. On a practical level, students in this course learn to use various tools, practices, and approaches found in Papua New Guinea's conservation and community development projects, as explained below.

In many parts of Papua New Guinea, non-Indigenous people are involved in resource use and extraction and often find their approaches contradictory to what local Indigenous people believe and practice. For example, in the northeastern Trans-Gogol area of Papua New Guinea, starting in the 1970s, a Japanese logging company, JANT Ltd, completely clear-felled timber. This created multiple, complex problems for the local people who lost their entire forest, which was the source of their very existence. Clear felling of trees is not a traditional practice. In Indigenous communities, extraction of timber for personal or communal needs follows a selective process whereby only mature trees are harvested for any timber needs. The Gogol River was inundated with sedimentation and debris, wildlife populations decreased, and local people felt disoriented and displaced (Bun, n.d.). Such scenarios are common in many parts of PNG such that many students taking Tiu's and Bozie's course at Goroka University have been exposed to similar situations.

The effects of the clear felling operation on the environment and the social aspects of life were felt throughout Madang and even throughout the country. Following the clear felling, the Gogol River and its tributaries changed forever due to heavy sedimentation and forest cover removal. Wildlife numbers dwindled and the landscape has changed completely from primary forest to secondary re-growths and shrubs. Many locals did not want to see the consequences faced by their neighbors living in the Gogol Naru timber area to come to their areas, which prompted local landowners' formation of the Madang Forest Resources Owners Association (MFROA) with the intention of harvesting their land in sustainable ways (pers com).

The implications for learning and applying TEK are that students must learn to recognize the existence of traditional or local ecological knowledge and, when faced with situations that disrupt or ignore TEK, be prepared to work with communities to facilitate non-Indigenous persons' or organizations' understanding of TEK. This can open conversations about how it may be possible to align resource extraction practices with local knowledge and practices.

Community engagement project

To fulfill course fieldwork requirements, students visit a local community or group that demonstrates self-determination and self-development. This follows lectures and tutorials on conservation, development, and community engagement processes. Students apply community engagement techniques and fact-finding about the types of conservation activities a community developed to promote TEK through sustainable management knowledge and practices. A community about five miles from the university was selected due to its efforts to address environmental degradation through community reforestation. A local population has been negatively impacting the environment with increased forest clearing for subsistence gardening or human occupation. Reforestation is a key approach because it enables animals and plants that may have diminished over the years to be replenished.

Prior to entering the community, students learn expectations about community protocols from course instructors. When students arrive at the community, each participating local family takes one or two students home, depending on the number of student arrivals. Students give a gift of food and other supplies to the community and to their family host. Additionally, students may choose to give personal gifts to the family, as this is acceptable in the Melanesian context. During the visit, students spend a day or two interacting with residents through informal discussions and data gathering from observations, interviews, and journal entries. Students also engage in host families' tasks, such as working in gardens, fetching water from a creek, storytelling around the fire, attending a village meeting, or participating in meal preparations.

Through engagements at each of these levels, students explore the community's use of TEK and how it is applied in activities such as food gathering, planting, consultation, and decision-making regarding sustainable resource management and use. Key learning for students includes recognizing community members' connectedness to their environment, use of TEK systems and approaches, and TEK-informed decision-making strategies for caring for their environments in ways that replenish what was lost or destroyed. Students express in feedback that they are re-establishing their own lost connections to TEK values, beliefs, practices, and knowledge systems, which their communities may have once practiced. Inspiration to apply learning to their own communities and future careers is another major response that students convey in course feedback. The community acknowledges the significance of the visit by letting students know that their contributions and rehabilitation work furthered the community's sustainable resource management efforts. Course assessments include students' journal entries used for debriefing and self-reflection, individual reports submitted to instructors, and presentations to course members.

Unit linking traditional ecological knowledge and bio-culture education

For second-year university students, a unit developed by Tiu and Susuke in 2019 focuses on making connections between Indigenous knowledge and conservation. The purpose of the unit is for students to develop ideas about how to improve conservation practices in contemporary Papua New Guinea. Topics covered in this unit include defining and identifying types of traditional knowledge along with making connections among paradigms of sustainability, traditional knowledge, and bio-cultural education, which integrates biology and culture. Additional topics include the significance of tribal art, education strategies for disseminating traditional knowledge, and ways to protect traditional knowledge. Overarching aims are for students to critically reflect on traditional knowledge systems in terms of core values and principles as well as gain respect for people, environments, and future generations. Students identify how they can use these knowledge systems to improve conservation practices in contemporary Papua New Guinea.

At Goroka University, the content of this unit has been recognized as significant in re-informing tertiary students about the value of their own traditional knowledge systems that promote sustainability. Students are now incorporating their learning in other disciplines at the university. For example, in other courses such as Heritage and Development Studies, due considerations are given to issues of Indigenous perspectives on sustainable resource development and management and protection, particularly of culturally significant sites.

Curriculum development for education of young children and their teachers

TEK is also influencing curriculum for children aged six to twelve years old. One of the key learning areas (KLA) of the National Curriculum Statement which supports this and reinforces the PNG Way at these levels is Culture and Community. The PNG Way is a concept that promotes the Indigenous Papua New Guinean way of life, such as continuous implementation of communal village lifestyles, cultural activities, use of tribal dialects, and other traditional and Indigenous ways. This PNG Way also consists of communal and consultative decision-making processes. In this context, teachers integrate moral stories and activities that reinforce TEK values so that children begin to recognize the importance of respecting, caring for, and taking responsible actions to protect people, other life forms, and environments. Teachers in more than forty schools in five provinces of PNG use teaching resources that specifically promote aspects of TEK in culture and environment as developed by Tiu, Betabete, Jimike, Mirisa, and Pochimel in 2015. The content of this resource material covers topics such as moral beliefs, values, and practices that reinforce sustainable principles, exploring environmental relationships for survival, and recognizing significant cultural and natural resources, threats to these resources, and actions that can be taken to protect them. There is great potential for more schools in these provinces to be involved in the use of this specifically developed resource focusing on aspects of TEK. The resource attracts numerous responses conveying teachers' concerns about the declining integration in the formal education system of traditional knowledge and practices for resource use and management. Education workshops for teachers are underway, with more planned in several provinces.

Policy influences

In another arena, Tiu and colleagues create and disseminate relevant policies capturing the importance of TEK as well as conducting ongoing capacity-building trainings that reinforce the use of TEK at different levels of the community. At the national level, consultation and review of policy development involves natural resource management. For example, objective three of the fourth pillar of the Papua New Guinea Protected Area Policy clearly states that "PNG's Protected Area Network will build upon traditional management and traditional ecological knowledge" (Independent State of Papua New Guinea, 2014, p. 15). The policy reiterates that decisions on the protected areas network will not only be based on scientific evidence, but also on traditional ecological knowledge. Such acknowledgement of TEK in a national document is instrumental in reinforcing the importance of TEK and reviving its values among present and future generations.

At the community level, ongoing capacity-building training workshops are conducted for different stakeholder groups that include villagers, Local Level Government and Ward councilors, teachers, farmers and any other interested individuals or groups. TEK values emphasize the salience of traditional and local knowledge, which can form the basis for sustainable community development efforts. For example, in the work with communities on building capacities of vulnerable communities for climate change adaptation, participants are taken through a reflective learning process to remind themselves how their ancestors viewed weather, seasons, and climate, and how these views have changed today. In the past, participants' ancestors monitored signs in nature like the fruiting season of certain plants, or the rising and setting of the sun, to predict the weather and seasons. Workshop participants note changes regarding when special plants are fruiting now as compared to the past. Also, the rising and setting of the sun occur at slightly different positions than before. Such observations prompt community members to make connections with what happened in the past, what is happening at the present time, and ways their local or traditional knowledge can inform decisions and actions for the present and future.

Conclusion

In view of prioritizing sustainability education, the value of respect for all life forms creates an ethic of care that can guide responsible actions to promote sustainable futures in Papua New Guinea and elsewhere. When students and community members encounter TEK through education and policy, they have the opportunity to develop relational awareness of the human-nature relationship, reciprocal care, and empathy. Immersion in local and traditional knowledge systems, values, and practices can foster change in students' and community members' attitudes as they observe or personally experience commitment to the well-being of individuals, communities, and their environments.

Fortunately, Papua New Guinea's national commitment to reviving traditional knowledge, values, and practices supports TEK implementation in both education and policy despite Western modernization and degradation of culture, lifeways, and environments. Reconnection with TEK values of respect, care, and responsible actions elevates approaches to sustainable livelihoods through sustainable management of natural resources, which is essential for mitigating environmental degradation and its impacts. It is vital for communities to reclaim their Indigenous knowledge and practices that protect the future health and well-being of waters, lands, and lives.

Course Planning

As communities evolve, they are often challenged to forego what they know and have practiced for generations in order to embrace the changes confronting them. Often the natural environment in which they live is affected by changes that result in the loss of species and habitats. Local or traditional knowledge associated with these environments is also threatened by this loss. This project challenges you to critically reflect on a rural or semi-urban Indigenous or tribal community to investigate changes that have impacted their way of life and led to loss of local or traditional knowledge and practices. Identify and analyze what actions they have taken to ensure continuity of their sustainable environments, lifeways, and livelihoods.

References

Bun, Y. A. (n.d.). *Community based forestry experience in madang, Papua New Guinea: Governance and decentralisation.* Retrieved from www.cifor.org/publications/pdf_files/events/documentations/yogyakarta/papers/paperyatibun.pdf

Cajete, G. (2015). *Indigenous community: Rekindling the teachings of the seventh fire.* St. Paul, MN: Living Justice Press.

The Earth Charter. (2000). Earth Charter International Secretariat. Retrieved from www.earthcharter.org

Independent State of Papua New Guinea. (2014). *Papua New Guinea policy on protected areas: Conservation & environment protection authority.* Waigani: National Capital District: Papua New Guinea.

MacDonald, M. (2001). Changing habits, changing habitats: Melanesian environmental knowledge. In J. A. Grim (Ed.), *Indigenous traditions and ecology: The interbeing of cosmology and community.* Cambridge, MA: Harvard University Press.

Mason, M. (2018). *What is sustainability and why is it important?* Environmental Science. Retrieved from www.environmentalscience.org/sustainability

Namunu, S. (2001). Melanesian religion, ecology, and modernization in Papua New Guinea. In J. A. Grim (Ed.), *Indigenous traditions and ecology: The interbeing of cosmology and community.* Cambridge, MA: Harvard University Press.

Posey, D. (2001). Intellectual property rights and the sacred balance: Some spiritual consequences from the commercialization of traditional resources. In J. Grim (Ed.), *Indigenous traditions and ecology: The interbeing of cosmology and community.* Cambridge, MA: Harvard University Press.

Tilbury, D. (2006). Environmental education for sustainability: Defining the new focus of environmental education in the 1990s. *Environmental Education Research, 1*(2), 195–212.

Tiu, S. A. (2007). *The role of Indigenous knowledge in biodiversity conservation: Implications for conservation education in Papua New Guinea.* Unpublished Masters Thesis, University of Waikato, Hamilton, New Zealand.

Tiu, S. A. (2016). *Traditional ecological knowledge in sustainable resource management in Papua New Guinea: The role of education and implications for policy.* Unpublished PhD Thesis, University of Waikato, Hamilton, New Zealand.

Tiu, S. A., Betabete, E., Jimike, I., Mirisa, S., & Pochimel, J. (2015). *Culture and environment: A resource book for elementary teachers.* Papua New Guinea: Research & Conservation Foundation.

Tiu, S. A., & Bozie, W. (2018). *Community conservation & development tools unit outline.* Papua New Guinea: University of Goroka.

Tiu, S. A., & Susuke, D. (2019). *Indigenous knowledge and conservation unit outline.* Papua New Guinea: University of Goroka.

United Nations. (2017). *United Nations sustainable development goals.* Retrieved from https://sustainabledevelopment.un.org

8

SUSTAINABILITY EDUCATION FROM AN INDIGENOUS KNOWLEDGE PERSPECTIVE

Examples from Southern Africa

Soul Shava

Introduction

The global environmental crisis, which includes climate change effects, biodiversity loss, environmental degradation, increased epidemics, and increased disparity between the rich and poor (see WEF, 2019), challenges us to seek new modes of thinking and living towards sustainability. There is an urgent need for sustainability education initiatives across all sectors of global society. However, sustainability education is mostly defined within universalized and hegemonic Western-Euro-Americentric approaches from the 'global north' that usually downplay (inferiorize, marginalize, invalidate, and exclude) sustainability practices and pedagogic approaches from indigenous communities from the 'global south' that have existed alongside them. The emphasis tends to be on the built environment and on greener technologies, which define dominant westernized notions of human development (see Dei, 2010; Knutsson, 2018), where we mainly experience the physical world through technology (Hallpike, 2018) and overlook the lifestyles of indigenous populations, particularly those in rural contexts, and their contribution to sustainable development. In a break from this pattern of Western epistemological hegemony, this chapter draws upon what Foucault calls the "insurrection of subjugated knowledges" (Foucault, 1980) by exploring the validity of some contextualized indigenous sustainability practices, cultural values, and environmental ethics from southern Africa. This is a decolonizing effort intended to situate indigenous knowledges in a dialogic encounter with other sustainability education discourses from across the globe.

Southern Africa has experienced its own share of environmental crises, of both local and global extent and/or origin. These include droughts and floods, food insecurity, disease epidemics (malaria, cholera, etc.), biodiversity loss, pollution, and land degradation. I contend that, while external approaches are undoubtedly useful, sustainability education responses need to be contextualized, acknowledge local circumstances, and respect the knowledge of the indigenous people. Indigenous communities have a strong relationship with and attachment to the land that constitutes their belonging to their lived environment. The examples presented below illustrate a range of sustainability practices in southern Africa which have universal relevance.

Indigenous sustainability norms, values, ethics, and practices

African indigenous communities embrace an ethic of care. In indigenous community contexts, emphasis is not on the individual, but rather on the extended family and the community. The individual's personality is defined by her or his relationship with and sense of responsibility to the family and community, as expressed in the Shona proverb "munhu vanhu" and its Nguni (Ndebele, Swati, Xhosa and Zulu group of related languages) equivalent "umuntu ngumuntu ngabantu", meaning a person is what s/he is because of the the the contributions of the people in the community. Strong family and community ties are evident in everyday livelihood activities, which are participatory, collaborative, cyclical, and reciprocal, involving the extended family or the entire village community (Hallpike, 2018; Dei, 1993). These livelihood practices reveal the existence of several communities of practice at extended family and village levels for activities such as child minding, livestock and crop husbandry, hunting and foraging, collecting water and firewood, and wedding and funeral ceremonies. Resources such as labor and draught power are pooled together and care is prioritized for the vulnerable members of the community, such as the young, orphaned, widowed, elderly, and disabled. These local communities of practice help to develop in the individual a strong sense of belonging, shared identity, values, beliefs, and practices. They also promote community resilience. Interestingly, the indigenous 'community of practice' approach provides a robust and sustainable model of community well-being that is gaining interest in industrialized countries through movements such as Transition Towns (Hopkins, 2008).

The indigenous ethic of care extends to care for the land. Ancestral land was viewed in the past as priceless in value and was not for sale. Today it continues to have symbolic cultural and spiritual significance and yet also supplies resources for everyday livelihood support needs of the community. Ancestral land is perceived to be an integral part of the indigenous community and identity, and imbues them with a sense of place, hence the Shona phrase "*mwana wevhu*" (a child of the soil). Rural communities' heavy reliance on the land for their survival establishes a reciprocal relationship with the lived environment. This makes it a living socio-cultural-ecological landscape (an ecological landscape inhabited by indigenous people that embodies their culture) filled with meaning and memory

(Makamure & Chimininge, 2015). Indigenous people believe that the land cares for them and that they should care for the land in return through caring for the various aspects of the lived environment, such as the streams, pools, rivers, wildlife, woodlands, and forests that sustain them. It is from within this relational foundation that indigenous environmental sustainability practices, culture, and ethics have emerged.

Indigenous environmental governance relies on traditional institutions, cultural norms, and values that guide people to utilize natural resources in sustainable ways. Such community-based conservation is heavily reliant on community cohesion, but this is now threatened. Modernization, urbanization, individualism, population growth, and westernized state governance usually disrupt and disempower traditional governance structures and take ownership of environmental resources away from local communities (Campbell et al., 2001; Mapedza, 2006). However, where community cohesion is still intact, indigenous governance systems play a significant role in environmental resource governance and these aspects could be promoted to enhance community identity and respect for the lived environment.

Traditional environmental management is a complex system of interconnected spiritual beliefs, taboos, cultural norms, and ethics. Community leaders play a significant role in cultural continuity through the maintenance and reinforcement of environmental rules and regulations as a moral obligation for community members. This is done mainly through ensuring that the community observes environmental taboos or avoidance rules (*zviera* [Shona], *ukuzila* [Nguni]), and maintains cultural norms and values as means of promoting desirable environmental ethics, behaviors, and practices. Such environmental sustainability management processes include taboos with regards to sacred natural sites, sacred animal and plant species, restrictions to hunting and gathering activities, and prevention of cruelty to non-human species (wildlife and plants), as discussed below.

Sacred natural sites

Sacred groves, forests, woodlands, and trees

Some natural habitats are considered sacred and are conserved and protected through local taboos and cultural norms and values (see Barrow, 2010; Mapara, 2016). For example, some woodlands and forest groves are believed to be the homes of ancestral spirits and are usually also used as communal burial sites. Their sacredness preserves the local biodiversity within them. Some tree species, such as the mobola plum (*muhacha/muchakata* [Shona], *umkhuna* [Ndebele] – *Parinari curatelifolia*) and the sycamore fig tree (*mukuy/muwonde* [Shona] *umkhiwa* [Ndebele] – *Ficus sycamorus*), are used as sites for spiritual rituals and ceremonies for households and villages. Other trees are associated with rain making and hunting spirits. These trees are protected on ancestral lands and are not to be cut down. The buffalo thorn (*muchecheni* [Shona], *umphafa/umlahlankosi* [Ndebele] – *Zizyphus mucronata*) and the confetti bush (*chizhuzhu/musosawafa* [Shona], *isihlangu* [Ndebele] – *Maytenus senegalensis*) are also protected as they are used for burial rituals.

Sacred pools, springs, and wetlands

A number of aquatic habitats are considered sacred and are conserved by indigenous communities through observance of religious and cultural customs. Most of these water bodies are believed to house water spirits and the vegetation surrounding them, particularly the riverine tree species (such as water berries [*Syzigium spp.*] and wild figs [*Ficus spp.*]) are protected through cultural customs. Similarly, aquatic indicator species, such as frogs and certain fish species and water birds, are traditionally protected. Killing or fishing these species is a taboo that, if broken, is believed to cause the water source to dry up. Agricultural activities are prohibited around water bodies, and trees within their vicinity are not to be cut down as it is claimed that such activities will cause the water body to dry up. The waterberry (*mukute* [Shona], – *Syzygium guineense*) is used as a reliable indicator for underground water sources and is never to be cut down. Additionally, the berries are edible and a source of fruit to the community.

Besides being habitats for aquatic biodiversity, the water bodies themselves are an important supply of water for livestock and domestic use and are therefore not to be profaned. When collecting water, certain taboos are observed that are important in the preservation of the water sources. Care is taken not to foul the water bodies. For example, no sooty or metal containers are to be dipped into the sacred water sources as it is maintained that this will cause the water body to dry up. Calabashes are instead used to collect the water and to fill the larger containers. Likewise, washing, doing dishes or laundry directly in the water bodies is culturally prohibited. Water is collected from the water source and these chores are done away from the water source. Scientifically, when the particles in soot and soap enter the water body they contaminate the water and darken it, increasing solar heating and water evaporation, which in turn could lead to drying of the water bodies (Mukwambo, 2017; Ndlovu & Manjeru, 2014). Such indigenous knowledge and practices can be incorporated into science lessons on water conservation in formal education processes.

Respect for places of spiritual significance by indigenous communities has directly contributed to biodiversity conservation. The exclusion of the spiritual dimension from westernized sustainability education discourses renders environmental sustainability a foreign concept detached from the lived realities of many indigenous learners. Re/introducing the spiritual aspects of indigenous sustainability practices in formal higher education processes has the potential to reveal their role in conserving environments and the value of perpetuating traditional beliefs.

Taboos for animals and plants

A taboo implies a prohibition, ban or restriction that is imposed on community members through cultural norms and customs in order to regulate resource use as a protective conservation measure. Taboos embody the hidden wisdom of indigenous peoples built through generations of interrelating with the lived environment and are integral to indigenous epistemologies. They play a significant role in the conservation of species and ecosystems and are worthy of consideration in modern biodiversity conservation practices. Certain animals and plants are revered for spiritual and other reasons and are not to be killed or destroyed.

Animal taboos

The killing and eating of certain animal species is taboo as they have spiritual significance. This includes the python as well as the pangolin, which has the status of food for the kings and chiefs and is a species prized by traditional healers. Certain ecological keystone species are also spiritually revered. These include the lion, which is considered a key ancestral spiritual species representing the spirt of the land (*mhondoro* [Shona]). Some predatory species, such as cheetahs, leopards, eagles, and the secretary bird, are likewise revered. Other predators, such as hyenas and owls, are protected because they are associated with witchcraft. Scavenging species, such as vultures and crows, are likewise protected by being considered too dirty to eat. Migratory bird species, such as storks, herons, swifts, and swallows, are traditionally protected as they are important indicators of seasonal changes, which define cycles of livelihood sustenance activities.

Other creatures (and some trees) have a special status because they are totem species (*mutupo* [Shona], *isibongo* [Ndebele]) for particular clan groups in the community. It is taboo for members of the clan to hunt, eat, or injure their totem species; doing so is believed to result in chronic illnesses as well as loss of teeth. In practical terms this ensured that not everybody would hunt the same species, which could lead to their extinction. Totems provide the identity of the clan and prevent incest and consanguineous marriages between close relatives in indigenous communities. Totems are expressed through praise poems that depict the character of the animal and of the clan. It is also common practice among the elderly to tell stories using animals and portraying them as people to either encourage or discourage certain characteristics and behaviors and to caution the young.

Plant taboos

Certain tree species are not harvested for firewood or timber because they are believed to bring bad luck to the home. These include the rain tree (*munyamharadzi* [Shona], *ichithamuzi/idungamuzi* [Ndebele] – *Lonchocarpus capasa*], whose wood was believed to bring quarrels in the home (Shava, 2000). This species has significance in that it produces droplets of water from its branches just before the rains due to an insect, the froghopper, which feeds on the sap of the tree and releases these water droplets. The fall of these drops of water is a sign of the start of the rainy season to the community. The tree is therefore traditionally protected as an important indicator of seasonal change.

Myths and proverbs

Indigenous myths

Myths have been employed by community elders to protect some sacred sites from environmental degradation or some species from extinction. Such myths include people being said to vanish, go mad, or see strange phenomena when they ventured into these sacred sites. Myths are closely related to taboos about sacred sites and are used to reinforce the conservation of these sites

Proverbs and Idioms

Indigenous proverbs (*tsumo* [Shona], *izaga* [Nguni]) are metaphors that depict wisdom or foolishness in indigenous social contexts and show the interaction of culture and nature. They can be employed to contextualize sustainability education. Here are two examples:

> "*Shiri yakangwara inovaka dendere rayo mvura isati yanaya*" (Shona) – "the wise bird builds its nest before the rains come." This proverb reveals observation of how birds prepare for the bad weather and is meant to caution and advise a person to plan and prepare in advance.
> "*Regai dziveshiri, zai harina muto*" (Shona) "let them be birds, eggs have no soup (*Also, "wadya zai wadya nhiyo yacho*" – "he who eats an egg eats the chick.") Embodied in this proverb is the conservation ethic of permitting the eggs to develop into adult breeding birds rather than eating the eggs. It is meant to caution an impatient person to persevere in order for better things to materialize.

Livelihood practices

Indigenous communities rely on diversified livelihood sustenance practices that relieve pressures on the land and reduce overexploitation of singular resources. Most of these livelihood substance practices reveal a conservation ethic.

Hunting of wildlife

Fishing, trapping, and hunting of wildlife was done through strict observance of breeding seasons in which such activities were prohibited by traditional leaders.

Hunting of pregnant or young baby animals was prohibited (Mapara, 2016). When large game was hunted, it was customary to share it among the hunters and the community. However, most traditional hunting practices have been abandoned as communities have lost their lands to the state, and hunting on communal lands is labeled as poaching.

Harvesting of wild food plants

Wild food plants provide an essential supply of nutrients to indigenous rural communities when in season. These plants include wild fruits, leafy vegetables, root and tuber plants, and mushrooms. Wild fruit trees are so valuable to indigenous communities that they are conserved even on cultivated land and in the grazing commons. Wild fruits are harvested only when they are ripe and throwing stones at them is prohibited (Risiro, Tshuma, & Basikiti, 2013). Harvesting ripe fruits not only prevents unnecessary wastage of wild resources but also ensures that the seeds in the fruits will be mature and able to germinate into new plants.

Firewood harvesting

Firewood is a primary source of energy for most indigenous rural communities in southern Africa. Indigenous wood harvesting practices in woodland and forest areas enable sustainability of the harvested wood species. When collecting firewood, deadwood from dry trees and dead branches is the first preference as it can be used immediately and is lighter to transport. Clearing deadwood gives the remaining vegetation better chances of flourishing. However, when deadwood is unavailable, live trees are used as a source of firewood and the wood is stored to dry. When trees are chopped down in the savanna woodlands, coppicing (leaving behind the base of the tree in the ground) and pollarding (removal of branches) are a common practice in Zimbabwe. This enables the regeneration of the trees. The most popular trees for fuelwood in the local savanna are the *msasa* (*Brachesytegia speciformis*) and *mnondo* (*Julbernadia globiflora*), which usually show vigorous regrowth after coppicing. Coppicing and pollarding increases harvestable wood biomass through the production of multiple stems

Medicinal plant harvesting

Most indigenous communities still heavily rely on traditional medicines for health and well-being. Traditional medical practitioners utilize several plant species as herbal remedies. Traditional healers use many approaches to conserve these plant species and ensure their sustainable use. These include leaving behind members of the same species when harvesting, leaving behind signs of harvesting to deter other traditional practitioners from harvesting from the same, harvesting bark from the east and western side of the tree to prevent ring barking, and not digging out all the roots when harvesting roots from a tree (Shava & Mavi, 1999; Edison, 2015; Mapara, 2016).

Farming and agriculture

Indigenous agricultural systems are local systems characterized by high species diversity (multi-cropping, multiple indigenous breeds), low chemical and energy inputs, high compatibility with the local environment (soils, climatic conditions), and diversity of adaptive strategies. These agricultural systems rely on the farmers' knowledge of their local macro and micro environments and reveal knowledge of ecological processes, such as the interconnectedness of environmental elements. The indigenous farming systems simulate the natural ecosystems, thereby making them ecological in nature.

Most indigenous farming systems are reliant on a diversity of indigenous crop varieties and indigenous livestock breeds, which are well adapted to the local environment context (including drought and flood resistant varieties) and they practice heirloom seed breeding and sharing. Such locally adapted species are important in local food sovereignty and security and contribute to the resilience and adaptive capacity of indigenous communities to climate change effects (Shava, Zazu, O'Donoghue, & Krasny, 2009; Nakashima et al., 2012). In southern Africa, indigenous crop species and varieties provide food security under adverse climatic conditions. These indigenous crops include drought resistant species, such as pearl millet, finger millet, and sorghum, which fare better during drought conditions than introduced staple cereals, such as maize, rice, and wheat.

Similar to indigenous crops, local indigenous breeds of goats, cattle, sheep, and chickens are hardy and able to withstand adverse conditions. Indigenous cattle breeds of southern Africa, such as the Hard Mashona in Zimbabwe, the Tswana cattle in Botswana, the Tonga cattle in Zambia, and the Tuli and Nguni cattle in southern Africa are naturally grazed, tolerant to dry weather and are disease resistant and they play an important role in providing meat, milk, manure, and drought power (Trail et al., 1977; Hoines, 1992; Rewe, Herold, Kahi, & Zarate, 2009; Tavirimirwa et al., 2013). Indigenous goats of southern Africa, such as the small Mashona Goat and large Matebele Goat in Zimbabwe, the Xhosa Lobed Ear goat of the Eastern Cape of South Africa and the Nguni Goat of KwaZuluNatal, are very hardy and drought tolerant breeds that are an important source of meat. Locally adapted sheep breeds in southern Africa include the Afrikaner sheep in the Cape Province of South Africa and the Damara sheep breed of Northern Namibia.

Raising awareness among indigenous communities of the importance of maintaining their indigenous agrobiodiversity and protecting their genetic pools instead of utilizing more popular introduced hybrid crops and livestock breeds will play a significant role in ensuring food security and sovereignty in the region. Globally, indigenous agrobiodiversity is important in averting the risk of reliance on a few staple food species against the background of environmental uncertainties such as climate change effects. Indigenous agrobiodiversity ushers forth a broad array of potential crops and livestock species and varieties that can enhance global future food security (Khoury et al., 2019). Teaching and research on the role of indigenous agrobiodiversity is an area that requires urgent attention in university agricultural curricula.

In addition to cultivating crops and keeping livestock, indigenous farmers practice selective conservation of wild plant species (fruits, wild leafy vegetables, medicines, shade trees, fuelwood trees) on their land (Campbell, Clarke, & Gumbo, 1991). Conservation of fruit trees is mainly due to their use as a source of food for livelihood sustenance. These wild, indigenous leafy vegetable and fruits contribute to the indigenous diet when in season. Selective conservation of wild plant species in communal areas increases species diversity on the land and attracts wildlife and pollinators as compared to modern intensive mono-cropping systems.

Indigenous mixed farming systems reduce the vulnerability that comes from a reliance on a few staple crops on animal breeds. Such farming systems enhance local food security. Aspects of indigenous agricultural systems are being incorporated into modern sustainable agricultural systems such as permaculture, agroforestry, and organic farming. Education on indigenous agrobiodiversity (indigenous heirloom seeds and indigenous livestock breeds) and its conservation, indigenous soil conservation practices, and indigenous agroforestry practices can play a significant role in sustainable agriculture education and in ensuring local food security and food sovereignty. This can be done through introducing participatory experiential and explorative case studies of indigenous sustainable agricultural practices in community contexts and researching their potential for modelling locally relevant sustainable agriculture.

Conclusion

This chapter illustrates how indigenous sustainability practices from southern Africa offer an alternative and complementary approach to conventional westernized sustainability education. Indigenous rural communities employ rules and regulations that protect biodiversity. Their values, ethics, and practices play a significant role in conserving resources and provide necessary knowledge for resilient adaptation to changing environment. The ethic of Earth care and a holistic notion of spiritual awareness are deeply woven into their culture. When a culture has beneficial attributes, it needs to be valued, revived, and promoted.

It is also important to indigenous peoples that their knowledges, cultures, values, and practices are seen as relevant to inform decision-making in all communities in the twenty-first century. If their practices are to be sustained, there is need to maintain or revive and restore a sense of community and belonging. It

TABLE 8.1 Course Content Guide

Conceptual Framework Dimensions	Lesson, Activity, or Project	Learning Informed by the SDGs (Goals 1.1 to 17.19) and The Earth Charter (Principles I.1 to IV.16)
Ethic of Care – Values – Attitudes – Behaviors	**1. Indigenous Ethic of Care** Plan a field trip to one or two local indigenous communities. Working in groups within an indigenous community context and in dialogue with indigenous community members, identify and describe the core aspects of their ethic of care. Reflect on the long-term implications (benefits and risks) of this ethic of care on ecological, social-cultural, and economic sustainability. Consider historic or global factors that may have impacted and can impact this ethic of care. Propose strategies for integrating aspects of an indigenous ethic of care in other community contexts.	4.7: By 2030, ensure that all learners acquire the knowledge and skills needed to promote sustainable development, including . . . through . . . appreciation of cultural diversity and of culture's contribution to sustainable development. 12.8: By 2030, ensure that people everywhere have the relevant information and awareness for sustainable development and lifestyles in harmony with nature. 1.5a: Ensure significant mobilization of resources from a variety of sources, including through enhanced development cooperation, in order to provide adequate and predictable means for developing countries . . . to implement programmes and policies to end poverty in all its dimensions.
Resilience & Regeneration – Knowledge – Skills	**2. Indigenous Resilience** Plan a field trip to one or two local indigenous communities. (If not possible, alternatively use detailed case studies of local indigenous communities that focus on their livelihood sustenance in relation to their lived environment). For each community, explore in detail aspects that contribute to its: community resilience (socio-cultural and economic); livelihood resilience (e.g. food security and sovereignty, health, etc.); and ecological resilience.	9.1: Develop quality, reliable, sustainable and resilient infrastructure . . . to support economic development and human well-being, with a focus on affordable and equitable access for all. 4: Ensure inclusive and equitable quality education and promote lifelong learning opportunities for all. I.2.: Care for the community of life with understanding, compassion, and love. I.2.a: Accept that with the right to own, manage, and use natural resources comes the duty to prevent environmental harm and to protect the rights of people.

Conceptual Framework Dimensions	Lesson, Activity, or Project	Learning Informed by the SDGs (Goals 1.1 to 17.19) and The Earth Charter (Principles I.1 to IV.16)
	Discuss how these aspects can be employed to transform other communities and contribute to the resilience of global society. Suggest innovative approaches that can be employed to share indigenous resilience practices.	II.8.b: Recognize and preserve the traditional knowledge and spiritual wisdom in all cultures that contribute to environmental protection and human well-being. III.12.c: Affirm the right of indigenous peoples to their spirituality, knowledge, lands and resources and to their related practice of sustainable livelihoods.
Advocacy for Life's Flourishing – Action – Critique – Reflection	**3. Learning as Connection** Identify key knowledge holders in the community context and the type of knowledge they possess. Propose how such knowledge holders can be engaged in interactions in formal sustainability education processes. Explore methods and pedagogies in which knowledge is transferred in an indigenous community inter-generationally as well as trans-generationally and suggest strategies for incorporating these in formal sustainability education processes. Discuss how indigenous knowledges can enable transformative learning and research processes. Working in groups in collaboration with a selected community, re-envision and share possible approaches of involving communities and students in co-engaged inquiry around local sustainable development knowledge and practices in formal education processes.	See also: I.1a, b; I.3.a, b; II.5.e; III.9.c; III.12.a, b, d; IV.14.d; IV.15.a, c. I.4.b: Transmit to future generations values, traditions, and institutions that support the long-term flourishing of Earth's human and ecological communities. II.7.f: Adopt lifestyles that emphasize the quality of life and material sufficiency in a finite world. III.14.d: Recognize the importance of moral and spiritual education for sustainable living. See also I.3.b; II.8.b; II.9.c; III.12.a, c, d. I.3.b: Promote social and economic justice, enabling all to achieve a secure and meaningful livelihood that is ecologically responsible. I.4.b: Transmit to future generations values, traditions, and institutions that support the long-term flourishing of Earth's human and ecological communities. III.12.b: Affirm the right of indigenous peoples to their spirituality, knowledge, lands and resources and to their related practice of sustainable livelihoods. See also: I.1.a, b; I.2.a; III.9.c; IV.14.d.

Source: An exploration of sustainability education from an indigenous knowledge perspective: examples from southern Africa

Soul Shava, Ph.D.

is also necessary to decolonize indigenous landscapes, thereby restoring a sense of place, where community members relate to and have ownership of the land and its resources. Many post-independent governments in southern Africa and the rest of Africa have retained centralized colonial environmental conservation and management policies and land tenure practices that alienate indigenous communities from the land and its resources, deprive people of land rights, and employ punitive measures when communities try to access natural resources for livelihood sustenance. Tourists are given access to these resources and hunt wildlife at costs that indigenous communities are unable to afford. National environmental management policies and systems should not alienate indigenous communities from conservation processes. Rather, they should recognize the centrality of indigenous communities in localized biodiversity conservation and should aim towards working with and learning from indigenous communities as custodians of their traditional lands, and complementary to national protected conservation areas (national parks and game/nature reserves and indigenous forest reserves).

Within urban contexts, community cohesion has largely dissipated and has been replaced by individualism and a lack of sense of belonging in the wake of modernity. Due to the impacts of western industrialization and modernization, people tend to focus on personal interests (their jobs, homes, and immediate families) at the expense of community cohesion and are alienated from the land, their lived environment. As a result, people are barely aware of the effects of their unsustainable actions on the environment and the community. There is a need to restore an inclusive community context and sense of place that can be passed down the generations. Rather than continue to be societies of strangers, community members in urban townships and suburbs should be encouraged to work together and to build relationships that develop a strong sense of belonging and care for the lived environment. This can be achieved through encouraging community participatory collaboration to address local environmental issues by promoting such initiatives as community 'greening' projects that utilize indigenous plants, thereby developing healthy and environmentally friendly neighborhoods. Such 'green' neighborhoods attract birds, insects, and other wildlife, making them biodiverse. An emphasis on indigenous fruit trees, shade plants, and medicinal plants provides much needed resources to the community while conserving indigenous species. Urban communities can benefit by learning from indigenous rural communities about localized biodiversity conservation practices through direct learning and sharing exchange visits between urban and rural communities and through relevant research, knowledge dissemination, and awareness by higher education institutions.

Indigenous communities provide a fertile ground for research into local sustainability practices and for the incorporation of the ideas that they embody into higher education curricula. This is particularly important in curriculum processes that are intended to be democratic and inclusive. I argue for higher education curricula that are relevant to the local people and that prioritize their issues by drawing upon local knowledge as much as they draw upon knowledge from other places and cultures. It is important to re-evaluate, reframe, re/contextualize, Africanize, and decolonize African higher education and to de-center Western-Euro-Americentric knowledge hegemony in formal higher education institutions. This opens up spaces for inter-epistemological dialogue and for reciprocal valorization of knowledges.

Course Planning

In charting the ways to future sustainability, there is need to recognize and critically engage with indigenous peoples and their knowledges, practices, and cultures that have occupied the margins of mainstream sustainability discourses. This calls for the creation of platforms that facilitate co-existence of wider ecological bodies of knowledge and encourage inter/multi-epistemological dialogue and reciprocal valorization of knowledges. Embracing the holistic and relational nature of indigenous knowledges requires consideration of the interrelatedness of persons with/in the community living in and from the land.

Guiding questions can include: What indigenous sustainability practices, ethics, and pedagogies exist in local indigenous community contexts? What approaches can be employed in dialogic engagements with indigenous communities on sustainability and environmental education processes? How do we recognize, value, or utilize indigenous environmental knowledge holders? How can we collaboratively and innovatively share indigenous environmental sustainability knowledge, ethics, and practices?

References

Barrow, E. G. C. (2010). Falling between the 'cracks' of conservation and religion: The role of stewardship for sacred trees and groves. In B. Verschuuren, R. Wild, J. A. MacNeely, & G. Oviedo (Eds.), *Sacred natural sites: Conserving nature and culture* (pp. 42–52). London, Washington D.C.: Earthscan.

Campbell, B. M., Clarke, J. M., & Gumbo, D. J. (1991). Traditional agroforestry practices in Zimbabwe. *Agroforestry Systems, 14*(2), 99–111. Retrieved from https://link.springer.com/content/pdf/10.1007%2FBF00045726.pdf

Campbell, B. M., Mandondo, A., Nemandwe, N., Sithole, B., De Jong, W., Luckert, M., & Matose, F. (2001). Challenges to proponents of community property resource systems: Despairing voices from social forests of Zimbabwe. *World Development, 29*(4), 589–600. https://doi.org/10.1016/S0305-750X(00)00114-5

Dei, G. J. S. (1993). Indigenous African knowledge systems: Local traditions of sustainable forestry. *Singapore Journal of Tropical Geography, 14*(1), 28–41. https://doi.org/10.1111/j.1467-9493.1994.tb00222.x

Dei, G. J. S. (2010). *Teaching Africa: Towards a transgressive pedagogy.* New York: Springer.

Edison, M. (2015). Managing natural resources and wildlife in contemporary society: Tapping into the traditional Karanga culture. *Scholars Journal of Arts, Humanities, and Social Sciences, 3*(1A), 41–48. Retrieved from http://saspjournals.com/wp-content/uploads/2015/01/SJAHSS-31A41-48.pdf

Foucault, M. (1980). *Power/knowledge: Selected writings and other interviews* (C. Gordon, Ed.). New York: Pantheon.

Hallpike, C. R. (2018). *Ship of fools: An anthology of learners' nonsense about primitive human societies.* Kuovola: Castalia House.

Hopkins, R. (2008). *The transition handbook.* Cambridge, UK: Green Books.

Hoines, D. H. (1992). *Mashona cattle of Zimbabwe.* Harare: The Mashona Cattle Society.

Khoury, C. K., Argumedo, A., Dempewolf, H., Guarino, L., de Haan, S., Wenzl, P. . . . van Etten, J. (2019). *With diversity at the heart: A 2050 vision for global food system transformation.* International Center for Tropical Agriculture (CIAT) (14 p.).

Knutsson, B. (2018). Green machines? Destabilizing discourse in technology education for sustainable development. *Critical Education, 9*(3), 1–18. Retrieved from http://ojs. library.ubc.ca/index.php/criticaled/article/view/186283

Makamure, C., & Chimininge, V. (2015). Totem, taboos and sacred places: An analysis of Karanga people's environmental conservation and management practices. *International Journal of Humanities and Social Science Invention, 4*(11), 7–12. Retrieved from https:// s3.amazonaws.com/academia.edu.documents/40651403/B04011007013.pdf?AWSA ccessKeyId=AKIAIWOWYYGZ2Y53UL3A&Expires=1552464446&Signature=4 R2KspJqdSfBOCPtyY03sN%2Bnpy4%3D&response-content-disposition=inline% 3B%20filename%3DTotem_Taboos_and_sacred_places_An_analys.pdf

Mapara, J. (2016). The environment as a significant other: The green nature of Shona indigenous religion. In F. Moolla (Ed.), *Natures of Africa: Ecocriticism and animal studies in contemporary cultural forms* (pp. 77–96). Johannesburg: Wits University Press.

Mapedza, E. (2006). Compromised co-management, compromised outcomes: Experiences from a Zimbabwean forest. *Africa Development, 31*(2), 123–146. Retrieved from www.ajol.info/index.php/ad/article/view/135742/125243

Mukwambo, M. (2017). *Exploring and expanding situated cognition in teaching sceiencecocnpets: The nexus of indigenous knowledge and western modern science.* Unpublished Doctor of Philosophy Thesis, Rhodes University, Grahamstown, South Africa.

Nakashima, D. J., Galloway McLean, K., Thulstrup, H. D., Ramos Castillo, A., & Rubis, J. T. (2012). *Weathering uncertainty: Traditional knowledge for climate change assessment and adaptation.* Paris: UNESCO and Darwin: UNU.

Ndlovu, C., & Manjeru, L. (2014, April). The influence of rituals and taboos on sustainable wetlands management: The case of Matobo District in Matabeleland South Province. *International Journal of Scientific and Research Publications, 4*, 4. Retrieved from https://pdfs.semanticscholar.org/aa87/890af8893c8097e5d28a2a74b4caad09b645.pdf

Rewe, T. O., Herold, P., Kahi, A. K., & Valle Zarate, A. (2009). Breeding indigenous cattle genetic resources in southern Africa. *Outlook on Agriculture, 38*(4), 317–326. https://doi.org/10.5367/000000009790422205

Risiro, J., Tshuma, T. D., & Basikiti, A. (2013). Indigenous knowledge systems and environment management: A case study of Zaka District, Masvingo Province, Zimbabwe. *International Journal of Academic Research in Progressive Education and Development, 2*(1), 19–39. Retrieved from http://hrmars.com/admin/pics/1442.pdf

Shava, S. (2000). *Tales of indigenous trees of Zimbabwe.* Howick: Share-Net.

Shava, S., & Mavi, S. (1999). Traditional methods of conserving medicinal plants in Zimbabwe. In R. O'Donoghue, L. Masuku, E. Janse van Rensburg, & M. Ward (Eds.), *Indigenous knowledge in/as environmental education processes: EEASA Monograph No. 3.* Grahamstown: Environmental Education Association of Southern Africa.

Shava, S., Zazu, C., O'Donoghue, R., & Krasny, M. E. (2009). Traditional food crops as source of community resilience in Zimbabwe. *International Journal of African Renaissance Studies – Multi-, Inter and Transdisciplinary, 4*(1), 31–48. https://doi.org/10.1080/ 18186870903101982

Tavirimirwa, B., Mwembe, R., Ngulube, B., Banana, N. Y. D., Nyamushamba, B., Ncube, S., & Nkomboni, D. (2013). Communal cattle production in Zimbabwe: A review. *Livestock Research for Rural Development, 25*(12), 1–16. https://doi.org/10.13140/2.1.3412.8009

Trail, J. C. M., Buck, N. G., Light, D., Rennie, T. W., Ruthford, A., Miller, M. . . . Cappter, B. S. (1977). Productivity of Africander, Tswana, Tuli and crossbred beef cattle in Botswana. *Animal Science, 24*, 57–62. https://doi.org/10.1017/S0003356100039209

WEF. (2019). *Global risk report 2019* (14th ed.). Geneva: World Economic Forum. Retrieved from www3.weforum.org/docs/WEF_Global_Risks_Report_2019.pdf

9

WALKING INTO THE HEART OF THE LANDSCAPE TO FIND THE LANDSCAPE OF THE HEART

Simon Wilson

This chapter takes a multidisciplinary approach to the issue of sustainability education. It emphasises the importance of co-creation of – and deep participation in – the environment as it appears to our senses. At its core is a concern that without actual personal experience of an intimate and heart-felt relationship with the world and with the heart of the world, any sustainability projects or plans may well be doomed to failure.

This amounts to a recognition that what *The Earth Charter*, in its first principle, calls 'love' (2006, p. 2) is essential to a living relationship, whether between people or between the Earth and its population. Tom Cheetham acknowledges this when he writes that it is "[w]onder and love [which] first draw us out into the world – a passion for things, for beauty, for discovery" (2015, p. 168). Love is in fact the polar opposite of the negligence, alienation, instrumentalisation, commodification, mechanisation, deadness, and indifference which have created the conditions for the current ecological catastrophe. It is, as Kallistos Ware writes, "the only true answer to our ecological crisis, for we cannot save what we do not love" (2013, p. 105). Without love, we and the world are laid waste.

Such thoughts are, to be sure, in no way novel. For example, one finds them too in the works of seventeenth-century poet and theologian Thomas Traherne:

> Lov is the true Means by which the World is Enjoyed. Our Lov to others, and Others Lov to us. We ought therfore abov all Things to get acquainted with the Nature of Lov. for Lov is the Root and Foundation of Nature . . . There are many Glorious Excellencies in the Material World, but without Lov they are all Abortiv.
>
> *(1958, p. 87) (sic throughout)*

If love is the root and foundation of nature, all living things depend on it. Remove it, as Traherne says, and everything in and of the world is stillborn, a dead thing.

The lesson is perhaps that sustainability education should actually be a praxis of love. If that is not the case, it will merely serve to accelerate the destruction of the natural world by attacking it at its very root and foundation.

Love, care, resilience, and advocating life

What is the significance of these reflections on a loving relationship with the world and the life of the world? One way to answer that question is certainly in terms of the guiding principles of sustainability explored in this book. Any true ethic of care must have love as its foundation, otherwise it degenerates into duty and ideology. Resilience requires it too, while the creativity necessary to foster regeneration under challenging circumstances is best fired by love. It fiercely motivates actions to ensure that life flourishes (including the social justice, gender equality, or respect of the integrity of the natural world the SDG requires in, for example, goals 5 or 16 [United Nations, 2015]). It resists commodification, and is always supremely personal, requiring complete freedom of the heart, but at the same time is by definition communal and shared, even across time (thus enabling harmonisation of "the exercise of freedom with the common good" for which *The Earth Charter* calls [2006, p. 4]). Finally, it is love which has the power to bring about the radical *metanoia*, the "change of mind and heart" advocated by *The Earth Charter* (2006, p. 4).

Love, in a word, is what animates care, resilience, regeneration, and advocacy practices, and prevents them from falling into abstract theory.

One aim of this chapter, then, is to describe methods of nurturing just such an orientation through sustainability education. It proposes practices perhaps not commonly associated with sustainability, based partly but not solely in the humanities (which, as Chara Armon points out in this volume, have often been overlooked in sustainability education). So this chapter will explore practices based in literature, imagination, local folklore, archaeology, and also a way of walking specific landscapes, which can be employed in or out of the classroom. The aspiration is to achieve a multidimensional and flexible experience, which addresses a range of ways of knowing and perceiving the world and the self. By describing what are in effect different perspectives or complementary approaches, I have tried to offer a view which is holistic and dynamic but which also tries to avoid a totalising vantage point. To that end, this chapter weaves spirals through and around its subject, rather than trying to proceed step-by-step along a straight path. Or, to employ a different metaphor, it is kaleidoscopic: it turns and turns, and while each turn rearranges its constituent elements in different ways, to form new patterns, the elements remain the same.

Such words, bare as they are, remain on the level of rather vague and abstract theory, which is counter to the living and wholly concrete connectedness to the environment which is my theme. I hope to move beyond description, to evoke in the reader the experiences, relationships, and transformations I am outlining. In that sense, the chapter does not provide a prescriptive model for other educators and students, but hopes to touch the heart, to inspire the reader to enter into a transforming relationship with the world, which they can pass on to others.

There can be no working through of a conceptual grid here, only an invitation to loving engagement.

Study

To start the journey proper, I would like to replace the words 'learning' or 'education' with 'study,' and to recover an enchanting but forgotten meaning of the latter word. If we turn to the *Oxford English Dictionary*, we find that its very first definition of the noun 'study' does not concern careful examination of objects, intense application of mind, or the cultivation of science. Rather, it reads: "Affection, friendliness, devotion to another's welfare; partisan sympathy; desire, inclination; pleasure or interest felt in something" (1989, p. 979). In other words, the primary meaning of study is a movement of the heart, a reaching out of the self to a world beyond the self. It is an active and loving engagement with other people and with the world, an outflowing of the deepest sympathy.[1] 'Study' was first used in this sense in the English language in around 1374, while the *OED*'s last citation is from 1697 (1989, p. 979). It thus appears that the Age of the Enlightenment put an end to this loving learning, along with much else which may be essential to life's flourishing.

If study is construed as affection, devotion, sympathy, or desire, it implies a reciprocal relationship between entities which are, in the fullest sense of the word, alive. In other words, to study something this way is an act akin to gazing at the face of someone we love. For, as the great Orthodox theologian Pavel Florensky wrote in a passage which seems perfectly to describe study,

> knowing is not the capturing of a dead object by a predatory subject of knowledge, but a living moral communion of persons, each serving for each as both object and subject. Strictly speaking, only a person is known and only by a person.
>
> *(1997, pp. 55–56)*

Our object of study, then, is our beloved, returning the gaze and drawing us ever further on, to know increasingly more of his or her infinite riches. Studying thus changes us and our relation to what (or, to be more precise, whom) we study. It changes the very aspect of what we study, renewing us and our beloved. It means an ever closer sympathy of two equals, in which there is distinction but no distance, and leads to what Chara Armon in this volume (drawing on the work of Thomas Berry) calls communion.

This intricately involved and dynamic relationship is no mere sentiment. The affection, sympathy, desire, and pleasure express the longing of the emotions, but also of the body, the mind, the spirit, and the soul, just as the word "heart", in many ancient spiritual traditions, describes the centre of a human's whole being, somatic, psychic, spiritual, imaginative, and more (see Cutsinger, 2002). Studying in fact offers the kind of holistic epistemology which David Selby and Fumiyo Kagawa call for, one which is

enriched through emotional, imaginative and creative entanglement with
the world, by spiritual and sensorial engagement with the close-at-hand
world, by embodied and somatic learning, by deep listening and intimate
observation, by action learning, by dialogic learning.

(2015, p. 278)

If love, then, is the enlivening centre of the guiding framework behind this
volume, study is the heart of sustainability education; or rather, sustainability
education *is* study.

One must also bear in mind that, like love, study can take many varied and
unpredictable – even surprising – forms. The transformations it works are not
amenable to control or manipulation by government or other bodies. Neither
can they be controlled or corralled by modish notions of 'outcomes' or 'bench-
marks.' The nature of study is always specific to the relationship between the
individuals studying (including the relationship between teacher and student).
Study thus becomes the rewilding of education, and pursuing it may lead to
the rewilding of the human/planet relationship. Finally, even if the approaches
described fall short of engendering fully transformative study, the worst they
can do is introduce people to fascinating literature, folklore, and archaeology,
while perhaps encouraging more physical exercise.

Literature and study

"The map is not the territory" we say, forgetting that the territory is not the
territory.[2] There is perhaps no landscape beyond our engagement with it. The
territory is imagined, walked, worked, loved into existence, and does not live –
is not truly alive – independent of our engagement with it. In turn, our imagination, our mind, our body, etc. are enlivened and informed by the world thus
responding to our sympathy, our devotion. Every act of perception, every glance
at the scenery, every inhalation of air, is in effect an act of co-creation, a response
which immediately calls out another response.

Such thoughts were common to the Romantic poets, who conceived of
"a bilateral transaction, a give-and-take, between mind and external object"
(Abrams, 1953, p. 61). In other words, they described and practised the co-
creation of self and world. The English poet Wordsworth rooted this co-creative
relationship in the love between mother and infant. In *The Prelude* he declares
that a loved infant is intimately linked with the cosmos, as child, mother, and
cosmos bring each other into being. Such an infant's mind is

creator and receiver both,
Working but in alliance with the works
Which it beholds.

(Wordsworth, 1985, p. 54)

It is this intricate relationship, this movement of loving responsiveness, which engenders life. Without it, the appearances of the world are dead, and so are we. Coleridge put it like this: "we receive but what we give,/And in our life alone does Nature live" (1974, p. 281). That is, if we do not go out of ourselves in love, devotion, sympathy, and pleasure – if we do not *study* the world – then nature's appearances start to seem independent of our gaze. Then the world dies; and something necessary to our beings dies too in a world which is held to be out there, objective, seemingly independent of us. We and the world are then dead things: a desert where a heart should be, a wasteland where fruit trees should grow. The important thing is that nothing can be sustained – there is perhaps nothing to be sustained – if we do not acknowledge that we and the environment come into being in a loving, dynamic, and endless act of co-creation.

It is not only the writings of the English Romantic poets which bear witness to these truths. In *As You Like It*, Shakespeare's imagination took the Forest of Arden of his home county and made it into a place of transformation for his characters, and this newly enchanted place in turn transformed and fructified his imagination. Similar transformations are wrought in and through the loving relationship between the writer Thomas Hardy and Wessex. Importantly, the works of such authors do not just describe a process, they initiate it too in the readers. They may lead us to give the world the special quality of attention Coleridge writes of, to thus transform it and be transformed by it. Our heart then goes out to the world and the world reaches out to our heart in a mutual embrace. Reading literature with this in mind may flood us and our environment with self-sustaining life.

Jocelyn Brooke country

The crucial influence on my own thoughts on these matters, however, was the comparatively obscure author Jocelyn Brooke, who invites us to share in the life and creation of a beautiful region of England known as East Kent. This area is especially dear to me as I live there, in a village called Bridge, close to the geographical centre of what he called his "mythopeoeic vision" (1981, p. 257). Brooke's writings, furthermore, are interesting because they reveal some of the strange pathways along which deep study of a landscape may lead one.

Jocelyn Brooke (1908–1966) lived much of his life in the little village of Bishopsbourne, some four miles or so southeast of Canterbury, just beyond my own home village. Bishopsbourne and its immediate surroundings inspired all his best writings. On long walks, Brooke experienced how this locality became intimately entangled with his soul. The reader of his writings, if he or she happens to live near Bishopsbourne anyway, can also participate in the mythic formation of the landscape in the same way, and be formed by it, so that it continues to live long after Brooke's death. Certainly that was true for me, as I would like to briefly outline.

Bishopsbourne began to take on mythopoeic qualities, Brooke tells us, from his earliest childhood. The transfigured village was a summerland of warmth and light and ease, a middle-class and very English Eden (Brooke, 1981, p. 26). Also woven into his vision, however, is a wider landscape encircling the village: sinister and horrific, this is a winterland preyed upon by strange subterranean elementals, dim demonic beings who live in tunnels and hellish caverns extending all the way down to Dover (Brooke, 1981, p. 171). As a boy, Brooke was tormented by the fear that he would be abducted by these creatures and carried off to their "infernal regions" (1981, p. 184).

Paradoxically what these demonic beings do is to nurture further the mythopoeic intertwining of land and Brooke's own being. By contrast, the very worst place in Brooke's strange geography is so terrifying not because it is inhabited by demons or evil presences but because it appears to be a collection of objects wholly external to himself, unresponsive to his gaze, independent of his consciousness, of sympathy, of love itself. As such, it is essentially dead, and it is from here that Brooke envisions the Third World War spreading into England (1950, p. 181).

This terrible place is called Clambercrown. The fields and woods around this forbidding area seem devoid of all meaning: "flat, lifeless symbols of themselves, without depth or significance" (Brooke, 1955, p. 193). It is, writes Brooke, "a waste land of the spirit," in which his interior world, too, is "emptied of life and meaning," subsiding into "an anarchic chaos of meaningless images" (1955, pp. 193, 196). He is possessed by the fear that, in such a place, his life must slip "into final negation, not-being, death-in-life" (1955, p. 196): a kind of zombie, or one of the undead, nightmarishly aping life but empty.

Essentially, Brooke is describing a kind of expulsion out of the entangled, co-creative mythic world into one in which phenomena appear to be wholly unconnected to his heart, objective as it were, seemingly opaque to his studying eyes, where the territory is the territory – a symbol of itself – and nothing else. Just a series of unyielding surfaces. This is a landscape – a wasteland as Brooke says – drained of mutual love, and it is perhaps the world most people inhabit in the global West. As we forget that we are intimately and reflexively connected to the world, our spirit too wastes away, and our mind becomes an arbitrary jumble of images, stripped of all quality: we too die. Under such circumstances, nothing is sustainable.

Walking the territory into life

It was reading Brooke which taught me that the life of the world depends on our loving, studious gaze, and that our life depends on the world returning that gaze, however unexpectedly. Transformation can only come, I learnt, when the lovers' gazes embrace. When I walked the local countryside, I walked partly in and through his mythopoeic land. I followed in his footsteps, and shared in his vision. My heart went out to this transfigured landscape, and its heart went out to me. The result was deep imaginative, spiritual, and somatic interweaving. Or, to put it another way, the result was life, and the dynamic and the ever-changing creative engagement life inspires.

Thus inspired, I began to move beyond Brooke's vision, to study the folklore and archaeology of the area, particularly of a hill between Bridge and Bishopsbourne (see figure 9.1).

I learnt that in the past the local inhabitants were not reliant on artists to create a living connection between self and land: it was common knowledge, embodied in stories and practices. It was especially fascinating to find that the stories seemed to single out the region as occupying a central role in the very life of England. I began to invite students and colleagues from Canterbury Christ Church University on my walks, and also began a private initiative, whereby local residents, too, accompanied me. My hope was to reweave them back into the landscape and to reweave the landscape back into them, so that all could be sustained, and we and England granted life again.

It was from Brooke that I first learned that the Nailbourne – the little river that runs through the Elham Valley – grants the locality national significance, as the place where England's fate is foreknown. It is an intermittent chalk stream, whose flowing is said to presage disaster both material and spiritual (see Brooke, 1946, pp. 25–27).

The first mention in writing of the Nailbourne's significance is in a fifteenth-century chronicle attributed to John Warkworth, which identifies the river as one of the five chief woe-waters of England, whose running "was a tokene of derthe, or of pestylence, or of grete batayle" (Warkworth, 1839, p. 24). One gathers that the meaning of the woe-waters had long been known to locals.

Even when it is not flowing, the Nailbourne haunts the landscape, invisibly moving below ground. The great film-maker Michael Powell, who was born just a couple of miles downstream of Bridge and Bishopsbourne, was entranced as a boy by the thought of the Nailbourne's hidden flow though underground channels and caverns (Powell, 1986, p. 20).

When walking, it seemed to me that its legend was not just about the potential disaster brought by flooding. Its story told of the interweaving of locals with a numinous, haunted landscape, and the terror that can occur when what should remain hidden in the pitch-black underworld is suddenly, openly, and horrifyingly displayed. The Nailbourne, like Brooke's demonic elementals, rises in the landscape and in the soul of the individual. Knowing and feeling its significance weaves the inhabitants of the valley into the landscape. Just as importantly, this deep knowing and engagement also offers some degree of protection, or at least mitigates the effects by weaving them into an endless tapestry of meaning, which includes past, present, and future. It offers, that is, sustainability, in the deepest sense.

We now live in a time which does not acknowledge this subtle intermingling. The Nailbourne's transformations are random, and speak of nothing. The result is inner and outer dearth, and pestilence, and battle.

The works of Brooke also revealed another piece of local folklore, which seems to confirm that the land of the Nailbourne is spiritually and materially crucial to the fate of England (see 1981, pp. 261–262). Half-way up Bridge Hill,

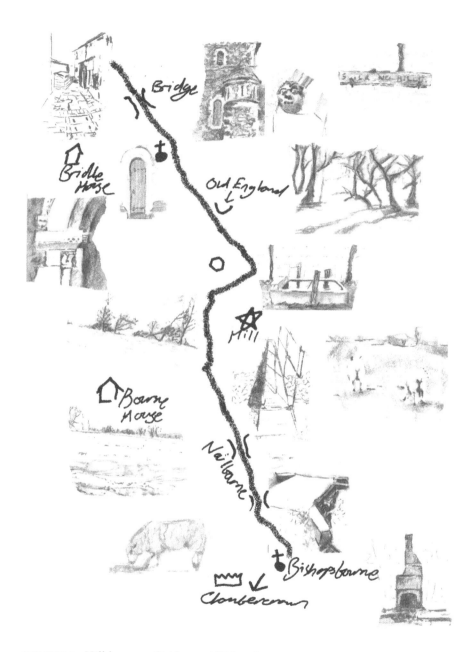

FIGURE 9.1 Hill between Bridge and Bishopsbourne

(*Source*: James Frost)

next to the road descending to cross the Nailbourne, is a feature called Old England's Hole. Tradition has it that local tribes dug in here in a literally last-ditch attempt to resist Caesar and his army in 54BC (Scoble, 2010, p. 7). Old England's Hole is thus associated with the romance of lost causes, the dream of what was lost when the Romans came, a 'Celtic' dream tinged with druidic mists, and enchanted by spells. The longing felt by many in Britain (and elsewhere) for the imagined past of faery, the Green Man, seasonal celebrations, and Avalon begins on the slope of Bridge Hill. In a way, this is a local and national version of the loss of Eden, the once and future loss which holds within it all losses (including the eventual invasion of the country by the Romans, some years after Caesar's incursion).

On the face of it this is an overblown claim to make about a relatively obscure part of a small corner of a not particularly large country. Yet it serves to emphasise the point that sustaining and sustainable relationships between humans and the world are always concrete, always specific, and thus always localised. We cannot love abstractions, and abstractions are exactly what the 'environment,' 'education,' or even 'the planet' remain unless experienced in particularities: particular places, particular cities, particular landscapes. Once we love them, though, we may come to love all nature to its roots and foundations. Elder Zosima, a monk in Dostoyevsky's *The Brothers Karamazov*, points this out: "Each leaf, each sunbeam of God, love it. Love the animals, love the plants, love every object . . . And at last you will love the whole world with an all-inclusive, universal love" (2003, pp. 412–413). What study nurtures is thus a kind of double vision: beholding a specific river, a specific hill or a specific hollow, and at the same time seeing the life that animates all the world.[3]

In the specific and yet unlimited case of Bridge Hill, the knowledge that Paradise had been lost there slowly brought with it the realisation that there, too, it could be regained, and so I went looking for it.

At the top of the hill is an ill-defined area which seems to have nothing to distinguish it, and yet it has its own name: Star Hill. Here, it seems to me, studious eyes may discover the centre of the cosmos, the place of pristine Creation, where the loving heart may go out and meet the heart of the world.[4] This is where Paradise may be regained. The fate of England and of the world may depend on having eyes to see what otherwise lies hidden on Star Hill

Such claims would of course be absurd if the same eyes did not also reveal that Star Hill can claim no exclusivity. As we all have a heart, the heart of the world is also everywhere, in every landscape and every cityscape. Having found the paradisiacal heart of the world on Star Hill, loving eyes may then see it in any and every place.

What I found on Star Hill are the concealed remains of a hexagonal structure, whose outline is only visible in especially dry years, from the air. Archaeological investigations, conducted 2003–2006, revealed it to be of Roman origin (Wilkinson, 2008, pp. 24–26). What enchanted me was its six-sided shape, for it is this which marks it out as the centre of the cosmos, the heart of the world. The number six, across many sacred traditions, has a variety of meanings, including reconciliation, peace, and the perfection of unblemished creation (see Guthrie, 1987, p. 323; Rooth, 2008, p. 311). Star Hill thus revealed itself to me as the place of mystical marriage, where heaven and earth kiss and intertwine, where apparent opposites are united, and participate in each other's being. It is a place of unspoilt creation.

The hexagonal shape itself stands for this mystical (re-)union. It is made by the union of two equilateral triangles, one pointing downwards and one upwards, forming within them the outline of a hexagon. This union symbolises the marriage of opposites (Rooth, 2008, pp. 322–323). The points of the triangles emerge from the hexagon to form a hexagram, or a six-pointed star. For those with eyes to see, a star surmounts Star Hill.

This is the culmination of my walk up Bridge Hill, past the Nailbourne and Old England's Hole. It is the final experience I try to offer those accompanying me, be they students, lecturers, or local residents. I hope, that is, that study, in the meaning I have tried to invoke in this essay, may lead the longing heart of the individual to profound and intricate entanglement with a way of being which reconciles the world and the divine, so that, necessarily, that reconciliation occurs both in the landscape and in the human person. This way of being is new in the sense of being very different from that which is cultivated in the contemporary world, but is simultaneously the recovery of the primordial state symbolised by Eden, in which divine and material are intricately entangled.[5]

Sustainability, indeed, may only be possible if our centremost self is, in every place, interwoven with the centre of the world, to foster a general renewal which is equally material, spiritual, and intellectual, and in which love calls to love. Without this lived experience of mutually responsive devotion and desire, we and the world will continue to fall apart into incomprehension, suspicion, and relentless mechanisation.

Other walks

I would like to mention briefly another form of profoundly experiential walking I have developed to invite students, colleagues, and others to study the world. As it is not always practical to go out for a longer walk, I have taken people on short walks of Canterbury Christ Church University's main campus. An ideal location has proven to be the small garden in front of Coleridge House, a particularly beautiful corner of the campus. My companions walk in pairs, one with eyes closed, the other guiding (see figure 9.2 for a map of such a walk).

We proceed at a snail's pace, every so often pausing to allow me to read a short text evoking a landscape or cityscape together with the figures which belong in it, such as Brooke, or Michael Powell, or Thomas De Quincey. The texts, aided by the slowly meandering course we take, weave new vision for the walkers, as other senses become heightened.

These walks last about 20 minutes. They are then followed by about the same length of time spent discussing the experience and any thoughts or feelings which may have arisen during it. This element is essential to the effect of

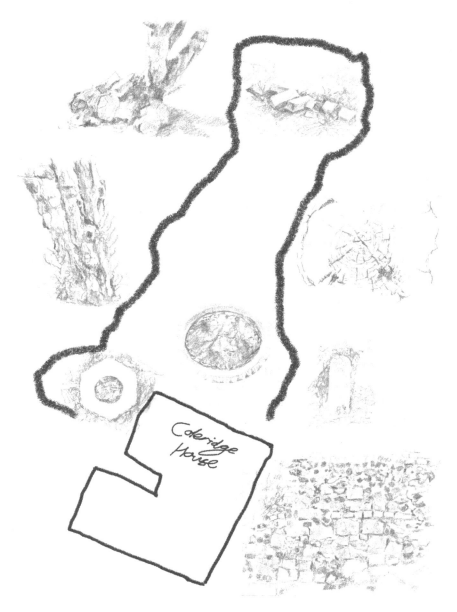

FIGURE 9.2 Map of Experiential Walking on Canterbury Christ Church University Campus.

(*Source*: James Frost)

the walks. It requires a tranquil space and the willingness, on my part, to do nothing but listen patiently, attentively and even lovingly. In a word, it requires studious listening. What happens cannot then be planned, but in my experience extremely personal and heart-felt associations arise, which indicate that a shift has occurred, a movement out of the kind of routine interactions which characterise life on campus. New and deeper relationships are fostered, between the participants and the campus and among the participants themselves.

Finally, participants are requested to write brief and informal notes as feedback. These speak of being "open to sensations, smells, feelings and touch," while the walk "took me to another mode of experiencing the campus surroundings." Others wrote of the way the walk opened "inner eyes of imagination" while being "a very sensory and erotic experience." One participant spoke of "place informing experience, and *vice versa*." I hope that something of this new sense of loving entanglement in the life of the world will remain with people.

"This walk should be part of classes," and "this should happen more often in life" are further comments I have received as feedback. I believe that *all* the practices described above are necessary to weave the individual back into the world (and *vice versa*), and thereby promote true sustainability. That weaving may begin with any of these modes and practices. My whole approach, however, has been informed by the need to foster study, which in turn I take to be the very heart of sustainability education, and necessary to nurture the dimensions of care, resilience, regeneration, and advocacy which give this volume its framework. Practices change as study deepens, and the experience of loving entanglement grows. It has been one of the arguments of the chapter that the precise form of that entanglement cannot be foreseen, calling into question notions of so-called outcomes in sustainability education. But still there is the hope that this studious journey may "end in lovers meeting."[6] And thus that it may never end.

Course Planning

It is not my intention to prescribe here any specific methods or learning outcomes: readers of the above chapter will find reasons enough why I am sceptical of their use in sustainability education. One additional justification for their absence is the context of the walks described below, which have been offered primarily as part of the MA Myth Cosmology and the Sacred, a course which values participatory and relational approaches to knowledge over 'evidence-based' methods. The feedback quoted in my chapter shows the transformative potential of these walks, and links them implicitly to the SDG and *The Earth Charter*. Commensurate with my interest in dynamic and experiential study, however, I leave it to the reader to identify the precise learning outcomes to which the feedback may point.

TABLE 9.1 Sustainability Education Grounded in the Sustainable Development Goals and The Earth Charter

Conceptual Framework Dimensions	*Activity*
Ethic of Care – Values – Attitudes – Behaviors **Resilience & Regeneration** – New knowledge – New relationships – Leadership – Strengthens communal bonds **Advocacy for Life's Flourishing** – Change of heart and mind encourages desire to bring about change in life and institutions	**Title: Walking the Campus into Life** **Place**: Main campus. **Aim**: To facilitate the kind of holistic heart entanglement with the environment which is at the centre of sustainability study. **Procedure**: Before the activity, a series of short texts (perhaps seven or eight) are prepared, describing and evoking a landscape or cityscape. I have often chosen passages derived from the works of writers, such as Jocelyn Brooke, John Michell, Elizabeth Bowen, or Thomas De Quincey. On the walk itself, students walk in pairs, one with eyes closed, the other guiding. They follow the organiser of the activity, who leads them slowly and carefully on a meandering and labyrinthine path through a specific part of the campus, occasionally pausing for him/her to read one of the pre-prepared texts. After the walk, an equally slow and meandering conversation is facilitated in a tranquil space, allowing students to share any thoughts, feelings, or associations which may arise during the walk. Finally, students are asked to write short and informal feedback. In my experience, this often centres on the way their relationship to the campus, learning, the university, and also to each other, has been changed. New somatic and imaginative modes of experience are recorded, along with the wish that these be embedded in curricula, and, more widely, in life outside the university.

Source: Course Content Guide: MA, Myth, Cosmology and the Sacred, Walking exercise, Dr Simon Wilson

Notes

1 See also Illich (1996, pp. 14–15). According to the *OED*, the word derives ultimately from the Latin *studium*, meaning "zeal, affection, painstaking study" (1989, p. 979).
2 The phrase was coined by Alfred Korzybski: see (1933, p. 58).
3 See also Ware on "double vision" (2013, pp. 94–95).
4 My view of this edenic point is influenced by René Guénon's conception of the 'Centre,' which I have discussed elsewhere (e.g. Wilson, 2015).
5 The primordial state is another idea derived from Guénon (Rooth, 2008, p. 93).
6 Shakespeare (2008, pp. 2.3: 42).

References

Abrams, M. H. (1953). *The mirror and the lamp: Romantic theory and the critical tradition*. New York: Oxford University Press.

Brooke, J. (1946). Month's mind. In *December spring: Poems* (pp. 25–27). London: The Bodley Head.

Brooke, J. (1950). *The image of a drawn sword*. London: The Bodley Head.

Brooke, J. (1955). *The Dog at Clambercrown: An excursion*. London: The Bodley Head.

Brooke, J. (1981). *The orchid trilogy*. Harmondsworth: Penguin Books.

Cheetham, T. (2015). *Imaginal love: The meanings of imagination in Henry Corbin and James Hillman*. Thompson, CT: Spring Publications.

Coleridge, S. T. (1974). Dejection: An ode. In J. Beer (Ed.), *Poems* (pp. 280–283). London: J.M. Dent & Sons.

Cutsinger, J. S. (Ed.). (2002). *Paths to the heart: Sufism and the Christian east*. Bloomington, IN: World Wisdom.

Dostoyevsky, F. (2003). *The brothers Karamazov: A novel in four parts and an epilogue* (D. McDuff, Trans.). London: Penguin Books.

The Earth Charter. (2006). Retrieved from earthcharter.org/invent/images/uploads/echarter_english.pdf

Florensky, P. (1997). *The pillar and ground of the truth: An essay in Orthodox theodicy in twelve letters* (B. Jakim, Trans.). Princeton, NJ: Princeton University Press.

Guthrie, K. S. (1987). *The Pythagorean sourcebook and library: An anthology of ancient writings which relate to Pythagoras and Pythagorean philosophy* (D. R. Fideler, Ed.). Grand Rapids, MI: Phanes Press.

Illich, I. (1996). *In the vineyard of the text: A commentary to Hugh's didascalion*. Chicago, IL: University of Chicago Press.

Korzybski, A. (1933). *Science and sanity: An introduction to non-Aristotelian systems and general semantics*. New York: Institute of General Semantics.

Oxford English Dictionary. (1989). (2nd ed., Vol. 16: Soot-Styx). Oxford: Oxford University Press.

Powell, M. (1986). *A life in movies: An autobiography*. London: Heinemann.

Rooth, G. (2008). *Prophet for a dark age: A companion to the works of René Guénon*. Eastbourne: Sussex Academic Press.

Scoble, C. (2010). *Letters from Bishopsbourne: Three writers in an English village*. Cheltenham: BMM.

Selby, D., & Kagawa, F. (2015). Drawing threads together: A critical and transformative agenda for sustainability education. In D. Selby & F. Kagawa (Eds.). *Sustainability frontiers: Critical and transformative voices from the borderlands of sustainability education* (pp. 277–280). Opladen: Barbara Budrich Publishers.

Shakespeare, W. (2008). *Twelfth night, or what you will* (K. Elam, Ed.). London: Bloomsbury.

Traherne, T. (1958). *Centuries, poems, and thanksgivings. Volume 1: Introduction and centuries*. (H. M. Margoliouth, Ed.). Oxford: Oxford University Press.

United Nations. (2015). *Transforming our world: The 2030 agenda for sustainable development*. Retrieved from https://sustainabledevelopment.un.org/content/documents/21252030%20Agenda%20for%20Sustainable%20Development%20web.pdf

Ware, K. (2013). Through creation to the creator. In J. Chryssavigis & B. V. Foltz (Eds.), *Towards an ecology of transfiguration: Orthodox Christian perspectives on environment, nature, and creation* (pp. 86–105). New York: Fordham University Press.

Warkworth, J. (1839). *A chronicle of the first thirteen years of the reign of King Edward the Fourth* (J. O. Halliwell, Ed.). London: The Camden Society.

Wilkinson, P. (2008). *The archaeological investigation of a hexagonal feature at Star Hill, Bridge, near Canterbury, Kent. 2003–6.* Retrieved from www.kafs.co.uk/pdf/Bridge.pdf

Wilson, S. (2015). René Guénon and the heart of the Grail. *Temenos Academy Review, 18,* 146–167.

Wordsworth, W. (1985). *The fourteen-Book prelude* (W. J. B. Owen, Ed.). Ithaca, NY: Cornell University Press.

10

THERAVADA BUDDHIST WAYS OF THINKING

Reflections on sustainability accounting education in a public university in Sri Lanka

A D Nuwan Gunarathne and Sasith Rajasooriya

Introduction

Notwithstanding the strenuous efforts of many individuals and organisations, education for a sustainable world has not yet received due attention owing to many interrelated structural aspects of education systems (Cortese, 2003). Most of these education systems around the world advocate a consumer-driven orientation, which influences students' subsequent behaviours and decisions. This exploitative behaviour poses many challenges for the implementation of the United Nation's Sustainable Development Goals (SDGs). Further, it directly threatens the Earth Charter's Principles for a sustainable way of life such as its Principle Seven, which promotes the adoption of production, consumption, and reproduction patterns that safeguard the Earth's regenerative capacities. This situation is also evident in contemporary business management education systems, including accounting. In the praxis of sustainability, accounting plays a crucial role in corporate sustainability performance by providing information for various stakeholders to make decisions. However, accounting education systems have not met the expectations of growing societal needs, and accounting graduates who one day become professional accountants are unprepared to face the emerging sustainability challenges. This calls for a more proactive role for accounting education whilst making major revisions to prioritize sustainability (Gunarathne & Alahakoon, 2017; Gray & Collison, 2002). In making these educational reforms, environmentalists and educators have made use of various religious teachings regarding the sustainability and human-nature relationships (Hitzhusen, 2007).

Although the impact of some religions, such as Christianity, on sustainability education systems has been discussed (Hitzhusen, 2007; Chansomsak & Vale, 2008), how oriental religious ways of thinking can inform business management education, accounting in particular, has received only limited attention. The purpose of this chapter is therefore to discuss how a sustainability management accounting [SMA] course introduced in a public university in Sri Lanka reflects Theravada Sinhalese Buddhist ways of thinking in enhancing the immediate and long-term pathways to sustainability-conscious decision-making.

Different religious viewpoints of the human ecological relationship influence sustainability education and hence students' behaviour and decision-making. In this context, sustainability education can be regarded as "a new way of thinking that is focused on learning and acting appropriately to improve or at least sustain the interrelationship between human and ecological communities" (Chansomsak & Vale, 2008, p. 35). As Sterling (2001) suggests, sustainability education evolves in three phases: accommodation, reformation, and transformation. The first stage, accommodation, considers the changes within the existing education paradigms and does not therefore challenge or change basic values. This stage is referred to as "education about sustainability" in which sustainability issues are added to existing policies and practices while treating sustainability as a separate subject in the curriculum. The second stage, reformation, takes place when participants of the education systems revisit, influence, and critically reflect the basic values and the concepts of sustainability. This stage, referred to as "education for sustainability," encompasses new content designed to change the value systems. The last stage, transformation, requires fundamental revisions in education systems while taking a cultural step forward towards strong forms of sustainability. This stage is referred to as "education as sustainability." Sustainability education should therefore aim to achieve higher levels of sustainability education evolution stages by changing knowledge, skills, and personality factors, such as attitudes and values and habits (Chansomsak & Vale, 2008).

The rest of the chapter is organized as follows: The first section "Theravada Buddhist thought on the human-nature relationship" provides an overview of the Theravada Buddhist thought on the relationship between sustainability, humans, and nature. The following section discusses the impact and application of Theravada Buddhist thought in Sri Lanka. The third section "Theravada Buddhist thought in sustainability accounting education" discusses the extent to which Theravada Buddhist thought is covered in the SMA course introduced by a public university in Sri Lanka. The last section presents reflections and future directions.

Theravada Buddhist thought on the human-nature relationship

The viewpoint of Theravada Buddhism on nature, humans, and relationships among all phenomena is described and analysed in depth in numerous discourses of the Buddha (suttas) and in the comprehensive analyses of the Theravada canon called "Abhidhamma." According to Theravada Buddhism, any observable existence and related phenomena are made up of a number of elementary corporeal and mental constituents. A set of these corporeal and mental elements together constitutes the "world." It is important to understand that the term "world" in Buddhism is taught and analysed in association with the individual. The entirety of the collective and conditioned existence of all the elements of the universe and its material and non-material substances are analysed in relation to the individual.

Theravada Buddhism highlights that being a human is an important and rare opportunity and, yet, emphasises that humans are yet one kind of being among innumerable other beings who are transformed from one form of "*nama-rupa*" (two main components, mental and corporeal aspects, respectively) or "*khand-has*" (aggregates) to another as per the rules of "*kamma*" (karma) and "*dhamma*" (Bodhi, 2000; Karunadasa, 1996). Such an elaboration indeed is distinct from many other teachings that argue human existence to be superior to others. Many monotheistic teachings teach or at least imply that the "world" or "nature" (including the surrounding environment and animals) is created by a supreme being (e.g. god) for humans. But in Theravada Buddhism, humans, animals, and all other such beings known or unknown are considered to be temporal states of the process of collective aggregates named above. Promotion of and emphasis on the well-being of animals and other beings in Buddhism is not defined relative to human well-being or goodness. But, instead, it accepts the freedom of all other beings, too, to live in the process.

Theravada Buddhism interprets the world as a set of conditionally existing infinite elements, neither created by some supreme being nor for some specific kind of species. Such an interpretation calls for coexistence. The world is ultimately what we perceive through our senses, including the mind (Samyuttanikaya 4:68 ChatthaSangayana Tipitaka). According to Theravada Buddhism, an individual is neither devoid of nature nor the nature and individual can be considered as two entities. An individual is not even just a part of nature. The individual and culture at large define what "nature" is ultimately. Nonetheless, we use the phrase "human-nature relationship" as a means of manoeuvring the discussion, still wondering whether it is appropriate to use the term "relationship"' according to Theravada Buddhist thought. As stated previously, Theravada thought on phenomena such as "human," "nature," "world," and "environment" is understood relative to the perspective of human mind and perceptive organs. Hence, it does not permit us to distinguish "human," "nature," or "world" as separate entities or independent entities. This deep viewpoint of Theravada Buddhism does not draw parallels with many other religious and philosophical viewpoints. Theravada Buddhism defines a conditional existence, in which the "world" or, in other words, "nature" is a conditioned existence and so is "human." In Theravada Buddhism, the external "world" and "I" (or myself) are just different ways of perception, which are not different entities of independent existence. These fundamental differences in Theravada Buddhism compared to many other religions give rise to several peculiar features in Theravada Buddhist culture. As

Stephen Scoffham observes in this volume, many faiths, including monotheistic religions, have considered the need for coexistence with nature in some way. However, the real challenge would be to develop a common basis to integrate all these teachings through an ideological foundation where such integration would work as a powerful force against the forces that exploit the earth. As Scoffham rightly emphasizes, a real solution that would make a difference in human–nature relationship is to have a "shift in thinking about our relationship to the environment and our sense of meaning." The authors believe that the Theravada thought of "world" discussed in this section would provide a foundation for such a shift.

Impact and application of Theravada Buddhist thinking in ancient and contemporary Sri Lankan society

Sri Lanka has been a Theravada Buddhist country for over 2300 years. After the formal introduction of Theravada Buddhism to Sri Lanka in 326 BC, for more than ten centuries the country's first kingdom, "Anuradhapura," played a major role in developing *Sinhalese Theravada Buddhist* culture while laying the foundation for its thought informed by the Theravada Pali canon.

Theravada Buddhist thought was disseminated for over two millennia among Sinhalese generations through various means. With the spiritual and religious leadership of Buddhist monks who preserved a rich written and vocal tradition of Theravada principles, Sinhalese generations are inheritors of the basic principles of Theravada Buddhism. Buddhist monks in Sri Lanka also preserved a long tradition of "dhamma preaching" for both novice monks and laymen. Higher education institutions in the Theravada tradition called "*maha-vihara*" were established where knowledge of both worldly and spiritual aspects of society were created and practised. Buddhist monks in the monastery in each village played the role of teachers. Under this leadership of Buddhist monks, villagers absorbed both knowledge and practice informed by Theravada Buddhist thought. Practically every worldly activity, including the production of food, trading, irrigation, industries, art, and architecture, was practised within the philosophical and spiritual guidelines of Theravada Buddhist thought. Relations between family members, parents and children, employer and employee, state and citizen, and personal acquaintances were shaped by the inherited and intrinsic understanding of Theravada Buddhist thought on nature, world, and life. Therefore, the Sinhalese were able to preserve and continue their harmony with nature without disturbing the natural flow of the environment.

Despite the influence of the Western ethos over more than five centuries of colonization and exposure to western modernity, science, and technology, the lifestyle of Sinhalese Buddhists even today manifests some sociocultural aspects of the Sinhalese Theravada Buddhist thought discussed above. A striking example of the sustainability, human–nature relationship is the Sinhalese irrigation system that has stood the test of time over two millennia. The tank system created and maintained by Sinhalese monarchs over thousands of years ago still contributes to agricultural production in Sri Lanka. The importance of this marvellous irrigation system lies in its natural flow of the water system itself without breaking or interfering with its pattern in an artificial way. Ancient tanks were built to support agriculture in both dry and wet zones in Sri Lanka, when water was insufficient for large-scale agricultural production. This system was supported by a massive network of tanks combining river, rain, geographical terrain, agricultural fields, and finally spiritual and physical aspects of the islanders (see Figure 10.1). The irrigation system did not consider agricultural production for human needs in isolation but also the co-existence or conditioned existence of all living beings, including animals and trees.

When tanks were built, due attention was given to the conservation and protection of wildlife. The canal system that connected the tanks had separate reserved areas for water supply over each mile or two for elephants and other animals, demonstrating the ancient concern for animals and nature. The surroundings of almost all the major tanks were dedicated sanctuaries by tradition and on specific occasions by law. Each Sinhalese village had a human-made small tank connected to a giant tank like Tissa Wewa (See Figure 10.1) in the province through a complex canal system. Paddy field, temple or monastery, tank,

FIGURE 10.1   An example of a tank system in Sri Lanka

Note: The most sacred monument of Theravada Buddhism, the Ruwanwelisaya (the Great Stupa) at Anuradhapura, Sri Lanka, stands behind the Tissa Wewa (tank), a living symbol of sustainable Theravada Buddhist culture. It is situated in the premises of the Maha Vihara (Great Monastary), which was the center of Theravada education and agricultural civilization of Sri Lanka for more than a millennium. During the Anuradhapura kingdom, irrigation-based civilization was developed along with hundreds of giant tanks such as Tissa Wewa.

Source: © Hiranya Malwatta

and cultivation area were among the key components of every village, while the villagers preserved the natural forest areas to ensure coexistence with animals and plants.

King Parakramabahu the Great (an ancient king whose reign is considered as the peak of ancient Sri Lanka's economic development) once declared that *"not a drop of rain water shall go to the sea without providing service to the world."* It is interesting to note that this king had not used the words "service to the human/ man" but instead "service to the world." The motive of the Sinhalese monarchs embedded in these words illustrates the effect of Theravada Buddhist thought on humans and nature. Even today, these ancient tanks manifest how Sinhala Theravada Buddhism encompassed the natural cycles of economic and social life.

Theravada Buddhist thought in sustainability accounting education

This section discusses how Theravada Buddhist thought does and does not reflect sustainability education by considering the first and only SMA course introduced in a public university in Sri Lanka. This university, the University of Sri Jayewardenepura, has a long history dating back to 1873. It was established by a Buddhist monk as a center for Oriental learning and today it is the largest university in the country in terms of student numbers.

Its SMA course was introduced in 2012 as an elective in its undergraduate degree (B.Sc Accounting honours degree, hereafter referred to as the degree program) by the Department of Accounting [DA] of this university. The students of DA usually become professional accountants shortly after graduation by obtaining membership in professional accounting bodies. They work in both private and public sector organizations locally and overseas, such as Australasia, the Middle East and Africa (Senaratne & Gunarathne, 2017). During the degree program, the students complete 40 course units in accounting, finance, management, and other related disciplines. This degree program is the first academic accounting degree introduced in 1991 into the university system of Sri Lanka. The degree program from its inception has always followed a high professional orientation to meet the requirements of the accounting profession (Senaratne & Gunarathne, 2010).

The introduction of the SMA course discussed here was a novel experience: it was the first time in an undergraduate accounting degree program in the country that a course of this nature was introduced. The motivation for this course was "to improve the accounting undergraduates' understanding of sustainability and to facilitate future thinking and praxis" (Gunarathne & Alahakoon, 2017, p. 399). A discussion of how the Theravada Buddhist thought is and is not reflected in this course can be carried out in two phases: a) course design phase and b) course delivery phase through practical applications.

Since the majority of the country's management and accounting graduates were not conversant with sustainability principles due to the neglect of sustainability education, this course at the design stage aimed to fill the lacuna among professional accountants capable of supporting organizational sustainability initiatives through planning, measurement, and monitoring. The Head of Department commented on the need to introduce a course of this nature as follows:

> *"At DA we had introduced some reporting aspects of sustainability some time back. However, we felt there was a need for accountants who can assist in [the management of] corporate initiatives on sustainability, not just reporting. . . . Therefore, we felt a course that discusses not only the reporting aspects but the management aspects was necessary."*

The focus of the sustainability reporting courses that were already in the curricula was to report the past performance of sustainability initiatives of an organization. However, this SMA course placed emphasis on the planning, measurement, control, and assurance aspects of sustainability, with the focus on modifying the corporate behaviour through trusted and targeted accounting information. For instance, this course introduced accounting for energy in which the role of accounting emphasises the energy efficiency of an organization by setting energy-related key performance indicators (KPIs), identifying the current energy flows and their associated costs, and evaluating alternative energy (renewable) sources.

At the design stage, this course considered the knowledge and skills that an accountant required to support the achievement of corporate economic objectives through corporate sustainability management. Therefore, Theravada Buddhist thought was not considered in the initial design as seen in the omission of any Theravada-related topics in the syllabus. The syllabus reflects Western orientations and origins as an antidote to modern unsustainable production and consumption patterns as is clearly evident in topics such as cleaner production, waste management, sustainability reporting based on the principles of the Global Reporting Initiative (GRI), and integrated reporting. These topics were market-driven as they reflected a prioritization of economic realities and were supportive of the conventional emphasis placed by Sri Lankan business organizations on typical measure-and-manage approaches to sustainability (see Abeydeera, Kearins, & Tregidga, 2016). This approach adopted at the design stage reflects the "accommodation" (or education for sustainability) phase of Sterling (2001) in which changes are made within the existing education paradigms by introducing sustainability as a separate subject in the accounting curriculum.

In addition, the underlying philosophy of the topics included in the course supported treating the environment as a separate entity that humans have to protect, which is not in line with the thinking of Theravada Buddhism. A close analysis of the topics taught in this sustainability course points to Elkington's (1994) triple bottom line concept that promotes economic, social, and environmental perspectives in sustainability. This is evident in the SMA course, which first separately discusses the accounting aspects pertaining to the economic, environmental, and social pillars of corporate sustainability and then the integration of these three separate aspects. Moreover, reporting aspects discussed in this course explicitly deal with the environment as a separate reporting dimension. For instance, in the GRI framework, environment is treated as a separate dimension of reporting while in the IIRC integrated reporting framework, environment is one of the six capitals an organization has to manage in its value creation process. This is not in line with the unified sustainability, human–nature relationship discussed in Theravada Buddhism.

Although the design and the topics in the course reflect much of the Western ethos of the sustainability, human–nature relationship, it is not totally devoid of some aspects of Theravada Buddhist thought. These aspects were incorporated in the course at the delivery stage through some of its practical applications. They are: a) field visits, b) case studies, c) guest seminars, and d) student centered learning approaches (see Gunarathne & Alahakoon, 2017; Gunarathne, 2018 for more details) (see Table 10.1).

An important reference to Theravada Buddhist thought was made during *field visits*, which were a compulsory learning requirement of the course. Although the main purpose was to visit business organizations, during the field visits the students also visited museums, temples, agricultural fields, and natural landscapes (see Figure 10.2). These visits facilitated discussions with external

FIGURE 10.2 A field visit made to a tea factory

Note: The students examining a waste treatment facility in a tea processing plant in the hill country of Sri Lanka. This plant is in the close proximity to a natural reserve and hence follows an environmentally friendly biological treatment process with minimum environmental impact.

TABLE 10.1 An Overview of the Practical Applications of the SMA Course

Practical application	What students engaged in	Objective	Arrangement	Where they occurred	Link to Theravada Buddhism
Field visits	Visiting business organizations, agricultural fields, and natural landscapes	To appreciate how sustainability management and accounting practices are carried out practically.	Visits to business organizations were arranged by making formal requests and other places were visited as visitors.	In business organizations and in fields	Students get opportunities to understand how Theravada Buddhist thought is reflected in individual thinking, human behaviour, and business processes and practices.
Case studies	Developing a case study on a sustainability management and accounting issue in a real-life organization	To improve the understanding of the organization-wide knowledge and to identify practical solutions to the sustainability issues encountered.	Students selected the case organizations; however, in some instances the course lecturer helped in finding suitable organizations through his personal contacts.	In business organizations	When they analyse organizational issues from a sustainability point of view, they can use Theravada Buddhist teachings to propose potential solutions.

(Continued)

TABLE 10.1 (Continued)

Guest seminars	Interacting with a resource person on a broad topic related to sustainability	To broaden the understanding of the multidimensionality of sustainability beyond the discipline of accounting.	Lecturer personally invited these resource persons to present a topic unrelated to accounting.	In classrooms	Students gain new insights into Theravada Buddhist teachings by blending Theravada Buddhist concepts with the resource person's viewpoints.
Student-centered learning approaches	Engaging in interactive, reflective and action-oriented learning activities	To enhance students' understanding of complex sustainability issues by promoting active and responsible participation in applying new knowledge and prior experience.	Lecturer played a facilitator role in promoting these learning approaches in class while some reflective discussions were made during the field visits.	In classrooms During field visits	Students deepen their understanding of Theravada Buddhist concepts and their application in modern sustainability practices through active participation.

parties, such as business sustainability managers, sustainability consultants and experts, Buddhist monks, historians, and agriculturalists who brought in different perspectives on the sustainability, human-nature relationship and the present environmental and social problems. Further, these visits allowed the students to experience and deliberate on (un)desirable corporate practices as well as social practices related to sustainability. These observations were often discussed in the classroom later on when the students were asked to express their views. These field visits and group discussions facilitated discussions of Theravada Buddhism among these students.

In *student-centered learning approaches*, especially when the concepts of sustainability were discussed, frequent reference was made to the ancient irrigation system and living patterns that exemplified a harmonious relationship with nature. Further, reflective discussions were held with the students on the current crisis of waste management in Sri Lanka and how and why it was not a problem in ancient times. As this course used group discussions as a part of its pedagogy, the students were asked to reflect on the concepts they had experienced, such as lakes and the ancient hydraulic civilization in relation to sustainable development. These examples would improve their understanding of how they should make decisions in a corporate setting or personal life guided by the ancient sustainable lifestyles. Further, they were instructed to reflect on the present-day problems associated with rapid development and what remedial action they should take as responsible citizens or future corporate leaders of sustainability.

In arranging *guest seminars*, the course lecturer paid special attention to inviting resource persons from different sustainability backgrounds. The topics covered in these interactive seminars included cleaner production, green architecture, and carbon management. These resource persons from different fields of expertise brought in novel views and practical concepts on various dimensions of sustainability outside the field of accounting. Although these seminars did not make explicit reference to Theravada Buddhist thought, they were useful for accounting students in broadening their knowledge of ecosystems, natural cycles, and the Earth's regenerating capacity, which provided a sound basis for understanding and relating Theravada Buddhist concepts later on.

Another practical application, *case study development*, also provide opportunities for students to apply their theoretical knowledge to a practical sustainability issue faced by an organization. This enabled them to interact with professionals from diverse backgrounds, such as engineering, production, procurement, marketing, and human resources. As the students proposed feasible solutions for the sustainability issues they identified, they were compelled to brainstorm and suggest alternatives beyond the knowledge obtained in classrooms. Like the seminars, this practical application also did not make explicit reference to Theravada Buddhist thought. However, identifying creative solutions and systematically evaluating them enabled the students to apply some of the observations made during field visits and the knowledge obtained through reflective discussions.

Some of these practical applications, such as field visits and student-centered learning activities, directly influenced students' critical reflections and value systems, indicating Sterling's concept of reformation (2001). The other two practical applications, namely, guest seminars and case studies, facilitated the reformation process among students. Being the first course of this genre, it fell short of the most advanced stage of Sterling, viz., transformation, which leads to fundamental revisions in education systems. In the future, graduates of the SMA course may return as guest speakers to describe, analyse, evaluate, and promote the impacts of Theravada Buddhist-oriented sustainability accounting in their workplaces, which may drive changes in the SMA program.

Reflections and future directions

As shown in this case, due to the high professional orientation of the degree program and the nature of the accounting discipline, the course design of the SMA course has been primarily driven by the Western ethos. However, the course delivery has facilitated broader discussion and reflective learning for the students while referring to some of the Theravada Buddhist precepts. This course can be viewed as one more inclined to the Western ethos in its design but adds Theravada Buddhist thought in its delivery. This suggests that when the market place demands employees to possess skills and knowledge to perform sustainability practices based on a Western orientation, sustainability education especially in disciplines such as accounting will have to be included in order to satisfy these market needs. However, in the course delivery, it is the role of the lecturer (or teacher) to engage the students in reflective discussion to provide a deeper understanding of the traditional value systems and how modern corporate practices deviate from them. This will provide a better footing for the students when they become practising managers to strike a balance between their private morals and workplace practices.

A contemporary sustainability-oriented accountant, who has understood the intricate human-nature relationship in Theravada Buddhism through practical living examples such as the irrigation system, would first change his personal behaviour by avoiding consumption or disposal patterns that would disrupt this natural flow in the environment, while preferring the products or service that attempt to maintain these natural cycles. For instance, in personal consumption behaviour, (s)he can switch to using a bag made out of linen than using single-use polythene bags. Then, these accountants can promote these practices in their workplace either by setting examples to peers or introducing workplace policies. In doing so, they can use some accounting tools and techniques such as life cycle analysis *[a systematic tool that evaluates the environmental costs and benefits associated with all the stages of a product's life cycle, such as raw material extraction, production, distribution, consumption, and disposal]* or environmental full cost accounting *[a method of costing which identifies all the possible economic, environmental, and social costs and benefits of a cost object such as a product or service]* as effective evaluation and communication

TABLE 10.2 Sustainability Education Grounded in the Sustainable Development Goals and the Earth Charter – Course Content Guide: Sustainability Accounting, Elective Course, Mr. Gunarathne

Conceptual Framework Dimensions	Lesson, Activity, or Project	Learning Informed by the SDGs (Goals 1.1 to 17.19) and The Earth Charter (Principles I.1 to IV.16)
Ethic of Care – Values – Attitudes – Behaviors	**Title: Case study development on sustainability accounting practices** [refer Burritt, Hahn, & Schaltegger, 2002 Framework for the analysis of sustainability accounting practices] *Steps* Each group selects one area listed above to focus on in consultation with the course lecturer. **I. *Study question & unit of analysis*** Demonstrate key competencies of system thinking to identify an issue in an organization or organizational unit in the above four areas.	**7.2** Increase the share of renewable energy in the global energy mix **7.3** Enhance the rate of improvement in energy efficiency **12.4** Achieve the environmentally sound management of chemicals and all wastes throughout their life cycle and reduce their release to air, water, and soil in order to minimize their adverse impacts on human health and the environment
Resilience & Regeneration – Knowledge – Skills	**II. *Data collection and analysis*** Demonstrate key competencies of system thinking, analytical and interpersonal, to collect the required data and analyze them in relation to sustainability accounting practices. **III. *Discussion and recommendation*** Demonstrate key competencies of strategic and critical thinking to explain the present practices and identify desired solutions.	**6.3** Improve water quality by reducing pollution, eliminating dumping, and minimizing release of hazardous chemicals and materials, reducing untreated wastewater, and increasing recycling and safe reuse **8.8** Protect labour rights and promote safe and secure working environments for all workers
Advocacy for Life's Flourishing – Action – Critique – Reflection	**IV. *Advocacy Outcomes*** Demonstrate key competencies of strategic and interpersonal competence with relevant employees to design and implement advocacy efforts that move current undesirable organizational practices along more sustainable paths. Coordinate with peer groups to present a collective advocacy statement for key decision-makers in each organization.	**12.2** Promote the sustainable management and efficient use of natural resource **I.7.** Adopt patterns of production, consumption, and reproduction that safeguard Earth's regenerative capacities, human rights, and community well-being.

(Continued)

TABLE 10.2 (Continued)

Conceptual Framework Dimensions	Lesson, Activity, or Project	Learning Informed by the SDGs (Goals 1.1 to 17.19) and The Earth Charter (Principles I.1 to IV.16)
	V. Reflection Outcomes: In your written and oral presentations, demonstrate key competencies of reflexivity, critique, and dialogue on how this case study development may or may not create significant change toward a desirable and sustainable future in: a) business organizations and b) your personal and professional life.	**II.10.c** Ensure that all trade supports sustainable resource use, environmental protection, and progressive labor standards. **11.10** Ensure that economic activities and institutions at all levels promote human development in an equitable and sustainable manner. **IV.14** Integrate into formal education and life-long learning the knowledge, values, and skills needed for a sustainable way of life.

tools to inform stakeholders. This enables them to serve as organizational change agents who promote and foster sustainability. Moreover, if the present organizational systems, including accounting are not capable of planning, measuring, and evaluating the present organizational practices in line with the Theravada Buddhist thought, they can introduce new accounting techniques.

These aspirations about contemporary sustainability-oriented accountants can only be achieved by moving sustainability education beyond the accommodation stage (Sterling, 2001) to more advanced stages, such as reformation and transformation. The students who have been educated in these more thorough stages of sustainability would critically evaluate the personal and organizational value systems, make revisions to organizational policies and practices, create more sustainable visions for organizations, and drive organizational actions in a sustainable manner. More specifically, in the accounting profession, these sustainability-oriented accountants can set policies and goals, make decisions, take follow-up actions towards more sustainable outcomes, and communicate the corporate sustainability information to the various internal and external stakeholders. Further, if the present accounting systems are not capable of overcoming the environmental and social issues, these sustainability-oriented accountants would (or should) devise new accounting practices and systems based on Theravada Buddhist thought, which are capable of providing better solutions or approaches than what is practiced at present. Equipped with these accounting and management practices, sustainability-oriented accountants can collaborate with other professionals who work in sustainability arenas to promote responsible production patterns as indicated in SDG 12 in their organizations. Moreover, they would not promote industries or business activities that impact the natural cycles in the environment by excessive resource use, degradation, and pollution along the whole life cycle that decrease the quality of life.

Despite the introductory application of Theravada Buddhist precepts to modern day corporate sustainability management in the Sri Lankan context, the authors see a positive side. Managers or accountants whose private value system is shaped by Theravada Buddhist thought provide a congenial environment for popularizing these modern sustainability-related concepts, such as environmental protection, equality, and social accountability even if their philosophical stance is not aligned to original Theravada Buddhist concepts. Thus, business organizations can make use of the sustainability-oriented thinking of future accountants to embrace new concepts akin to their value system (Gunarathne & Senaratne, 2018). In addition to the business organizations, educators in management and accounting disciplines and policymakers can capitalize on this favourable attitude of accountants to foster a better world (Gunarathne & Alahakoon, 2016). This would lay the foundation for mitigating the consumer-driven orientation, which results in exploitative behaviour and decision-making of the consumers including students. This is paramount, as allaying greed is the key to the achievement of the UN SDGs and Earth Charter's Principles for a sustainable way of life.

If proper sustainability education mechanisms can be formulated, changing some of the personal and professional behaviour patterns of the (management) students such as evaluation and decision making, consumption and disposal would not be challenging in a country like Sri Lanka that provides a congenial environment for contemporary sustainability concepts to take off. Thus, policy level support is necessary if the education system is to move forward to advanced stages of sustainability education such as reformation and transformation. This could be materialized through university-led initiatives such as conferences, forums, and discussions that bring policymakers, faculty members, students, and university administrators together to deliberate on the benefits of Theravada Buddhism-oriented sustainability thinking in the corporate workplaces and civil society. This should then lead to the introduction of novel courses or curriculum reforms in the future that are built on the principles and value system of Theravada Buddhism.

Course Planning

In this Elective Course, our class will discuss how sustainability accounting practices are applied by a selected Sri Lankan business organization and how far they reflect Theravada Buddhist thought. This exercise will enable you to appreciate the practical validity of the sustainability management and accounting concepts learnt in the subject and assess to what extent they exhibit Theravada Buddhist concepts. For this purpose, you are required to visit and analyze the sustainability management practices of an organization. A case study should be developed based on the organization you visit (see Yin, 2009). In developing this case study, you are required to form groups of *four to six* members with one member as group leader.

When developing the case study, you need to select one area out of the following four areas for analysis: 1) energy (or carbon) analysis, management, and renewable energy; 2) waste disposal and chemical management; 3) water consumption, recycling, and management; and 4) employee welfare, equity, and occupational health and safety (see Table 10.2 above for more details).

References

Abeydeera, S., Kearins, K., & Tregidga, H. (2016). Does Buddhism enable a different sustainability ethic at work? *Journal of Corporate Citizenship*, *6*, 109–130. https://doi. org/10.9774/GLEAF.4700.2016.ju.00013

Bodhi, B. (2000). *A comprehensive manual of Abhidhamma*. Seattle, WA: BPS Pariyatti Editions.

Burritt, R., Hahn, T., & Schaltegger, S. (2002). Towards a comprehensive framework for environmental management accounting: Links between business actors and environmental management accounting tools. *Australian Accounting Review*, *12*(2), 39–50. https://doi.org/10.1111/j.1835-2561.2002.tb00202.x

Chansomsak, S., & Vale, B. (2008). The Buddhist approach to education: An alternative approach for sustainable education. *Asia Pacific Journal of Education*, *28*(1), 35–50. https://doi.org/10.1080/02188790701850063

Cortese, A. D. (2003). The critical role of higher education in creating a sustainable future. *Planning for Higher Education*, *31*(3), 15–22.

Elkington, J. (1994). Towards the sustainable corporation: Win-win-win business strategies for sustainable development. *California Management Review*, *36*(2), 90–100. https://doi.org/10.2307/41165746

Gray, R. H., & Collison, D. (2002). Can't see the wood for the trees, can't see the trees for the numbers? Accounting education, sustainability and the public interest. *Critical Perspectives on Accounting*, *13*(5–6), 797–836. https://doi.org/10.1006/cpac.2002.0554

Gunarathne, A. D. N. (2018). Developing graduate competence in sustainability management. In P. M. Flynn, T. K. Tan, & M. Gudić (Eds.), *Redefining success: Integrating sustainability into management education* (pp. 86–96). Oxon: Routledge.

Gunarathne, A. D. N., & Alahakoon, Y. (2016). Environmental management accounting practices and their diffusion: The Sri Lankan experience. *NSBM Journal of Management*, *2*(1), 1–26. http://doi.org/10.4038/nsbmjm.v2i1.18

Gunarathne, A. D. N., & Alahakoon, Y. (2017). Integrating futures thinking through transdisciplinarity into sustainability accounting education: perspectives from Sri Lanka. In P. B. Corcoran, J. P. Weakland, & A. E. J. Wals (Eds.), *Envisioning futures for environmental and sustainability education* (pp. 397–405). Wageningen, The Netherlands: Wageningen Academic.

Gunarathne, A. D. N., & Senaratne, S. (2018). Country readiness in adopting integrated reporting: A diamond theory approach from an Asian Pacific economy. In K. H. Lee &

S. Schaltegger (Eds.), *Accounting for sustainability: Asia Pacific perspectives* (pp. 39–66). Cham, Switzerland: Springer.

Hitzhusen, G. E. (2007). Judeo-Christian theology and the environment: Moving beyond scepticism to new sources for environmental education in the United States. *Environmental Education Research, 13*(1), 55–74. https://doi.org/10.1080/13504620601122699

Karunadasa, Y. (1996). *The dhamma theory: Philosophical cornerstone of the abhidhamma.* Kandy: Buddhist Publication Society.

Senaratne, S., & Gunarathne, A. D. N. (2010). *A case of an accountancy study programme in Sri Lanka to improve relevance and quality of undergraduate education: A new dimension on institutional view.* Paper presented at the 1st International Conference on Business and Information, University of Kelaniya, Sri Lanka.

Senaratne, S., & Gunarathne, A. D. N. (2017). Excellence perspective for management education from a global accountants' hub in Asia. In N. Baporikar (Ed.), *Management education for global leadership* (pp. 158–180). Hershey: IGI Global.

Sterling, S. (2001). *Sustainable education: Re-visioning learning and change.* Schumacher Briefing No. 6. Dartington: Green Books.

Yin, R. (2009). *Case study research: Design and methods.* Thousand Oaks, CA: Sage.

11

EDUCATION FOR SUSTAINABILITY IN EARLY CHILDHOOD EDUCATION

Sustainability transformation through collaboration

Nicola Kemp and Polly Bolshaw

Introduction

Early Childhood Education (ECE) has been relatively slow to engage with Education for Sustainable Development (ESD) and lags behind other educational phases in both practice and research. Encouragingly, the last ten years have seen a rapid growth in international interest and Early Childhood Education for Sustainability (ECEfS) is now a recognised area of study. This chapter explores the collaboration between postgraduate students and lecturers on a newly validated Masters level module in ECEfS at a UK university. There are at least two ways to engage with the chapter. Firstly, from the perspective of higher education as a case study of embedding sustainability within an academic programme; and secondly, from the perspective of early childhood education as examples of sustainability in practice. However, these are not independent perspectives. Rather, this collaboratively authored chapter explores the connections between the postgraduate students' own engagement with sustainability and that of the children and the practitioners with whom they engage. In the UK 'practitioners' is the term used to refer to the adults working with young children in Early Childhood Education settings.

Sustainability in higher education

There is a long-standing, global recognition of the role education can play in contributing to sustainable development (see for example, World Commission on Environment and Development, 1987). In 2015, the UN Sustainable Development Goals placed education centre stage within the international policy discourse about creating a sustainable future. Responses from across the higher education sector have been varied and there is a clear division between those who adopt a 'strong' and those who have a 'weak' view of educational purpose in relation to sustainability. The 'strong' view sees education as a secure process with guaranteed and guarantee-able outcomes, and it suggests that education can develop sustainable citizens of the future by engendering a particular mindset. From this perspective, sustainability is the endpoint of ESD – something which comes after education. The assumption is that once all individuals have received a good enough education (based on knowledge and understanding), sustainable development will follow. This has provoked concern about how a commitment to the principles of sustainability might affect academic freedom since it is based upon the transmission of a pre-defined body of knowledge (Jones, Selby, & Sterling, 2010). This was highlighted in a recent report in the United States for the National Association of Scholars in which Peterson and Wood (2015) refer to sustainability as higher education's 'new fundamentalism.'

However, there is an alternative, 'weak' way, of understanding the relationship between education and sustainability which draws upon the thinking of educational philosopher Gert Biesta (2013). Biesta argues that far from being strong and secure, the process of education is risky and the connection between educational input and output is necessarily uncertain. The task of the educator, therefore, is not simply to transmit bodies of knowledge but to enact a 'pedagogy of interruption' that supports and sustains 'grown-up' ways of being in the world. This means that educators need to foster exploration of the key educational question, 'Is what I desire desirable – for myself, for my life with others and for the planet?'

The research highlighted in this chapter was conducted at a university where a critical (weak) approach to sustainability has been developing over the past ten years. The focus is on the design and implementation of a new unit of study (module) within a master's level programme in Early Childhood Education. We argue that critical engagement with sustainability in the way articulated here raises several challenging educational questions – questions about educational purpose, participation in practice, and praxis – that must be addressed when developing the curriculum. The distinctive nature of ECE provides particular insights that apply to other educational phases (Kemp, 2017).

Designing the module

A question of purpose – framing the module

In designing the module, the first question to be considered was that of educational purpose, since it is only after purposes are established that other decisions can be made about appropriate content and relations. Biesta (2015) proposes a multi-dimensional model of educational purpose which identifies three interconnecting domains – qualification, socialisation, and subjectification. We considered each of these domains in turn. Since the module was part of a master's programme, the domain of qualification was clearly important – students would be assessed individually and their marks would contribute to their final degree award or grade. This meant we had to devise a module that was academically challenging and engaging. We were also really interested in the domain of socialisation. In England, the curriculum for Early Childhood Education recognises Personal, Social & Emotional Development as one of three prime areas for

0–5-year olds but such issues are rarely considered within the context of higher education.

Biesta's third domain, that of subjectification, is arguably the most challenging to describe but is of particular relevance to sustainability. Biesta uses the short-hand of "taking responsibility for our responsibilities" to describe what he means by this concept and he explains that it is in subjectification that the promise of transformation is revealed as it can "reconfigure the existing order of things" (Biesta, 2013, p. 84). We were inspired by the idea of creating educational spaces in which subjectification could emerge and this meant keeping the module as open and flexible as possible.

A question of participation – framing the module

We wanted to prioritize relationships within the module to create spaces for participation. This is a 'weak' form of education which necessitates opportunities for students to participate both (a) in directing the content of the module and (b) as members of a learning community. It also permits a potentially different type of relationship between the postgraduate students themselves and the children and families with whom they work. We decided to adapt a loose framework commonly used to promote participation and democratic values in early childhood settings called the '*intento progettuale*' (which can be translated as 'intended projects'). The *intento progettuale* framework is used in the Reggio Emilia programme of early childhood education in Northern Italy and was pioneered by the Italian education philosopher, Loris Malaguzzi. At the start of the academic year, practitioners draw up a document listing topics and themes that they intend to introduce to children throughout the months ahead. The topics are developed in conjunction with children, their parents, and the local community and there is a firm expectation that the topics will become more complex as time goes on.

There are many ways that the framework can be used in practice but we were particularly influenced by Macdonald's (2015) work with early years teachers to develop children's understandings of sustainability at an early years centre. Here she developed the concept of the *intento progettuale* by identifying shared pedagogic values. At the start of the module, the postgraduate students were asked to develop their own *intento progettuale* to frame their research. To create this, they were asked to complete two activities. In the first activity, they were placed into three small groups to examine Schwartz's (1994) fifty eight universal human values and work collaboratively to identify the five values that they recognised as fundamental for early childhood education in the twenty-first century. This provoked lively discussion and debate. After that, the students negotiated as one large group to agree upon a final set of collective values which would form the foundations of the group's *intento progettuale*.

Secondly, again in small groups, the graduate students were guided to discuss what types of action they could take to develop Early Childhood Education for Sustainability. De Bono's (2009) thinking hats exercise was used to help them consider what would be appropriate and to identify feasible types of participatory action which they could lead. In this exercise participants are invited to adopt a range of different perspectives or 'thinking hats,' such as creative responses (green hat), optimism (yellow hat), and feelings (red hat). Four overlapping themes emerged through this activity (see Figure 11.1).

The group's *intento progettuale* contributes to participation on two levels. Firstly, it supports the postgraduate students to take part in a piece of action research as a joint endeavour with other university students, by identifying common values and intended projects. Secondly, it supports children's participation within the projects that the students choose to undertake. This is exactly what Malaguzzi intended for the *intento progettuale* framework.

A question of praxis – responding to the framework

One of the advantages of adopting the *intento progettuale* framework was that it offered a way of connecting the individual projects the graduate students would develop. A key theoretical influence for informing the individual student projects was Stephen Kemmis' (2009) notion of action research as a means of individual and collective transformation. Kemmis (2009) describes three types of action research – technical, practical, and critical and argues that critical action research is required if practices are unsustainable in any of five ways: discursively; morally and socially; ecologically and materially; economically; or personally. Critical action research can provide a means of transforming practices (doings), understandings of these practices (sayings), and the conditions in which they practice (relatings). Understood in this way, critical action research is a way of moving towards values-based

Collective Value	Theme 1 Awareness Raising	Theme 2 Development of Resources	Theme 3 Change to Setting	Theme 4 Issue-Based Intervention
Social Justice				
Creativity				
Sense of Belonging				
Being Part of Nature				
Broadmindedness				

FIGURE 11.1 The framework or *intento progettuale* developed by the postgraduate students

practice (praxis) and so fits with the values-based approach of the module. All post-graduate students were required to undertake a piece of critical action research as their assessment task for the module. As they developed their thinking, they were asked to map their project onto the larger framework (the *intento progettuale*) and to consider the synergies and connections with their peers' projects.

From theory to practice: case studies

This section presents examples of the postgraduate students' research projects. All the students within the group were given the opportunity to contribute. The following case studies each illustrate one of the four themes which the group had identified earlier (awareness raising, development of resources, changes to setting environments, and issue-based interventions). It is interesting that the projects engage with both global and local issues. They have been written by the students in their own voices.

Theme 1 awareness raising

The UN sustainable development goals by Hilary Welland

My contribution to the *Intento Progettuale* has been to develop a resource to promote community participation based around the UN Sustainable Development Goals (SDGs). The resource, a circular display board, features the seventeen SDGs, presented as a jigsaw to exemplify the interconnection and relatedness of each goal and their significance to global society. Cut out areas on each goal create space for a community to place photographs, illustrating ways they have engaged with each SDG (see Figure 11.2). Although a simplistic device, this offers an interesting and creative way to encourage community awareness and involvement in the SDGs. The intention is that the resource could be displayed in community locations, such as a village hall in which different groups meet.

The catalyst for the project was my attendance at an inter-university conference on sustainability, where I was introduced to the SDGs. On my return, I included images of the SDGs as a provocation within undergraduate teaching modules in the early childhood directorate where I work. Whilst the modules were not specifically related to sustainability, using these SDG images ignited rich conversations, engagement, and deep exploration of current issues. I realised that my colleagues were only vaguely aware of the SDGs. This lack of knowledge, combined with limited resources to support engagement, may account for why many practitioners don't engage young children in sustainability-related issues. My research indicated the need for creative ways to raise greater awareness, and became the impetus to cultivate a resource incorporating the SDGs to be used to ignite interest in sustainability within the early childhood sector.

The more I explore and work with the SDGs, the more worth I find in them. Engagement with the goals offers individuals and communities opportunities to go beyond their original purpose and to interpret them according to local

FIGURE 11.2 The UN SDGs jigsaw for use by local community groups
(*Source*: Hilary Welland)

circumstances. It is an anticipatory hope, that this modest, yet important, 'ripple effect' of growing awareness and interest in the SDGs will gather momentum – there will be continuity beyond this research and that the resource will be used to facilitate 'communities of practice' (Lave & Wenger, 1991) focused on sustainability.

Theme 2 development of resources

Developing 'the process model' by Caroline Lampard-Shedden

I wanted to develop a practical and approachable ECEfS resource aimed at early childhood practitioners. Initially, the enormity and complexity of this task felt overwhelming and I saw the intangibility that surrounds sustainability, coupled with the existing requirements placed on early years settings, as potential barriers to practitioner engagement. I realised early in the research cycle that the role of teaching resources is not simply to teach children *about* sustainability topics. Instead, they are part of the *process* by which children and practitioners engage with sustainability education. My ideas were influenced by several educational theories such as Dewey (1916, 1938), Sterling (2001) and the Reggio Emilia approach (Edwards, Gandini, & Forman, 1998). I identified the following principles as central to the development of my framework

- *Collaboration* – creating an environment in which genuine co-construction of knowledge is possible and positioning children as equal and not subordinate in the process.
- *Participation* – this principle has its foundation in children's right to participation within all the social contexts they inhabit. It challenges traditional paradigms of childhood and positions children as social actors.
- *Documentation* – utilising pedagogical documentation as a tool to accurately represent children's voices and the learning process provides a platform through which tokenism can be avoided.
- *Connectivity* – the setting specific way in which sustainability topics can, and indeed should, be addressed. Thus, making the learning deeply relevant to the children.

Having identified these principles a tangible method of exploration was still required. I drew upon Katz and Chard (2000) and Ji and Stuhmcke (2014) for ideas about project-based learning and adapted them into a model which could be used in ECE settings to develop sustainability awareness. I decided to call this *The Process Model* (Figure 11.3). The non-prescriptive nature of the model allows practitioners to discuss and identify a sustainability topic relevant to them. The cyclical approach introduces topics in an accessible way through storytelling (using picture books or practitioner created stories), explores what is currently happening, works towards and implements a change, and shares the learning with the wider community. It also recognises that the learning is never complete and allows for continual reflection and learning to take place.

To gain feedback about the model, I conducted semi-structured interviews with practitioners. The findings from these interviews highlighted two significant considerations. Firstly, the difficulty of translating a theory-based model into practice and secondly the absence of explicit reference to sustainability within the early years' curriculum. I aim to address these barriers, along with exploring the potential and limitations of *The Process Model*, in my forthcoming master's dissertation.

Theme 3 change to setting

Through the eyes of the child by Julie Cordiner

I was interested in exploring the question 'how can we nurture environmental stewardship in early childhood education?' My method of research involved

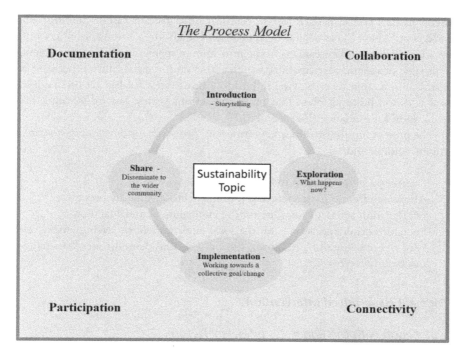

FIGURE 11.3   The Process Model for engaging with sustainability in ECE settings
Source: Caroline Lampard Sheddon

privileging the child's voice and ensuring that they were viewed as researchers in their own right. This was achieved by using a 'mosaic' type approach (Clark & Moss, 2001) as a unique way of listening to and tuning in to young children. Using pupil conferencing and naturalistic observations, children were empowered to unlock their own ideas for change and transformation.

The study investigated what pupils would like to do to improve their nursery outdoor garden. Letting the children drive the change process gave them a sense of ownership and importance. It also encouraged them to collaborate and engage in dialogue. Ultimately, the process created a new consciousness within the children, one in which they were writers of their own stories, who could effect change on their world. They metamorphosed into holders and agents of power enabling them to transcend the UN image of children as those whose rights must be protected by others (Convention on the Rights of the Child, 1989), to active citizens who dynamically participate in their own decision-making.

Affording children the agency to change their world ensured that that their participation was genuine and not tokenistic (Hart, 1997). This led to increased care and concern for the small creatures in the environment and for the environment itself. The children were observed saving spiders, watering plants, and problem-solving ways to support growing plants, equally their collaborative communication with each other increased. Throughout the project, they were involved in a constant cycle of expectation, initiative, decision-making, and reflection. Agency was a vital ingredient in the children's transformation into decision-makers and custodians of the non-human species in their environment. This type of agentic participation, which allows children to build a repertoire of caring action, appears to be vital in building future stewardship action in adults as it is our childhood selves that build the actions which our future adult self relies upon for guidance (Biesta & Tedder, 2007).

The project highlighted four key important processes for developing stewardship in young children.

- Create space for children to act in an agentic way.
- Allow children to participate and lead the decision-making process.
- Let the adult act as an advocate for the environment and a facilitator.
- Focus attention and actions on the local environment or setting, effectively "dig where you stand" (Maguire, 1987, p. 15). This demonstrates that change can be achieved.

Theme 4 issue-based interventions

It all began with the Robin . . . by Helen Turton

The idea for my research began from the awe and wonder displayed by a group of three- and four-year olds when they spotted a robin perched in a tree. During and after this visit to the woods, they talked excitedly about the robin and later eagerly told their parents. After further discussion with the children and practitioners, it was decided to use this opportunity to talk with the children about local ecosystems within their immediate environment, thus encouraging them to be active learners of biodiversity, specifically wild birds. This approach to early education utilises the children's interests as a starting point for future learning, reflects the learning theory of John Dewey (1916, 1938) and supports Montessori's (1989) claim that education is not only what is taught but is also what is experienced from the environment.

The research project involved children, parents, and practitioners. Firstly, the children and their families took part at home in the 'Big Garden Birdwatch' organised by the Royal Society for the Protection of Birds (RSPB, 2017). In the nursery setting, a bird feeder was then erected and discussion undertaken with the children about the different types of food that birds like to eat. To extend their learning further and to consolidate family links, children and practitioners created bird feeders that they could take home for use in their gardens. In addition, bird identification books were created and placed at an indoor birdwatching station in the nursery along with binoculars and mark making materials. The birdwatching station became a focal point with children spending long periods of time observing the birds. They used the identification books to work out which birds they could see visiting the bird feeder and after a few weeks', children were naming the birds freely without the support from the identification cards or practitioners. The children actively used the mark making materials to represent the birds they could identify, creating further opportunities for discussion with the practitioners and supporting children's thinking.

The project has also supported transformative learning from nursery to home, further extending children's opportunity to connect to nature. It highlights the importance of using the local environment for early childhood education for sustainability.

Discussion

In the following discussion, we return to the three questions we raised in the introduction. These focused on (1) educational purpose (2) participation, and (3) the transformation of practice (praxis). We explore the ways in which the case studies can help answer these questions and shed a light on what sustainability education means for those in higher education as well as early childhood practitioners.

Educational purpose

Feedback from the postgraduate students revealed that they felt the module had been transformational; that it had changed the way they understood sustainability and enlarged their ideas about how it might be implemented in practice. It provides an example of the student advocacy and activism Patty Born Selly calls for in this volume whereby tutors offer tools which support students in challenging and changing dominant (and unsustainable) power structures and systems. Kemmis' (2009) definition of praxis as the transformation of practices (doings), understandings of these practices (sayings), and the conditions in which they practice (relatings) offers a way to uncover deeper meanings in the case studies.

The primary focus for one student working full-time in an ECE setting was on the transformation of practices (doings). Helen noted the children's excitement at observing a robin and this provided the impetus for her research reinforcing the importance of starting with the child. Sustainability seems like such a global concept it can be overwhelming to engage with at a practical level. These case studies demonstrate the importance of starting small and seeing opportunities through the eyes of the child. They also show how conducive environments can foster new opportunities – a small-scale example of how immersion in the natural world can help to build an ethic of care.

Hilary's SDG jigsaw provides a connection between such setting-based practice and the bigger global picture. It offers a way of transforming understandings of practices (sayings) through raising awareness of the global goals. Her focus on creating a resource for a shared community space is a way of promoting inclusive engagement and advocacy that could easily be adapted to other contexts. Indeed, the university where the researchers currently work is now exploring ways of developing this resource for use on campus.

Both Julie and Caroline were concerned with transforming the conditions in which they practice (relatings). Julie talks powerfully about how giving children permission to share and develop their own ideas about how to improve the nursery garden privileged their 'voice.' Caroline outlines a cyclical approach that introduces sustainability topics in an accessible way through storytelling, explores what is currently happening, and works towards implementing change and sharing the learning with the wider community. Both Julie and Caroline identified challenges with existing practice and wanted to explore what pedagogy based upon sustainability principles that are aligned with an ethic of care might look like in practice. For them, relational awareness is central to sustainable education and they offer important insights into what this might look like.

Participation

In the introductory section, we considered the question of participation and the ways in which the postgraduate students were supported to contribute to designing the structure of the module. In turn, this shaped the participatory action research that they undertook on an individual level. For example, the notion of participation was central to Julie's case study, in which she recognised that it was necessary to go beyond tokenistic recognition of children's rights towards what Davis and Elliott (2014) term agentic participation when planning developments in early childhood settings. Thus, she firmly scaffolded children to take the lead in deciding and driving change, with the aim of giving them agency. This enabled them to become in her words "writers of their own stories, who could effect change on their world."

We argue that whilst agentic participation is one step on from traditional foundational rights to participation, the notion of collaboration transcends this. Whilst agentic participation considers the individual, collaboration draws out the notion of a community-based collective. This concept features most explicitly within Caroline's project. She identified collaboration and participation as central principles noting the difference as follows: whilst *participation* is concerned with the rights of the child and demonstrates a shifting perspective of childhood, *collaboration* develops this through the "genuine co-construction of knowledge" and a view of children as equal to that of adults. Her process model demonstrates how collaboration underpins advocacy within an educational setting. Yet she also acknowledges that enabling children's collaboration is not easy or straightforward; systemic barriers, such as organisational structures, curricular pressures, and a lack of practitioner confidence exist which need to be overcome for the Process Model to become a core feature of early childhood practice.

Transformation of practice

This chapter started with an assertion that it could be read at two levels; firstly, from a higher education perspective focusing on learning experiences and secondly, from an early childhood perspective focusing on teaching experiences. This is based on the mirroring and reciprocity that we have observed between the experiences of the postgraduate students as learners and as practitioners. We feel that this reciprocity has been at the heart of the transformation process. The move towards praxis (or values in practice) seems to require both conceptual exploration and practical application in constant dialogue. This is perhaps most strongly demonstrated in Caroline's case study where her 'process model' designed for use in ECE settings closely mirrors the action research cycle she herself was engaged in. It also emphasises some of the pedagogic principles that influenced us when designing the module. This is significant because it emphasises the importance of process rather than content in sustainability education. The delivery of the module was based around an exploration of collective values and principles, and it is interesting that there is again a mirroring of this in Julie's case study – her four pedagogic principles reflect our own thinking as we were designing the module. This suggests that role-modelling principles and values might be an important aspect of sustainability education. It also suggests that there is untapped potential for transferring thinking about ways of relating between educational phases, or, to put it another way, that higher education could learn from early childhood and vice versa.

It is interesting to observe the way in which the students (who came from a range of contexts) experienced this mirroring differently, although we suggest that in all cases it contributed to the observed transformation. Hilary works as a lecturer of early childhood undergraduates and for her, it was becoming aware of the SDGs that was the catalyst for change in both her research and her teaching. She specifically noted the "reciprocal relationship between teaching and learning." This highlights the importance of sustainability education being 'applied' rather than simply an academic exercise and of the concept of praxis as a way of understanding the application.

Conclusion

Although Early Childhood Education for Sustainability is an emergent field, sustainability thinking is deeply rooted in ECE philosophy and practice. Early childhood philosophers have long espoused an ethic of care both in relation to people and places. As Friedrich Froebel, the nineteenth century pioneer of the kindergarten put it, early years pedagogy is about fostering all the potentialities 'inherent in a human being' and it is a process which must be 'rooted in natural relationships and conditions' (Lilley, 1967, p. 18). These ideas are explored in the case studies presented. In this chapter we argue that there are lessons that Higher Education can take from ECE. Firstly, that the most conducive environments for an ethics of care to thrive are often those where "we stand" – in this chapter these are the University and ECE settings. Secondly, when thinking about advocacy for life's flourishing, there is value in moving the focus from the individual towards the collective and from participation to collaboration. Thirdly, that resilience and regeneration can be supported by drawing upon values, practices, and ideas from other times and places since these can provide fresh perspectives

TABLE 11.1 Course Content Guide: Early Childhood Education for Sustainability Module, Dr. Nicola Kemp

Conceptual Framework Dimensions	Lesson, Activity, or Project	Learning Informed by the SDGs (Goals 1.1 to 17.19) and The Earth Charter (Principles I.1 to IV.16)
Ethic of Care – Values – Attitudes – Behaviors	**Lesson, Activity, or Project Title:** **Activity: Developing an *intento progettuale* – framing the module (part 1)** The *intento progettuale* framework for the module is developed in two stages. In the first activity, students are placed into three small groups to examine Schwartz's (1994) fifty-eight universal human values and work collaboratively to identify the five values that they recognise as fundamental for early childhood education in the twenty-first century. After that, the students must negotiate as one large group and agree upon a final set of collective values which will form the foundations of the group's *intento progettuale*.	*All SDGS are introduced but students are particularly encouraged to think about SDG4 (quality education) and SDG 17 (partnership for the goals)* *All SDGS are introduced but students are particularly encouraged to think about SDG4 and SDG 17*
Resilience & Regeneration – Knowledge – Skills	**Activity: Developing an *intento progettuale* – framing the module (part 2)** Secondly, again in small groups, the students discuss what types of action they could take to develop Early Childhood Education for Sustainability. De Bono's (2009) thinking hats exercise is used to help them consider what knowledge and skills they hold collectively.	*Students will identify which SDGs most closely align with their own action research.*
Advocacy for Life's Flourishing – Action – Critique – Reflection	**Activity: Developing participatory action research** The assessment for this module is a piece of participatory action research focusing on a sustainability issue pertinent to early childhood education. Action research is a way of moving towards values-based practice (praxis) and so fits with the values-based approach of the module. All students are required to undertake a piece of critical action research as their assessment task for the module. Each individual piece of research is mapped onto the *intento progettuale* and students are encouraged to reflect on synergies and connections with their peers' projects.	14. Integrate into formal education and life-long learning the knowledge, values, and skills needed for a sustainable way of life 14a. Provide all, especially children with educational opportunities that empower them to contribute actively to sustainable development

and different ways of thinking. At a time of growing international support for sustainability education, particularly through UN Sustainable Development Goal 4.7 (UN, 2017), we believe that this chapter provides some insights which could inform both theory and practice in higher education.

Course Planning

This module aims to explore the notion of sustainability and to identify philosophical and practical connections with early childhood education. Drawing on critical theory and conceptions of young children as active citizens capable of contributing to and creating change, the module considers the potential of early childhood education to contribute to sustainable development. It encourages students to develop their thinking about sustainable futures, to challenge assumptions and to seek creative alternatives within the context of early childhood education.

References

Biesta, G. (2013). *The beautiful risk of education*. London: Paradigm Publishers.

Biesta, G. (2015). What is education for? On good education, teacher judgement, and educational professionalism. *European Journal of Education*, *50*(1), 75–87.

Biesta, G., & Tedder, M. (2007). Agency and learning in the lifecourse: Towards an ecological perspective. *Studies in the Education of Adults*, *39*(2), 132–149.

Clark, A., & Moss, P. (2001). *Listening to young children: The mosaic approach*. London: National Children's Bureau for the Joseph Rowntree Foundation.

Convention on the Rights of the Child. (1989). Treaty no. 27541. *United Nations Convention on the Rights of the Child*, 1577: 4–14. Retrieved October 29, 2019 from https://downloads.unicef.org.uk/wp-content/uploads/2010/05/UNCRC_united_nations_convenion_on_the_rights_of_the_child.pdf?_ga=2.119561160.1753319808.1496413662-596175726.1496413662

Davis, J., & Elliott, S. (2014). *Research in early childhood education for sustainability: International perspectives and provocations*. London: Routledge.

De Bono, E. (2009). *Six thinking hats*. London: Penguin Books.

Dewey, J. (1916). *Democracy and education*. New York: The Free Press.

Dewey, J. (1938). *Experience and education*. New York: Touchstone.

Edwards, C., Gandini, L., & Forman, G. (Eds.). (1998). *The hundred languages of children: The Reggio Emilia approach – Advanced reflections* (2nd ed.). Westport: Ablex.

Hart, R. (1997). *Children's participation: The theory and practice of involving young citizens in community development and environmental care*. London: Earthscan.

Ji, O., & Stuhmcke, S. (2014). The project approach in early childhood education for sustainability: Exemplars from Korea and Australia. In J. Davis & S. Elliott (Eds.), *Research in early childhood education for sustainability* (pp. 158–180). London: Routledge.

Jones, P., Selby, D., & Sterling, S. (Eds.). (2010). *Sustainability education: Perspectives and practice across higher education*. London: Earthscan.

Katz, L., & Chard, S. (2000). *Engaging children's minds: The project approach* (2nd ed.). Westport, CT: Ablex Publishing.

Kemmis, S. (2009). Action research as a practice-based practice. *Educational Action Research*, *17*(3), 463–474. https://doi.org/10.1080/09650790903093284

Kemp, N. (2017). Early childhood education for sustainability. In S. Powell & K. Smith (Eds.), *An introduction to early childhood studies* (4th ed.). London: Sage

Lave, J., & Wenger, E. (1991). *Situated learning: Legitimate peripheral participation.* Cambridge: Cambridge University Press.

Lilley, I. (1967). *Friedrich Froebel: A selection from his writings.* Cambridge: Cambridge University Press.

MacDonald, M. (2015). Early childhood education and sustainability: A living curriculum. *Childhood Education, 91*(5), 332–341.

Maguire, P. (1987). *Doing participatory research: A feminist approach.* Amherst, MA: Center for International Education, University of Massachusetts.

Montessori, M. (1989). *Education for a new world* (The Clio Montessori Series). Oxford: ABC-CLIO Ltd.

Peterson, R., & Wood, P. W. (2015). *Sustainability: Higher education's new fundamentalism. National Association of Scholars.* Retrieved from www.nas.org/images/documents/NAS-Sustainability-Digital.pdf

Royal Society for the Protection of Birds (RSPB). (2017). *Big garden birdwatch.* Retrieved from ww2.rspb.org.uk/get-involved/activities/birdwatch

Schwartz, S. H. (1994). Are there universal aspects in the structure and contents of human values? *Journal of Social Issues, 50*(4), 19–45.

Sterling, S. (2001). *Sustainable education: Re-visioning learning and change.* Cambridge: Green Books.

UN. (2017). *Sustainable development goal 4: Targets and indicators.* Retrieved March 27, 2018 from https://sustainabledevelopment.un.org/sdg4

World Commission on Environment and Development (WCED). (1987). *Our common future.* Oxford: Oxford University Press.

12

BOUNDARY-CROSSING LEARNING IN ESD

When agricultural educators co-engage farmers in learning around water activity

Tichaona Pesanayi

Introduction

This chapter shares experience from the 'Amanzi [Water] for Food' project (www.amanziforfood.co.za), established as a response to rural farmers' needs in the Eastern Cape, South Africa, who were given back land after the apartheid period, but who had no access to water to grow food. The project established a learning-centered innovation involving a wide range of actors from different activity systems, all working together around *developing* and *using* rainwater harvesting and conservation (RWH&C) productive demonstration sites as activity sites for learning about sustainable agricultural water. The research program that this project forms part of (Lotz-Sisitka et al., 2016), in which I was a leading co-engaged formative researcher (Pesanayi, 2019), involves a number of graduate researchers, students, and lecturers from universities and agricultural colleges working together with communities to develop co-engaged learning approaches for agricultural learning systems (see Lotz-Sisitka, this volume). In this program we use the concept of 'activity' to identify collective, purposeful actions that people choose to do together, and the specific people doing these. The 'Amanzi [Water] for Food' project involves the Water Research Commission (WRC) of South Africa, Rhodes University, the University of Fort Hare, the Fort Cox College of Agriculture, and local learning partners, such as the local economic development unit of the local municipality, extension services, farmers, and farmers' associations.

The co-learning that I describe here was supported by a number of mediated co-learning processes. The mediated processes that I worked on included: 1) establishing insight into the need state of the farmers who were suffering from not being able to bring water to their crops, which included historical and ethnographic analysis of the practices and associated activity systems; 2) facilitating the formation of a social learning network involving multi-actors in the agricultural learning system; 3) implementing a training of trainers (ToT) course on rainwater harvesting and conservation to activate the network; 4) engaging in formative intervention research using change laboratories for productive demonstration site development; and 5) using social media and community radio to communicate information on RWH&C. These mediation processes were conceptualized out of graduate research that I was involved in (i.e. as a graduate PhD scholar I was co-designing these mediated processes – see Pesanayi, 2019). I was doing this with senior professors at two universities, college lecturers at an agricultural college, and with students from these two higher education institutions. The students involved were both graduate students and undergraduate students. As students and academics involved in the project, we saw ourselves as co-learners, recognizing that we can all learn from each other how to generate and contribute to sustainability. Important to this case study is that I, as graduate researcher, was able to co-lead such a process in collaboration with others, and via this we were also able to level the power gradient and divisions that normally exist among academics, students and communities.

To accomplish this, I examined the inter-related activity systems of universities, college, farmers, extension services, local economic development offices, and farmers' associations and how they were either supporting (or not) smallholder farmers who were desperate for solutions to their agricultural water problem. They were given back land in post-colonial land reform processes, but were not given access to water to farm the land. I found the activity systems to be dynamic, with much potential for interaction around the object of farmers' concerns (i.e. sustainable agricultural water). I also, however, found that they were not as engaged as they could be around the farmers' concerns, given a history of bifurcation between university and community/college and community, and I also found that students were not engaging in practicing agricultural water techniques as practices had been lost in an over-emphasis on theory in agricultural colleges. I also found a colonially produced dualism between small holder farmer and industrial farming, with the latter being the only one valued for livelihood development (Pesanayi, 2019).

I therefore, via my early consultations with the various activity systems, and via sharing knowledge between and across them (i.e. mediating between them), was able to reveal the potential for these to become interacting activity systems, each with a contribution to make in what was revealed as a complex agricultural learning system (Pesanayi, 2019). This formed the foundation of developing a co-engaged and functional social learning network when all actors agreed to collaborate on trying to resolve the farmers' difficulties, while also contributing to their own changing practices. The learning network that formed in 2014 met regularly around the five mediation processes outlined above over a five-year period (still ongoing). It was ongoing interaction in this learning network, centred around the farmers' interests and matters of concern, that allowed a substantive collective learning process to emerge over time, shared in brief below (the full detail of which is captured in Pesanayi, 2019; with earlier detail captured in Lotz-Sisitka et al., 2016).

Contexts influencing (un-)sustainability practice at the small-scale farmer level

Sustainability of small-scale farming in southern African drylands has generally been a low priority issue for various reasons that include domination of the agricultural sector by large-scale conventional agriculture, corporate greed, and poor resource allocation by governments. Small-scale dryland farming has a history of displacement of colonized or marginalized peoples by dominating classes (McIntyre, Herren, Wakhungu, & Watson, 2009). This history has stigmatized the value of small-scale farming as unimportant in the economy, and yet it has been known to contribute considerably to both household and national food security (ibid.). Taking South African and Zimbabwean case studies as examples, it has been shown that sustainable agricultural water for food has not been prioritized in mainstream agricultural research, extension, and education (Pesanayi, 2019).

Agricultural curricula in both South African and Zimbabwean contexts foreground irrigation as the formal and most effective way of provisioning water to crops and pastures and virtually ignore alternative water provisioning for small-scale farming contexts that have no access to dams or lack the capacity to develop them. The result is that the universities and agricultural colleges produce farmers and extension workers who are unprepared for dryland farming nor have the capacity to advise farmers farming in dryland areas (ASSAf, 2017). Government extension services therefore become dysfunctional institutions when it comes to servicing small-scale farmers, and fall short of government promises to develop small-scale farming through water development. The growing impact of climate change and climate variability, which include rainfall variability and increased drought conditions, have worsened this problem.

Another context is the privileging of industrial large-scale farming and the undermining of small-scale farming by the agricultural learning system. Again, agricultural curricula in agricultural training institutes and universities focus on production systems of large-scale commercial and industrial farming from a national economic perspective, and hardly address household food security. One university lecturer described this problem as follows:

> "We design courses according to our expertise, and they are approved by Higher Education . . . I am to teach what is approved, then I cannot come and change the curriculum as [X] and say I should put household issues into that. So that is the major problem".
>
> *(Lecturer, personal communication, May 11, 2016)*

Schools in South Africa have played and are playing a role in perpetuating unsustainable agricultural education practice. During the pre-1994 apartheid period, the problem was characterized by commission, whereby agricultural curriculum content in the racially segregated social-engineering project of the apartheid state education system was geared towards educating Black people as elementary level agricultural workers, in order to create a labor force for White commercial farming. This stigmatized agricultural education and made it less popular among young Black students, who had aspirations of escaping pre-determined categories of menial labor that were constructed via the education system. The post-1994 democracy period that ushered in a democratic government with transformational objectives for equity and redress, has, however, paradoxically created a problem of omission, whereby primary schools have no agricultural education at all, and secondary schools only have it almost mid-way through the system (Pesanayi, Khitsane, & Mashozhera, 2016).

One of the results of this stigma-laden history and subsequent omissions is that farming is generally deplored as an occupation by young African students in schools and colleges, especially the younger generation. By way of example, in my research (Pesanayi, 2019), one male farmer described how he was discouraged by friends from farming, another described youth apathy in farming, and a young farmer admitted to a change in attitude among most young people in the Amathole District of the Eastern Cape Province:

> "Why don't you hire someone to do your farming instead of doing it yourself? Your wife is a nurse so why trouble yourself with engaging in farming labor. You could do something else instead."
>
> "The garden space and the land is big enough and available for other people . . . There are many youths in the village that are just doing nothing, staying at home."
>
> "I would agree . . . sometimes, as youth we want to see results now, now. . . . something that takes a long time to achieve discourages us, we have a negative attitude towards that . . . gardening is a process that needs time."

More widely, the political systems of the developing world also betray small-scale farming by allowing trade agreements that end up flooding markets with cheap, subsidized products from more economically powerful countries (AFSA, 2019).

Theoretical and conceptual framing

This chapter is based on my PhD study (Pesanayi, 2019) that worked with a cultural-historical activity theory (CHAT) frame (Engeström, 1987). CHAT considers that human activity is culturally mediated by artefacts, concepts, tools, or instruments that facilitate learning about and in the world, in relation to an object such as sustainable agricultural water, in this case. Building on Vygotsky's

(1978) concept of activity, in which the subject (human), her/his object, and the mediation tool were sufficient to describe the activity, his colleague Leont'ev added dimensions of rules, community, and division of labour, which were clarified by Yrjo Engeström (1987). Engeström (1987, 2016) further argued that an activity system usually interacts with other activity systems, and in this case the small-scale farming activity system interacts with the extension activity system and the agricultural education activity system among others, forming a constellation called third generation activity. This chapter is concerned with the common object of sustainable agricultural water being pursued by the different activity systems considered. CHAT methodology involves carrying out change laboratory workshops, which are carefully mediated workshops that incorporate data from interviews and ethnographic work with participants (mirror data). Using this data, participants reflect on their work and identify gaps and areas where they are unable to move forward to resolve problems in their activity. Through a technique called double stimulation (Sannino, 2015 in Hopwood & Gottschalk, 2017), research participants go from one stage to another as their object of activity and their learning expand to provide them with opportunities to model new solutions and conceptualize how to implement these (i.e. double stimulation is a generative mechanism that potentially triggers reflection and volitional agency). Via these processes, the object changes with time and transforms as participants move towards their desired new model, which emerges through co-engaged activity, rather than being pre-determined. As Bhaskar (1993) has noted, human life is concept and activity dependent; hence, changing social life requires changes in both concepts (mediating tools) as well as activity.

The focus on change in concept and shared activity via co-engaged emergence in social-ecological change processes is an important insight for sustainability education, which in this case is described as sustainable agricultural education that is inclusive of lecturers and college students who co-engage with the situation of small-scale dryland farmers. It is also integrated in extension planning and activity, and in agricultural education curricula that are geared towards supporting small-scale dryland farming. Such education, therefore, recognizes the creative co-engagement potential of college students, also respects the dignity of small-scale farmers, and is endogenously socially acceptable, economically viable, ecologically sound, and technically feasible, being congruent with smallholder farming practices in traditional African societal contexts (Brescia, 2017; Pesanayi, 2019). This means such education needs to listen to the voices of farmers, such as their demands for agro-ecological farming practices, and respond by incorporating relevant curricula, training programs, and demonstrations. Agro-ecological farming is an agri-food system capable of nurturing people, societies, and the planet (Brescia, 2017) and offers a response to the social and ecological impacts of monoculture, industrialized agriculture. Following sustainability principles, it consciously privileges smaller-scale local economies, healthy food, diversity, and ecological integrity in the food production system.

Sustainability education in small-scale dryland farming communities: farmers at the center of learning networks around their concerns

For small-scale farming systems, sustainability education must be relevant to the context, such as dryland farming systems that are predominant in such areas, and must address concerns, such as learning to live with climate change and variability and how to improve water for food production. These aspects of sustainability are largely lacking in the approaches of extension advisory services, which tend to be top down and imposing (Pesanayi, 2019). The Academy of Science of South Africa (ASSAf, 2017), in their review of agricultural curricula, recognised a gap between small-scale farmers, researchers, educators, and extension, and proposed what they called a 'knowledge triangle' that places farmers at the center, with researchers, educators, and extension services all contributing to the learning and practice of farmers.

Historically, education in agricultural colleges in South Africa was based on an economic model that ignored the socio-ecological systems at play in small-scale farming systems. However, through the co-engaged formative intervention work carried out in the Amanzi for Food program (Pesanayi, 2019), this thinking, in the case study, was seen to shift gradually to incorporate the social and ecological dimensions of small-scale farming systems in drylands. Lecturers from the two universities concerned, together with a group of lecturers from the Fort Cox Agricultural College, and their students, started understanding small-scale farmer contexts of work by having co-engaged dialogues with them in change laboratory sessions, and visiting farmers' plots.

The process of placing farmers at the center was not easy, as lecturers were used to having their knowledge at the center, instead. However, the development of empathy among the lecturers helped to permeate the knowledge and conceptual boundaries separating them from farmers' contexts of work. Developing empathy occurred when the lecturers and students realized that elderly women farmers were struggling to bring water to their fields as they were forced to carry heavy buckets of water from a local dam because the pump and other options for bringing water to the fields had failed. This was painful for them.

As noted above, in order for the subjects of the different activity systems to mobilize around a common object of activity, prior ethnographic work involving both historical and contemporary analysis was carried out through interviews, observations, focus group discussions, and working with the research participants involved (Pesanayi, 2019). Over fifty research participants were involved in total and the common result they expressed was the gap in their intersectional work, and the need to work together through dialogue and collaboration. This occurred when they developed a deeper understanding of the elderly women farmers' plight, as mentioned above. One of the key gaps revealed was that the different agricultural actors (subjects of activity systems) were working in silos that were creating and perpetuating unsustainable farming practices, excluding the small holder farmers. It was starkly revealed that farmers felt misunderstood by extension advisors and agricultural colleges regarding how they were working with water issues in dryland areas. One farmer described this gap and need as follows, " . . . there must be something that is relevant from these institutions . . . That is what we are crying for".

In response, participants decided to form a learning network in the Eastern Cape Province (Amathole District), to enhance collaboration and coordination of their learning efforts towards sustainable agricultural water. The learning network provided a non-hierarchical forum to facilitate new learning interactions and agency. It was found that empathy played an important role in motivating agricultural educators to consider themselves as co-learners with those they were normally used to training in top-down fashion (Pesanayi, 2019). An important process in supporting the learning network formation was a co-engaged training of trainers (ToT) program that allowed all actors from the different activity systems to deliberate different rainwater harvesting and conservation options, and to expand their engagement with each other via productive demonstration site development (encouraged in the network formation process and course), thereby activating the learning network practices. Changing from a top-down approach to a co-engaged approach required tact and humility, as expressed by one agricultural educator,

> "I had also been given a scribing role and the chairing of the planning meeting due to the nature of work I do. I think the fact that I am a lecturer has made other members to sit back and judge themselves as being less knowledgeable. I believe that my profession has clouded the judgement of other team members. This in a way might have compromised the strength and potential of other farmers . . . There were times when I would be quiet and just pose a question to encourage discussions from the farmers. So I would just take their comments."

The learning networks that were formed at district and local levels were very important in facilitating collective learning and 'identifying with' each other's contexts, especially the context of the smallholder farmer. Identification was an important boundary-crossing indicator, as initially described by Akkerman and Bakker (2011) and Engeström, Engeström, and Kärkkäinen (1995). In my study I found that this identification occurred via the empathy formation process that allowed for identification with the farmers' plights by others in the network.

Co-engaged formative intervention processes were carried out in successive boundary-crossing change laboratory sessions that involved the core group of agricultural actors from the different activity systems, leading to a number of different outcomes. A key outcome was the development of productive demonstration sites at the elderly women farmers' plots through the participation of agricultural educators, small-scale farmers, students, and agricultural extension advisors who helped to develop the production demonstration sites (small ponds and furrows) for the women. A second outcome was change in the college curriculum, knowledge, and practices of college lecturers and their students, described below.

Sustainability-oriented curriculum changes emerging from the farmer-centered learning network approach

Following the demonstration site development in the elderly women's cooperative garden, a second stage was use of the sites for teaching purposes, which took place at Fort Cox College and at two farmers' plots. The changes outlined in Table 12.1 indicate curriculum innovation outcomes in one lecturer's practice as a result of the boundary-crossing change laboratory workshops, participation in the ToT program that supported development of productive demonstration sites and the learning network activation, and the actual co-engaged productive demonstration site development that took place.

The changes shown in Table 12.1 were a result of collective learning in the Amanzi for Food program. As can be seen from Table 12.1, through being part of these co-engaged dialogues and visits to farmers' plots, lecturers developed agency in sustainable agricultural water teaching and practice. The agency the college lecturers developed out of the co-engaged learning process is seen in the new curriculum innovation approaches (see Table 12.2) whereby they integrated RWH&C and other principles of sustainable agriculture/agro-ecology relevant to small holder farmers into their course outlines, and their lectures and practical work, which they did not do before the intervention of the Amanzi for Food project and the research upon which this chapter is based.

Course content guide (agricultural training institutes)

The course content guide shared below in Table 12.2 is based on curriculum innovation work done by agricultural colleges as they participated in the Amanzi (Water) for Food Programme. The table shows typical courses taken across different years of study. Additional or modified course content is provided in bold italics. It reflects the way in which the curriculum transformed towards sustainability and inclusion of smallholder farmer needs.

Such curriculum innovation is much needed in Africa, as smallholder farming is an important source of livelihoods and income for the majority of farmers in Africa (Pesanayi, 2019). It also responds to the ASSAf (2017) demand for more relevant, farmer-centered curricula, the Earth Charter's ethics for social and ecological care, and the demands of the Sustainable Development Goals, which argue for quality education that meets the needs of people (www.globalgoals.org).

TABLE 12.1 Changes Made in one Lecturer's Practice at Fort Cox College (Showing the Interconnections That Emerge When Farmers Are Placed at the Centre)

• Enhanced knowledge of RWH&C and integration of knowledge into the planning of productive demonstration sites as sites for intermediary action and co-learning	• The lecturer's knowledge of RWH&C was enhanced considerably as he claimed to have known very little at the beginning of the learning network formation. His engineering background contributed to his prior knowledge and emphasized large-scale irrigation farming practices. • A diagram developed by the lecturer to plan RWH&C productive demonstration sites during his participation in the Amanzi for Food ToT programme, showed use of concepts developed with others combined with sustainability knowledge from Water Research Commission RWH&C materials, which combined RWH&C techniques, in this case a farm pond, solar panel to power water pump, elevated water tank, and gravity conveyance to drip irrigation system. • In planning and setting up the productive demonstration sites (see below), the lecturer successfully integrated irrigation principles and structures (drip irrigation fed by raised reservoir) already in the curriculum, with newly modelled RWH&C practices of farm dam and mulching (meaning placing dry grass on the surface of the soil to retain moisture). He developed these ideas from the Change Laboratories and in three Amanzi for Food training of trainers' assignments where all participating in the networked ToT programme were oriented to a range of RWH&C practices to expand their knowledge and experience.
• Actual contribution to development and sustainability of productive demonstration sites for teaching and learning	• His expanding knowledge via the co-construction of productive demonstration of RWH&C is evidenced below: *"The use of photographs and videos was one step towards a true learning experience. These were employed for the teaching of farm ponds as a RWH technique to college students. Of utmost importance was the demonstration site erected at Fort Cox College of Agriculture and Forestry. College students, high school students, agricultural professionals, and farmers all converged at this site for an extraordinary learning experience in the construction, observation, guided manipulation and use of the site. The demonstrations included all the technicalities involved in the construction of farm ponds as well as the setting up of an irrigation system. College students conducted practical and experimental projects from this site, which were included under formal assessments of student achievement of the diploma qualification"* (Lecturer 1, March 22, 2015).

(Continued)

TABLE 12.1 Continued

	• Mulching was also implemented and made a huge impact during the drought of 2015/2016, sustaining a spinach and gooseberry horticulture plot for over two months covering a holiday period where rainfall and watering were absent.
	• Knowledge developed from boundary-crossing learning was further applied in a number of other demonstration plots, including a teaching garden developed on Fort Cox College campus near lecture rooms; in local farmers' plots; and other places.
	• Additionally, the lecturer led a team made up of colleagues from a local agricultural research institute, a farmer, and students to help other farmers identify suitable productive demonstration sites in the local area, and also initiated the construction of these productive demonstration sites process by facilitating cooperative agreements to help set up the productive demonstration sites with other local partners on the college site, and on farmers' plots.
	• With the winter rains that fell in the last two weeks of July, 2015 the farm pond was filled with water, which the lecturer and the students monitored for water retention/ infiltration, which allowed them to share this knowledge more widely with other framers who were developing small farm dams as RWH&C approach.
• Changes made to college curriculum	• Following these initial engagements, the lecturer was appointed coordinator of the Amanzi for Food processes at Fort Cox College of Agriculture and Forestry.
	• The lecturer continued this work, working with second-year diploma students to do trial experiments on water conservation on grass-covered areas and cleared areas as controls. He stated at the time *"There lies a good opportunity to engage more students in experimental projects that are RWH&C related. The fact that the experimental projects and the Soil and Water Conservation course are done in the second semester (which culminates in the rainy season) is an advantage that can be manipulated in the teaching of the RWH&C since practical engagement can most conveniently be carried out during this period."*
	• The course notes developed by the lecturer now contain detailed diverse RH&C practices.
	• The lecturer furthermore liaised with the Head of the Department of Agriculture to ensure that the five-year curriculum review process at Fort Cox College of Agriculture and Forestry incorporated the capturing and use of rainwater harvesting more explicitly. The lecturer is leading a process of incorporating curriculum innovation changes into the wider college curriculum review process that now profiles the smallholder farmer's needs, which previously were absent.

• Expanded community interaction and links with other universities and knowledge partners.	• After the first year of innovations in the college, the lecturer continued to operate in and lead an expanded community of practice where the lecturer interacts with University of Fort Hare on curriculum development matters, and also with farmers and extension workers.
	• He was elected chairperson of the learning network in 2015 and in 2016. This expanded community grew to include other farmer innovators and partners, and a new practice called 'illima', which is a traditional isiXhosa (local African group) practice of 'working together'.
	• Since then, students have regularly assisted farmers with 'illima' events, such as sharing leaf litter for mulch, offering advice on RWH&C designs, and construction of tunnel gardens, among others. Students are also supporting a youth cooperative farming group with RWH&C practice development in the local community.
	• Other lecturers in the college have also become involved in the productive demonstration site development in the community, and in the regular 'illima' events, which are ongoing (into 2019).
	• The lecturer has also participated actively in national water symposia, national and international conferences, and workshops sharing agricultural water learning, and the learning network concept has been expanded to other provinces in the country, where the lecturer has been able to share his experience of developing these practices at Fort Cox College with other agricultural colleges and universities in South Africa.
	• Members of the learning network now also serve on the College Curriculum Innovation Committee, which has brought farmers and local stakeholder views into the college decision-making about curriculum.
	• Materials from the Water Research Commission on RWH&C have now also been included in the college library and are used regularly for teaching.
	• The work of the lecturer and co-engaged learning partners has also been shared on a number of radio broadcasts, and in other social media, especially via a WhatsApp group, Facebook, and the Amanzi for Food website updates.

TABLE 12.2 Exemplar of Courses and Course Content for Sustainable Agricultural Water (adapted from Fort Cox Agricultural and Forestry Training Institute, 2019)

Year	COURSES AND COURSE CONTENTS			
1	**INTRODUCTION TO AGRICULTURAL ECONOMICS Course Outline** Introduction to economic concepts, production factors, the function of economy, structure of economy (circular flow, agriculture in the economy, *the role of small-scale farming in national agricultural production and household food security*, introduction to agricultural production economic theory, the production function, cost functions, input and output optimization	**SOIL AND WATER CONSERVATION Course Outline** Soil Erosion (types, causes, prevention, and control), Reclamation of degraded lands, Soil conservation techniques (contours, ridges, terracing, etc.), *State of water and agriculture allocation*, Water conservation techniques.	**INTRODUCTION TO AGRICULTURAL ENGINEERING Course Outline** Draft power: Animal traction as a power source; . . . *'gelesha' soil preparation using animal traction.* Seedbed preparation: Primary and secondary tillage; . . . *minimum and no-tillage.* **Instruction** Lectures, practicals; . . . *a study visit to a farm using animal traction and gelesha*	**INTRODUCTION TO CROP PRODUCTION Course Outline** Origin, classification, and nomenclature of economic crops *and traditional crops* **Instruction** Lectures and practicals (identification of different crop seeds, fertilizers, herbicides, and pesticides; *manure, compost, integrated and organic pest management*).
2	**HORTICULTURE 1 (VEGETABLE PRODUCTION) Course Outline** Vegetable production systems; . . . *diversity of traditional leafy vegetables, socio-ecological role.*	**SOIL AND WATER CONSERVATION Course Outline** Rainwater harvesting (infield and outfield), and Loss of water in the field. **Instruction** Lectures, practicals (mulching, soil moisture measurements, constructing, constructing water conservation structures, determination of evaporation)	**IRRIGATION PRINCIPLES Course Outline** . . . *RWH&C farm dams* **Instruction**. . . . *construction of farm dams*	**FIELD CROP PRODUCTION Course Outline** Crop production systems, . . . management practices of different field crops (maize, sorghum, *millets*, wheat, potatoes, and pulses)
3		**SOIL AND WATER CONSERVATION Course Outline** Rainwater harvesting (infield and outfield), and Loss of water in the field. **Instruction** . . . *farm-based co-teaching by farmers doing RWH&C.*		**ADVANCED CROP PRODUCTION Course Outline** . . . tillage systems, . . . genetically modified crops, organic farming, *open pollinated varieties (OPVs)* **Instruction** . . . *develop seed bank of OPVs of crops.*

Conclusion

As shown in the sections above, learning around farmers' concerns for agricultural water was able to bring people from different agricultural learning activity systems to learn together in novel and effective ways. These people were agricultural educators training young agriculture graduates and practicing farmers in modern farming systems in agricultural colleges, rural development centers, and universities; agricultural extension advisors produced by these agricultural training institutions; and small-scale farmers operating in dryland farming systems. Traditionally trained to work in mandates confining them to their sectoral silos, through formative intervention methods, they were able to cross knowledge, institutional, and conceptual boundaries that previously kept their values, practices, and interventions apart. As outlined in the chapter, this occurred through a farmer-centered approach that generated empathy and led to formation of a multi-actor learning network, which used in-field change laboratories and collaborative productive demonstration site development to seed ESD curriculum innovation around rainwater harvesting and conservation praxis. It can be concluded that mediated co-engagement of small-scale farmers with agricultural educators and extension advisors in formative interventions that generate empathy can lead to new learning that is significant for scaling sustainability education practice in and across agricultural learning activity systems.

Acknowledgements

I would like to acknowledge the Water Research Commission of South Africa for providing funding for the Amanzi for Food project from which this chapter derived its data (Lotz-Sisitka et al., 2016; Pesanayi, 2019). I also acknowledge the farmers, lecturers, students, and other colleagues who participate in the Amanzi for Food learning network.

Note

This chapter was written by Dr Tichaona Pesanayi shortly before he graduated with his PhD on 11 April 2019. He sadly passed away one week after obtaining his PhD, on 17 April 2019. He was a much-loved leading figure in Environment and Sustainability Education in Southern Africa, leading the Southern African Development Community Environmental Education Programme across 12 countries for a number of years, and contributing to the re-orientation of agricultural education towards sustainability across the southern African region. The chapter was concluded by Professor Heila Lotz-Sisitka, his colleague, research supervisor, friend, and mentor.

References

Academy of Science of South Africa (ASSAf). (2017). *Revitalising agricultural education and training in South Africa.* Pretoria: ASSAf.
Alliance for Food Sovereignty in Africa (AFSA). (2019). *African Civil Society statement on EU-Africa-Europe agenda for rural transformation.* Retrieved from https://afsafrica.org/african-civil-society-statement-on-eu-africa-europe-agenda-for-rural-transformation/

Akkerman, S. F., & Bakker, A. (2011). Boundary crossing and boundary objects. *Review of Educational Research, 81*(2), 132–169.

Bhaskar, R. (1993). *Dialectic: The pulse of freedom.* London: Verso.

Brescia, S. (2017). *Fertile ground: Scaling agroecology from the ground up.* Food First. Retrieved from www.foodfirst.org

Engeström, Y. (1987). *Learning by expanding: An activity-theoretical approach to developmental research.* Helsinki: Orienta-Konsultit.

Engeström, Y. (2016). *Studies in expansive learning: Learning what is not yet there.* New York: Cambridge University Press.

Engeström, Y., Engeström, R., & Kärkkäinen, M. (1995). Polycontextuality and boundary crossing in expert cognition: Learning and problem solving in complex work activities. *Learning and Instruction: An International Journal, 5*, 319–336.

Hopwood, N., & Gottschalk, B. (2017). Double stimulation "in the wild": Services for families with children at-risk. *Learning, Culture and Social Interaction, 13*, 23–37.

Lotz-Sisitka, H., Pesanayi, T., Weaver, K., Lupele, C., Sisitka, L., O'Donoghue, R. . . . Phillips, K. (2016). *Water use and food security: Knowledge dissemination and use in agricultural colleges and local learning networks for home food gardening and smallholder agriculture. Volume 1: Research and development report.* WRC Research Report No. 2277/1/16. Pretoria: Water Research Commission.

McIntyre, B. D., Herren, H. R., Wakhungu, J., & Watson, R. T. (Eds.). (2009). *International assessment of agricultural knowledge, science and technology for development (IAASTD): Agriculture at a crossroads, global report.* Washington, DC: Island Press. Retrieved from www.unep.org/dewa/agassessment/reports/IAASTD/EN/Agriculture%20at%20a%20Crossroads_Global%20Report%20(English).pdf

Pesanayi, V. T. (2019). *Boundary-crossing expansive learning across agricultural learning systems and networks in southern Africa.* Unpublished PhD Thesis, Rhodes University, Grahamstown, South Africa.

Pesanayi, V. T., Khitsane, L., & Mashozhera, F. (2016). Teaching and learning of "Water for Agriculture" in primary schools in Lesotho, South Africa and Zimbabwe. *Southern African Journal of Environmental Education (SAJEE), 32*, 133–144.

Sannino, A. (2015). The principle of double stimulation: A path to volitional action. *Learning, Culture and Social Interaction, 6*, 1–15. http://doi.org/10.1016/j.lcsi.2015.01.001

Vygotsky, L. S. (1978). *Mind and society.* Cambridge, MA: Harvard University Press.

13

A FUTURE THAT IS BIG ENOUGH FOR ALL OF US

Animals in sustainability education

Patty Born

Introduction

Aiming for "inclusive engagement," this book urges readers to explore multiple perspectives, value systems, and relationships, so that we may act in new and equitable ways involving all life forms on the planet. This chapter provides a framework for that goal and is grounded in the proposition put forward by Barrett et al. (2017) that "recognition of and engagement with the more-than-human as agential and communicative beings is at the core of a *transformative sustainability learning*" (Barrett et al., 2017, p. 132; italics mine).

In a move toward this recognition and engagement with animals, this chapter offers an examination of narratives, practices, and systems that influence our everyday relations with animals. Then I turn to the role of animals specifically within environmental and sustainability education. Following that is a critical evaluation of the placement of animals in two germinal documents in environmental and sustainability education: the UN Sustainable Development Goals and the Earth Charter. Throughout each section of this chapter are provocations: prompts for shifting awareness, behavior, and thinking toward a future predicated on sustainable relations with animals. Finally, the chapter concludes with a tool that educators and students can use to reflect on and challenge those foundational assumptions and begin to renew animal-human relations.

Author's note and terminology

My positionality: I am a white, cis-gendered, heterosexual vegan woman from the United States of America with settler-colonial ancestry. I recognize that my privilege and positionality have shaped my understanding and experience of environmental and sustainability education, nature, and animals, as well as offering me significant access, choice, and safety in relation to same. As an educator, I aim to be an ally and to work to alleviate suffering and oppression where I can. Part of that work is to interrogate the human-animal relationship.

Animal: I refer to non-human animals as simply "animals" with a caveat: the linguistic separation of human from animal may alienate humans from nature (Cronon, 1991; Myers, 1998; Serpell, 1986) implying, as it does, that we are separate from those who aren't humans. Well-intentioned efforts to dismantle the human/animal or human/nature binary employ terms such as "non-human," "more-than-human," or "other-than-human." These terms suggest that to be "human" is preferred, and other beings are simply "not us." Acknowledging this issue, I nonetheless make the linguistic distinction for the simple sake of brevity.

Pronouns: When referring to animals, many people use object pronouns such as "which," that," or "it" instead of "who" or "she/he" – further perpetuating objectification and distancing themselves from animals through language. Noting how important pronoun use is in gender studies, Gruen (2011) reminds us that the words we use (or do not use) have "implications far beyond grammar" (p. xvi). Words can misrepresent or erase the identity of individuals. To avoid erasing animal identity, then, I use he or she to describe individual animals, except when gender is not known, in which case I use the gender-neutral pronoun "they."

Sustainability education, environmental education: though the two disciplines have some clear distinctions in theory and in practice, both disciplines exhibit what Ferreira (2009) describes as "a shared goal of . . . a sustainable society" and a shared belief that "the goal of education is to enhance the capacities of individuals so they can bring about personal and social change" (p. 608). I use the acronym ESE to refer to both environmental and sustainability education, although I acknowledge the disciplines have numerous differences in theory, practice, and goals.

The anthropocene and human exceptionalism

Generally speaking, at least in so-called developed countries, [shaped by western, white, male, settler-colonial] ideologies have driven human practices, behaviors, and habits. These ideologies have had devastating consequences to Earth and its inhabitants. Estimates of the rate of animal extinction (including insects and arthropods) range from 200 to 100,000 species lost to extinction annually (World Wildlife Foundation, 2017). Scientists have described this mass extinction event as "unparalleled in 65 million years" (Ceballos, García, & Ehrlich, 2010), noting that more than 30,000 species of mammals and amphibians are currently considered critically endangered, endangered, or threatened.[1] At the time of this writing, over one-third of land vertebrates are experiencing population declines "of a considerable magnitude" (Ceballos, Ehrlich, & Dirzo, 2017, p. E6089), and some research suggests a likely decline in insect species by 40%

(Sánchez-Bayo & Wyckhuys, 2019) over the next few decades. At the time of this writing, the United Nations has warned that over a million animal species are threatened with extinction in the near future, possibly within a few decades (Diaz et al., 2019). Scientists have termed this geological epoch the "Anthropocene" to acknowledge the human impacts on natural systems, landscapes, and processes (Crutzen, 2002, Lewis & Maslun, 2015).

Humans have participated in and perpetuated animal suffering through erasure, objectification, commodification, and theft of freedom and habitats. Their activities may ostensibly be to benefit animals, such as inspiring pro-environment behavior. However, closer examination reveals a "human exceptionalism paradigm" (Catton & Dunlap, 1978, p. 42) which places [usually white, western, settler-colonial] human needs, desires, and well-being above that of many other humans and of all other species. This paradigm has driven much of human behavior and consumption, leading to harmful practices of entitlement and dominion, which have been problematic to animals (as well as many humans). An additional limitation of this paradigm is that it precludes relational understanding: if humans are superior to (and therefore separate from) all other beings, we are not interdependent on or connected to any other beings or systems of life on Earth, and therefore cannot engage in authentic relations with others. (Plumwood, 2002, as cited in Lupinacci & Happel-Parkins, 2016) Bearing this in mind, if the goal of sustainability education is true *transformative sustainability*, it's imperative that educators are aware of and able to recognize the pervasiveness of this paradigm of human exceptionalism and its impacts on our relations with animals.

Factors shaping our relations with animals

The human exceptionalism paradigm or anthropocentric mindset drives many of the *narratives*, *practices*, and *systems* in which many humans either tacitly or directly participate. Rarely does one factor occur in isolation For example, the *narrative* that tells caregivers that cow's milk is critical for young children drives the *practice* of Americans consuming enormous quantities of milk daily. Both the narrative and the practice are outcomes of the *system* that is the dairy industry – part of the animal-industrial complex. The dominant assumption driving this is that cows' milk is ours to take. Space prevents an exhaustive exploration of these factors, but the activity template accompanying this chapter provides a process for identifying additional examples of each and for identifying ways to challenge them. Beneath the practices and the narratives that influence our relations with animals are large-scale systems that are deeply foundational to our western consumer society. In many cases, the systems depend on human complicity or ignorance of harm toward animals in order to exist (Adams, 2009), such as the following:

Animal captivity: Lloro-Bidart and Russell (2017) and Warkentin (2011) analyze the hidden curriculum that is found in edutainment ventures that rely on animals as resources (such as zoos, aquaria, and ecotourism). Here, the ostensible agenda is human entertainment, education, and discovery, but another, less obvious story being told is that animals are biocommodities (to further human financial interests and to satisfy a human desire for pleasure or entertainment) Lloro-Bidart, 2014.

Meat and other products we consume: Animals are particularly objectified and commodified in the "animal-industrial" system (Noske, 1989; Safran-Foer, 2010). This system depends on the killing and confinement of billions of animals annually to provide humans with meat, eggs, and dairy products for food. It also includes the "by-products" of those animals: the leather, fur, and feathers used for clothing and other human comforts; as well as the beaks, hooves, bones, organs, and other body parts that are used for animal food, adhesives and waxes, cosmetics, medicines, preservatives, and other consumptive purposes. The dominant assumption here is clear – these animals, their bodies, and the things that come from their bodies are required for human consumption.

Medical, scientific, military research: Although in the United States, federal laws purportedly aim to safeguard the well-being of animals (Adams, 2009), they are still harmed in significant numbers every year in weapon testing and scientific experimentation; their tissues are used for medical products, devices, and preservatives. In school settings, animal dissections are often simply accepted as a necessary part of science education, even for young children. While many argue that these sacrifices are important and necessary in order to ensure human education, safety, and health, there is no denying that the system relies on the suffering and death of animals. In this case, a dominant assumption is that human life is more important and that some animal suffering is justified in the name of human well-being.

The point of these examples is to provide a context in which dominant, anthropocentric assumptions dictate the terms of our relations with animals. Other contexts are not quite so clear.

Animals in ESE

In ESE, animals are used as pedagogical tools for a number of outcomes (i.e, Kahn & Humes, 2009; Maina-Okori, Koushik, & Wilson, 2017). ESE curricula and programs typically aim to increase care and interest in animals, nature, and "the environment" writ large. Animals are used as "hooks" to engage people in pro-environment behavior (Kellert, 2002); for example, think of the images of marine animals suffering from ingesting ocean plastic, which are used in popular media to encourage people to use less plastic. Elsewhere, they are used as "living sentinels" (Wikelski, 2016): markers of climate change or deforestation, the modern day "canary in a coal mine." A popular image of a starving polar bear provides a poignant testimony to the effects of climate change. Arguably, these programs sometimes lead to pro-environment behavior change (Lloro-Bidart, 2017), but even so, this practice uses animals as pedagogical tools that reinforce human exceptionalism: our needs, desires, and well-being are the ultimate outcome of such programs.

Elsewhere in ESE, particularly in reference to environmental literacy or science education, we find the [historically white, western] focus on science and its "almost exclusive concern with cognition of facts and systems" (Spannring, 2017, p. 66). The reductive nature of science, which values ordering, naming, and classifying, reinforces human exceptionalism by positioning the human species as the only species with the right and capacity to name, order, and identify the value of others. Within media, animals may be anthropomorphized, stylized, and deterritorialized (Almiron, Cole, & Freeman, 2015; Karniol, 2012; Timmerman & Ostertag, 2011). Outcomes associated with many ESE programs suggest that humans are stewards, caretakers, conservators, appreciators, and managers of the natural world. The ultimate "reason" for making sustainable choices is human well-being and maintenance of a system of commerce and education that perpetuates human exceptionalism.

Toward sustainable relations with animals

Acknowledging animals as more than tools, symbols, or objects of study, instead as "living beings with their own experiences, perceptions and interests, as actors and individuals with an intrinsic value" (Shapiro, 2002, cited in Spannring, 2017) challenges the discourses that allow for and perpetuate the subjugation of animals within ESE and other contexts. But how do we do that? So many of our economic systems, cultural norms, and physical needs are served by the practices that rely on animal suffering or use, it can seem an impossible task. One way to move toward transformative sustainability learning (Barrett et al., 2017) begins with simply recognizing animals with their own individual lives and experiences (Gruen, 2009) Ethical consideration of animals is a challenging idea for some. Some scholars suggest that certain animals should be given moral consideration over others (Donovan, 2006) based on their capacity to feel pain, their value to humans, perceived ability to think, and so on. Others (i.e Birch, 1993) call for an environmental ethics that affords moral consideration to all beings rather than focusing on specific criteria. Thomas (2016) argues for a conception of animal agency and autonomy that recognizes their abilities to "make decisions and direct their actions based on reasons" (p. 5), and that animals have desires, preferences, and intentions. To what degree these qualities exist and how they are demonstrated is not the question being taken up by this chapter, but I assume that readers are willing to acknowledge the validity of this argument.

Ethical consideration of animals means that one must be willing to behave in ways that acknowledge and support animal well-being, and avoid causing harm where possible. Becoming aware of and willing to interrogate harmful narratives, practices, and systems is one way of doing so. In multispecies interactions,

Warkentin urges "a praxis of paying attention" (2010, p. 101), in other words, being attentive to animals' gestures, behavior, and body movements. This is but one way to renew relations.

Animals in the U.N. sustainable development goals and the earth charter

The United Nations Sustainable Development Goals (SDGs) and the Earth Charter (2010) seek to establish and secure a sustainable future through the elimination of social problems, such as poverty, lack of education, and other inequalities, and to create systems that support human rights. Focused on human well-being, neither document explicitly attempts to articulate explicitly what a sustainable future might look like if animal well-being were prioritized along with human well-being. This section offers a critical evaluation of the documents with an eye toward attentive, sustainable relations with animals. Students' responses to the prompts provided in this section can be used to help them repair and re-center their own relations with animals. In articulating their understanding of interspecies relations, they will begin to transform their own sustainability education by more consistently considering and prioritizing animal well-being.

As their title suggests, the UN Sustainable Development Goals prioritize development as the way to ensure human well-being. If transformative sustainability education is to include sustainable relationships with animals, though, this position is somewhat problematic. First, because many harmful things have been and continue to be done to animals in the name of "development," and second, because the focus on human well-being clearly reinforces a paradigm of human exceptionalism, and therefore positions animals as resources to which humans are entitled. Although there are 17 goals, only three of them (Goals 12, 14, and 15) mention animals at all, and even then, animals are described as mere resources. For example,

> Goal 14 states, "*Conserve* and sustainably *use* the *oceans, seas, and marine resources for* sustainable development" and Goal 15 reads: "*Protect, restore, and promote* sustainable *use* of terrestrial ecosystems, *sustainably manage forests*, combat desertification, and *halt and reverse* land degradation and *halt biodiversity loss.*"

These two goals offer a good example of how language frames animals and their value to us. In the statements above, animals as living beings are essentially erased from the picture. Animals and their habitats *are* directly addressed in Goal 15, with its associated targets serving as calls to action for humans to protect habitats and preserve biodiversity:

> "take urgent and significant action to reduce the degradation of natural habitats, halt the loss of biodiversity and, by 2020, protect and prevent the extinction of threatened species,"

"take urgent action to end poaching and trafficking of protected species of flora and fauna and address both demand and supply of illegal wildlife products."

Each of these statements seems to imply a concern for animal well-being. However, looking deeper, Goal 15's ultimate aim is stated as the "sustainable use" of Earth's life systems. Other targets associated with this goal contain human-centric language referring to biodiversity (animals and their homes) as "resources," and state the need to "use" biodiversity and ecosystems "and their services" sustainably. Animals, plants, and other non-human beings are thus valued (and included in this goal) as resources to humans.

> *Do these goals prioritize animal well-being alongside human well-being? Why or why not? How do you know? What would you say is the outcome for each of these goals? Who is best served by the outcome? Does describing animals and nature as "resources" make them more valuable to humans, and thus, more worthy of consideration and care?*

Of particular note is "Goal 12: Ensure responsible consumption and production patterns." It too explicitly mentions animals in one of its targets, stating:

"By 2030, ensure that people everywhere have the relevant information and awareness for sustainable development and lifestyles in harmony with nature."

This reference to harmony with nature is notable because of all the targets associated with the SDGs, it is the only one that implies a relationship between humans and nature that is not solely based on human needs. Unfortunately, none of the actions or targets associated with this goal suggest how this "harmony with nature" is to be achieved, nor is the idea described further.

> *What does "harmony with nature" look like? Is it the same for everyone? What is the human relationship with animals in this vision? What might "harmony with nature" be for an owl, a dolphin, an endangered toad, or a cockroach? What is YOUR vision of "harmony with nature"? Once you've articulated your vision, describe how the SDGs align (or not) to your vision of a harmonious lifestyle. Do the SDGs offer effective steps to creating this harmonious lifestyle? Why or why not?*

Earth charter

Compared to the SDGs, the Earth Charter more deeply considers animals and their well-being outside of their relationship to humans. The preamble to the Earth Charter states:

> "The resilience of the community of life and the well-being of humanity depends on preserving a healthy biosphere" and additional principles found within the document refer to animals.
>
> The first principle of the Earth Charter states:
>
>> "Recognise that all beings are interdependent and every form of life has value regardless of its worth to human beings."
>>
>> *(Principle 1b)*

The Earth Charter contains four main themes, two of which implicitly acknowledge the intrinsic value and importance of animal life:

> Principle 1: "Respect and Care for the Community of Life" and Principle II: "Ecological Integrity." For example, point 2 in Principle 1 is
> "Care for the community of life with understanding, compassion, and love. Accept that with the right to own, manage, and use natural resources comes the duty to prevent environmental harm and to protect the rights of people."
>
> *(2000)*

While ostensibly a guide to caring for the community of life as a whole, noting the specific need to protect the rights of *people* leaves out many other lives: another example of how language (or the lack thereof) can serve to erase individuals or groups. Who is included in the Earth Charter's "community of life"? The reader is left to decide.

Some questions that educators can ask their students that will help to call out the human exceptionalism paradigm evident in this language include:

> *Who has the right to own, manage, and use natural resources? Has that changed over time? Is it the same no matter one's geography? Who has the right to exist? What is meant by "natural resources"? What is meant by "environmental harm"? Why did the authors of this statement address only the rights of people? What rights do you think animals should have?*

Principle 2, "Ecological Integrity," however, reflects a position more inclusive of animals as beings with agency. Point 5 of principle 2 is to:

"Protect and restore the integrity of Earth's ecological systems, with special concern for biological diversity and the natural processes that sustain life." Several sub-points related to this principle specifically address protection and preservation of animals. Here, animals are recognized as valuable in their own right rather than as "resources" and humans are called upon to act in ways that help and support other species:

5b. Establish and safeguard viable nature and biosphere reserves, including wild land and marine areas, to protect Earth's life support systems, maintain biodiversity, and preserve natural heritage.

5c. Promote the recovery of endangered species and ecosystems."

While the Earth Charter acknowledges that humans consume "resources" for survival, it diverges from the UN SDGs in how it "rejects the widespread modern view that the larger natural world is merely a collection of resources that exists to be [exploited by] human beings" (Rockefeller, 2006, p. 622). The Earth Charter's focus on reverence, compassion, and love as pathways to achieve harmony and justice implies a responsibility for the well-being and ethical treatment of all species. In contrast, the SDGs foreground economics and development. Both have their merits, but neither frames animals as sentient beings with experiences and biographies of their own, worthy of empathy, consideration, respect, or rights. Evolutionary biologist Marc Bekoff recognizes that "We need a new mind-set and social movement that is transformational and centers on empathy, compassion, and being proactive" (p. 56).

Educators who wish to rethink and challenge dominant human exceptionalism paradigms for sustainability education can use these documents to help guide critical reflection about the role of public policy or compacts such as these in shaping behavior.

> *Can documents like these sway public sentiment? Is education alone powerful enough to move the needle on sustainability? Is a change in public sentiment all that is needed in order to transform our relations with animals? Does everyone in a society have to have the same values or opinions about animals in order for a truly sustainable future? Why or why not?*

Conclusion

Advocacy as pedagogy: seeking renewal

If, as educators, we believe it is important to work toward a sustainable future, we need to supply our students with a variety of tools to change the dominant power structures and systems that have led to this place of global crisis. As Lupinacci and Happel-Parkins state, "this is a battle that must be fought on multiple fronts in an effort to overcome anthropocentrism both immediately and for future generations" (2016, p. 17). For many people, it is neither possible nor reasonable to abandon all of these systems and practices. However, by recognizing the impact and pervasiveness of these systems, we have already begun to deepen awareness of the counternarrative: that animals are individuals with their own lives and experiences. Having identified several narratives, practices, and systems that perpetuate human-animal separation, as well as ideas and provocations for disrupting them, we can commit to restoring and renewing our relationships with animals now and for the future. We can commit to engaging in behaviors and practices that prioritize animal well-being whenever possible, recognizing that as a relational practice, which may look different in different contexts, and for different people. We can start by simply watching animals more closely, considering the ways in which their agency might be expressed. We can change our language and consumptive practices, more mindful of the impacts they have on animal lives and bodies, aiming to reduce participation in systems that perpetuate or rely on animal suffering.

Educators are in a very important position to support and facilitate change. Teacher educators in particular, can focus their attention on the many dominant assumptions in education that undermine animal well-being and perpetuate suffering as well as a human-animal split. Moving toward a sustainable future that prioritizes animal well-being requires educators to identify, challenge, and disrupt narratives and practices that are harmful to animals. Simply put, if our future is going to include all living communities and relations, we must be mindful of the damage done by our anthropocentric paradigms. We must work to alleviate suffering and violence where we can, and choose not to participate when possible. Critical reflection on how we want to engage in ethical relationships with animals is an important step toward transformative sustainability education. Only through doing so can we move toward a future that is truly inclusive and just.

Course Planning

As people invested in a truly sustainable future, we need to recognize, and challenge, implicit assumptions that maintain an anthropocentric hierarchy (Kahn, 2007). This activity challenges students to critically evaluate common practices and settings in which animals are used and/or oppressed in the service of human well-being. Through this activity, they begin to re-think their relations with animals and create shifts in their own thinking that will move them toward sustainable relationships that are just, compassionate, and ethical. They will practice the skills of critical evaluation and "unpacking" narrative, practices, and systems to identify dominant assumptions. These skills will aid them in understanding how pervasive oppression can be. As they gain fluency with these skills and continue to apply them, they will begin to use them to better understand the relational nature of sustainability.

TABLE 13.1 Course Content Guide: Animals, Ethics and ESE

Conceptual Framework Dimensions	Project for Student Groups	Learning Informed by the SDGs (Goals 1.1 to 17.19) and The Earth Charter (Principles I.1 to IV.16)
Ethic of Care – Values – Attitudes – Behaviors	**Title: Indentifying the factors that shape our relations with animals** **I. Narratives, practices, and systems identification:** Articulate an example of each of these ideas, providing evidence for your conclusions and grounded in the theoretical framework of this chapter and/or additional resources. **II. Toward a sustainable future together** Identify necessary steps to challenge and dismantle harmful narratives, practices, and/or systems to co-create a desirable and sustainable future that situates all animals as deserving of care, respect, and consideration.	*Re-word SDGs to better reflect human-animal relations. How would you change them while preserving the integrity of the original intent? Is it possible?* **Goal 16.7**: Ensure responsive, inclusive, participatory, and representative decision-making at all levels. *Note that animals communicate and express their experience in ways very differently than do*
Resilience & Regeneration – Knowledge – Skills	**III. Advocacy Outcomes –** Design and communicate efforts and strategies that shift human-animal relations away from harmful/unsustainable to sustainable paths. These might be major shifts, or they might be smaller. Coordinate with peer groups to present to your colleagues a collective advocacy statement to guide thinking about narratives, practices, and systems, describing and maintaining a vision of human-animal relations as peaceful and sustainable.	*humans. This goal is included here to provoke you to think about what animals MIGHT decide to do/say/choose if their fates weren't in human hands.* Ib. Recognise that all beings are interdependent and every form of life has value regardless of its worth to human beings
Advocacy for Life's Flourishing – Action – Critique – Reflection	**IV. Exhibition Outcomes –** Create and share cohesive whole-group approach to steps toward changing the narrative, practice, or system; and: provide strategies, solutions or ideas for moving away from perpetuating animal suffering and toward a new way of interrelating with them **V. Reflection Outcomes:** In your written and oral response, dialogue about how this assignment may or may not create significant change toward a desirable and sustainable future grounded in renewal of relations with animals. How will these changes move you and others toward a renewed relation with animals?	**I.2**. Care for the community of life with understanding, compassion, and love. **II.3.b**. Promote social and economic justice, enabling all to achieve a secure and meaningful livelihood that is ecologically responsible. *And ethical towards animals.*

Source: Typical students/participants: teacher education students, environmental studies students

Procedure

Examine the factors that impact animal well-being and shape human-animal relationships. Investigate a setting in which animals are featured prominently: a zoo or aquarium, a farm or petting zoo, etc. You may consider an animal auction, hatchery, or breeding/teaching facility, butcher shop or farmers' market. Take notes and abide by all laws. Consider the following: What animals are here? What is their housing or shelter like, if any? What role do humans have? How do you imagine animals are experiencing this setting? What leads you to that belief?

In this setting, identify one example each of narrative, practice, and system. In doing so, you'll be structuring an understanding of how human-animal relationships are impacted by and dependent on these narratives, practices, and systems. Can you identify manageable ways to dismantle harmful practices leading to an inclusive, sustainable future? How would this setting be different if animal well-being were prioritized?

What is the *narrative* of this setting? Which animals are present? Why them? Whose agenda is served? What are the overt and covert stories being told about these animals? What is the human relationship story regarding these animals?

What are the *practices* employed in this setting? Are animals used directly or indirectly to meet human needs or desires? Are animals being erased, objectified, manipulated, or enclosed? What are humans doing to or with animals? Are there identifiable interaction patterns? If multiple species are present, do humans behave differently (actions, tone of voice, language,) across species? Detail what is happening. How much agency do animals have, and how is it demonstrated? How might an animal in this setting resist (or consent to) what is happening? Finally, make notes about how YOU are interacting or engaging with animals in this setting.

Finally, the context you have chosen is part of a *system* that supports, perpetuates, and relies heavily on humans to maintain a certain relationship with animals. Is it a system that commodifies animals? Are animals being harmed in this system? How? For what purpose? How do humans benefit from this system? Are there ways that animals benefit from this system?

In conclusion, identify ways these narratives, practices, or systems could be changed to demonstrate an ethic of care, to re-vision a new human-animal relationship that considers sustainability for all living beings. Consider some ways that humans could interact with animals in this setting that might honor their agency, their individual biographies, and their rights to exist.

Note

1 Note that this number doesn't include birds, reptiles, fishes, insects, or arthropods.

References

Adams, C. J. (2009). Chapter Three. Post-meateating. In Animal encounters (pp. 45–72). Lieden, Brill.

Almiron, N., Cole, M., & Freeman, C. P. (Eds.). (2015). *Critical animal and media studies: Communication for nonhuman animal advocacy.* New York: Routledge.

Barrett, M. J., Harmin, M., Maracle, B., Patterson, M., Thomson, C., Flowers, M., & Bors, K. (2017). Shifting relations with the more-than-human: Six threshold concepts for transformative sustainability learning. *Environmental Education Research, 23*(1), 131–143. https://doi.org/10.1080/13504622.2015.1121378

Bekoff, M. (2014). *Rewilding our hearts: Building pathways of compassion and coexistence.* Novato, CA: New World Publishers.

Bell, A. C., & Russell, C. L. (1999). Life ties: Disrupting anthropocentrism in language arts education. In J. P. Robertson (Ed.), *Teaching for a tolerant world, grades K-6: Essays and resources* (pp. 68–89). Urbana, IL: National Council of Teachers of English.

Bell, A. C., & Russell, C. L. (2000). Beyond human, beyond words: Anthropocentrism, critical pedagogy, and the poststructuralist turn. *Canadian Journal of Education/Revue canadienne de l'éducation*, 188–203.

Birch, T. (1993). Moral considerability and universal consideration. *Environmental Ethics, 15*, 313–332.

Bosselmann, K., & Engel, J. R. (2010). *The earth charter: A framework for global governance.* Amsterdam, The Netherlands: KIT Publishers.

Catton, W., & Dunlap, R. (1978). Environmental sociology: A new paradigm. *The American Sociologist, 13*, 41–49.

Ceballos, G., Ehrlich, P., & Dirzo, R. (2017). Population losses and the sixth mass extinction. *Proceedings of the National Academy of Sciences Jul 2017, 114*(30). E6089-E6096. https://doi.org/10.1073/pnas.1704949114

Ceballos, G., García, A., & Ehrlich, P. (2010).The sixth extinction crisis loss of animal populations and species. *Journal of Cosmology, 8*, 1821–1831. Retrieved from http://journalofcosmology.com/ClimateChange100.html

Cronon, W. (1991). *Nature's metropolis.* New York: W.W. Norton

Crutzen, P. (2002). Geology of mankind. *Nature, 415*, 23. https://doi.org/10.1038/415023a

Díaz, S., Settele, J., Brondízio, E., Ngo, H., Guèze, M., Agard, J., ... & Chan, K. (2019). Summary for policymakers of the global assessment report on biodiversity and ecosystem services of the Intergovernmental Science-Policy Platform on Biodiversity and Ecosystem Services.

Donovan, J. (2006). Feminism and the treatment of animals: From care to dialogue. *Signs, 31*, 305–329.

Ferreira, J. A. (2009). Unsettling orthodoxies: Education for the environment/for sustainability. *Environmental Education Research, 15*(5), 607–620.

Foer, J. S. (2010). *Eating animals.* Penguin UK.

Gruen, L. (2009). Attending to nature: Empathetic engagement with the more than human world. *Ethics and the Environment, 14*(2), 23–38.

Gruen, L. (2011). *Ethics and animals: An introduction.* Cambridge: Cambridge University Press.

Kahn, R. (2007). Toward a critique of paideia and humanitas: (Mis)education and the global ecological crisis. In I. Gur-Ze'ev & K. Roth (Eds.), *Education in the era of globalization* (pp. 209–230). New York: Springer.

Kahn, R., & Humes, B. (2009). Marching out from Ultima Thule: Critical counterstories of emancipatory educators working at the intersection of human rights, animal rights, and planetary sustainability. *Canadian Journal of Environmental Education, 14,* 179–195. Retrieved from https://cjee.lakeheadu.ca/article/view/895/558

Karniol, R. (2012). Storybook-induced arousal and preschoolers' empathetic understanding of negative affect in self, others, and animals in stories. *Journal of Research in Childhood Education, 26,* 346–358.

Kellert, S. (2002). Experiencing nature: Affective, cognitive, and evaluative development in children. In P. H. Kahn & S. Kellert (Eds.), *Children and nature: Psychological, sociocultural, and evolutionary investigations.* Cambridge, MA: Massachusetts Institute of Technology.

Lewis, S., & Maslun, M. A. (2015). Defining the anthropocene. *Nature, 519,* 171–180. https://doi.org/10.1038/nature14258

Lloro-Bidart, T. (2014). They call them "good-luck polka dots": Disciplining bodies, bird biopower, and human-animal relationships at the aquarium of the pacific. *Journal of Political Ecology,* 389–407. http://doi.org/10.2458/v21i1.21142

Lloro-Bidart, T. (2017). Neoliberal and disciplinary environmentality and "sustainable seafood" consumption: Storying environmentally responsible action. *Environmental Education Research, 23*(8), 1182–1199. https://doi.org/10.1080/13504622.2015.1105198

Lloro-Bidart, T., & Russell, C. (2017). Learning science in aquariums and on whalewatching boats: The hidden curriculum of the deployment of other animals. In M. P. Mueller et al. (Eds.), *Animals and science education: Environmental discourses in science education* Springer, Cham (pp. 41–50). https://doi.org/10.1007/978-3-319-56375-6_4

Lupinacci, J., & Happel-Parkins, A. (2016). (Un)Learning anthropocentrism: An ecojustice framework for teaching to resist human supremacy in schools. In S. Rice & A. G. Rud (Eds.), *The educational significance of human and non-human animal interactions: Blurring the species line* (pp. 13–30). London: Palgrave Macmillan.

Maina-Okori, N. M., Koushik, J. R., & Wilson, A. (2017). Reimagining intersectionality in environmental and sustainability education: A critical literature review. *Journal of Environmental Education,* 1–11. https://doi.org/10.1080/00958964.2017.1364215

Myers, O. E. Jr. (1998). *Children and animals.* Boulder, CO: Westview Press.

Noske, B. (1989). *Human and other animals.* London: Pluto Press.

Plumwood, V. (2002). *Feminism and the Mastery of Nature.* London: Routledge.

Rockefeller, S. (2006). Earth Charter Ethics and animals. in Waldau, P., & Patton, K. (2006). *A communion of subjects: Animals in religion, science, and ethics.* New York: Columbia University Press. pp. 622–628.

Sánchez-Bayo, F., & Wyckhuys, K. (2019). Worldwide decline of the entomofauna: A review of its drivers. *Biological Conservation, 232,* 8–27. https://doi.org/10.1016/j.biocon.2019.01.020

Serpell, J. A. (1986). *In the company of animals.* Oxford: Blackwell.

Shapiro, K. (2002). Editor's Introduction: The State of Human-Animal Studies: Solid, at the Margin!. *Society and Animals, 10*(4), pp. 331–338.

Spannring, R. (2017). Animals in environmental education research. *Environmental Education Research, 23*(1), 63–74.

Timmerman, N., & Ostertag, J. (2011). Too many monkeys jumping in their heads: Animal lessons within young children's media. *Canadian Journal of Environmental Education, 16,* 59–75.

Thomas, N. (2016). *Animal ethics and the autonomous animal self.* London. Palgrave MacMillan.

Warkentin, T. (2010). Interspecies etiquette: An ethics of paying attention to animals. *Ethics and the Environment, 15*(1), 102–121.

Warkentin, T. (2011). Interspecies etiquette in place: Ethical affordances in swim-with-dolphins programs. *Ethics and the Environment, 16*(1), 99–122.

Wikelski, M. (2016). Living sentinels for climate change effects. *Science, 352*(6287), 775–776.

World Wildlife Foundation. (2017). *How much is being lost?* Retrieved from wwf.panda.org/our_work/biodiversity/biodiversity/

14

DEVELOPING A CURRICULUM FOR SUSTAINABILITY EDUCATION

Lesson planning for change

Mary F. Wright and Florence A. Monsour

Introduction

Teacher education programs train teacher candidates to write and deliver curriculum using a pragmatic approach to disciplinary content area lesson planning. However, educating undergraduates to teach children and youth in the era of climate change calls for pedagogies that inform rather than ignore sustainability-oriented curricula. This chapter calls for a balance between training teacher candidates to plan content area lessons and the need for cultivating sustainability-based lessons using a transdisciplinary approach. Lesson planning for real-world problem-solving involves using engaging pedagogies to provoke thought and action toward addressing sustainability (Sterling, 2001). Modeling a variety of resources and artful pedagogies, candidates design lessons to promote cross-disciplinary connections inviting students to participate in collaborative, inquiry-based activities to achieve praxis toward positive change.

Siloed disciplines housed within colleges may hinder a holistic view of sustainability, but the sustainability dilemma belongs to all and can bridge the disciplinary divide. Teacher education programs have opportunities to resist teacher training that perpetuates the status quo by exposing teacher candidates to artful ways of curriculum development (Wright, Cain & Monsour, 2015). As the sustainability crisis looms larger, and arrives sooner than predicted, the fields of "engaged pedagogy" (hooks, 1994), ecocomposition (Dobrin & Weisser, 2002), place-based critical pedagogies (Gruenewald, 2003 a & b), and arts-based performative pedagogies (Greene, 1995; Ellsworth, 1997, 2005) intersect as fundamental to teaching for deep and transformative learning.

For teachers and teacher educators, a tension exists between the art and science of teaching. Education is a human science; it cannot be reduced to a prescriptive scientific method. The science of teaching involves pragmatic components of lesson planning and assessment to measure academic achievement; the art of teaching, on the other hand, considers the context of teaching and learning, and the developmental, social-emotional needs of learners. The art of teaching embraces deep engagement, including the arts and aesthetics, in addition to utilizing content area techniques in the classroom. Contemporary public schools often sacrifice lesson fluidity, focusing on test-driven curriculum, particularly standardized testing, which has escalated in the last decade in answer to federal accountability and local administrative measures. Teachers delivering a prescriptive curriculum focus on math and reading skills to boost test performance scores. Locked within the constraints of top-down mandates that influence what teachers should teach and what students should know, teacher autonomy fades, limiting freedom to create curriculum that includes interdisciplinary or transdisciplinary concepts (Apple & Beane, 1995).

Within our coursework, we embrace the art of teaching and resisting prescriptive methods of teaching and learning in favor of transformative sustainability-based pedagogies that include what hooks terms "engaged pedagogy" (1994, p. 15). Lesson planning as ecocomposition with engaged and arts-based performative pedagogies fosters a discourse of hope for striving towards a sustainably just world.

Engaged pedagogies

ESD, or education for sustainable development, as articulated by UNESCO (2017), ". . . empowers learners' informed decisions and responsible actions for environmental integrity, economic viability and a just society for present and future generations" (2). ESD draws upon a premise that teachers can gain awareness of how to integrate sustainability into curriculum. This involves broadening disciplinary curriculum to include sustainability-related concepts, readings, and activities. Sustainability education blends cognitive thinking (knowledge) and affective learning (personal feelings and empathy). Teacher candidates need to appreciate different dimensions of sustainability, sometimes described as 'pillars:' ecologic (e.g., water quality), economic (e.g., energy costs) and social (e.g., poverty). Candidates need to encounter and practice pedagogies that will engage early years, primary, and secondary education students in mindful interaction and inquiry regarding sustainability. Finally, candidates need to acquire skills to write sustainability into content area lesson and unit plans. The goal of ESD is transformative sustainability learning, or TSL (Sipos, Battisti, & Grimm, 2008), a holistic approach to teaching and learning that introduces dimensions of sustainability literacy. The term sustainability literacy has evolved from a purely ecologic or environmental view to an expanded notion that includes looking at sustainability knowledge, skills, and practices to constitute an ecologic, economic, and social justice lens (Stone & Barlow, 2005). In addition, sustainability literacy in education pedagogy embraces critical and creative thinking, and social opportunities for dialogue, that together invite action towards positive change.

Ecocomposition

We draw from the field of ecocomposition, specifically looking at how it influences the lesson planning process to promote change. At the heart of the lesson plan, essential questions challenge learners to become change agents by interacting with the sustainability issue under study. Reframing the lesson planning process as ecocomposition aligns with Dobrin and Weisser's (2002) notion that the intellectual work that goes on at the university level is inseparable from "the "public," and that ecocomposition, ". . . sees the university as the public, all part of the same system, all the same place" (91). Teachers influence many lives and their students will join the citizenry, likewise influencing our world. The lesson plan and its enactment in the classroom provide opportunities for discourse that encourages critical self-awareness about active ways to problem solve for the greater good of society. Within ecocomposition, "Rhetorical choices, invention strategies, and writing processes are all part of a writer's ecology that influences their worlds" (ibid, p. 110). In a lesson on climate change, for example, candidates as writers choose essential question(s) to guide learning objectives and activities within the lesson to support students in answering the essential question. In an elementary teacher candidate's idea for teaching water quality, for example, essential questions scaffold sustainability learning and the subsequent writing of the lesson plan: "How does water become polluted?" "How do I contribute to water pollution?" "What can I do to stop water pollution and improve water quality?" Candidates then write an interest approach or hook to engage learners, and a step-by-step description for lesson enactment.

Engagement within a lens of ecocomposition extends experiences beyond the classroom. Derek Owens' "Bee Vision" of the curriculum (referred in Dobrin & Weisser, 2002, p. 135) presents an interconnected systems thinking approach to curriculum writing as a ". . . reshaping of composition away from a writing-based discipline to a discipline that uses writing as a vehicle through which sustainability is promoted" (ibid, p. 137). Candidates design lesson activities that engage students in exploring sustainability issues, stimulating dialogue and working towards change. Candidates writing a lesson on hydroponic or aquaponic farming, for example, plan inquiry-based lab experiments simulating contexts such as urban rooftops, in the desert, or home. Within the simulation, students collaboratively create a hydroponic system using media such as perlite, rockwool, peat moss, or vermiculite.

Place-based critical pedagogies

Place-based writing and reflection serve as a prelude to analyzing real-world issues, and as a critical pedagogy encourages students to view writing as a vehicle for change. Students write to reach public and political arenas, including service learning to bring about awareness to issues. This corresponds with hooks' view of "engaged pedagogy" in which teaching is service: "The teacher who serves continually affirms by his or her practice that educating students is the primary agenda, not self-aggrandizement or assertion of personal power" (2002, p. 91). Sustained or mindful reflection embedded in curriculum purposefully connects students to a sense of place. Biologist Stephen Jay Gould argues that we cannot save species and environments without "forging an emotional bond between ourselves and nature as well – for we will not fight to save what we do not love" (1991, p. 9). Place-based writing is grounded in reflection, reconnecting students with the land. To effectively develop a critical pedagogy of place, educators need to resist accountability measures that prevent them from expanding their ". . . inquiry and practice to include the social and ecological contexts of our own and others' inhabitance" (Gruenewald, 2003b, p. 10).

Place-based writing to inform lesson planning begins when teacher candidates find a place that is special to them on campus or community in which to silently commune with nature while taking note of sensory perceptions. Reflecting through writing provides candidates with an immediate connection to and reverence for place, and a platform to begin re-framing their understanding for "being in the world" (Danvers, 2014) as a *part of* rather than *apart from* it. Danvers notes that, "By paying close attention to the sensual world around us. . . . learners can begin to grasp the unboundedness of being-in-the-world – a mode of being that could help us achieve a sustainable future" (ibid, p. 190).

Place-based lesson planning has challenges. Contemporary sustainability curriculum scholarship advocates that ecological literacy (Orr, 1992) move further toward a bioregional curricular approach (Hensley, 2011) recognizing the need to connect teaching and learning to a deep sense of place. Orr (1992) discusses obstacles facing the teaching of ecological literacy in schools. Besides addressing limitations of a narrow-minded western culture of thought, he emphasizes lack of experiential curriculum within the limitations of indoor education. An expanded view of place-based education evolves from an individualistic to a cultural and community approach (Pinar, 1975; Gruenewald, 2003 a & b, 2007; Smith, 2007; Dobrin & Weisser, 2002).

Arts-based performative pedagogies

Teacher education programs that re-frame the teacher within the metaphor of artist coincide with the need to generate authentic reflection about sustainability issues. Perrone uses three metaphors of teaching: teaching as naturalist, as researcher, and as artist, explaining that ". . . the conception of the teacher as artist emphasizes the connection between creative and fully functioning individuals who are in touch with their own learning in exciting and stimulating classrooms" (as cited in Zeichner, 1996, p. 58). Imagination in teaching gives students agency, opening pathways for transformation, as the conscious participation required stimulates ". . . growth and inventiveness and problem solving . . . the hopes of felt possibility" (Greene, 1995, p. 132). The Earth Charter (2000) addresses transformative learning, calling for the ethical and spiritual dimension of sustainability education to be integrated into curriculum. Arts-based ESD (UNESCO, 2012) pedagogies support this dimension by encouraging critical thinking, social critique, and analysis of local contexts using pedagogical practices that often draw upon the arts (Dewey, 1934) using drama, play, music, and design as opportunities for engagement in deep reflection. Engaging students in reflection and contemplative practices fosters awareness for living mindfully in ecological and socially just ways.

Sustainability lesson design: writing for change

The lesson plan is the creative roadmap for teachers, serving as a guide for implementing ESD. Framed within ecocomposition, the lesson plan becomes a living guide designed to engage thinking about sustainability issues in the early years, primary (early years and primary in British school systems) and secondary (lower and upper secondary in British systems) classrooms. Texts cultivate an ethic of care (Noddings, 2003) through values, attitudes, and behaviors. Students might read "Thinking Like a Mountain" from Leopold's *Sand County Almanac* (1949) to support an appreciation for humans' interconnectedness to the ecosystem. In the writing workshop (Atwell, 1998), an iterative approach to the writing process is established through drafting, editing, revision, and publishing writing while conferring with peers and the instructor. Finally, we focus on designing lessons with pedagogical praxis that moves students toward sustainability-oriented change.

A traditional lesson plan is rigid, separating required components into confined cells, diffusing the gestalt of the lesson, as candidates focus on minutia rather than the goal the lesson seeks to accomplish. In traditional lesson plan writing, candidates must use the headings: context for learning, goals and objectives, state and national standards, essential questions, informal formative and summative assessments, academic language and its demands, motivational set, procedures and activities, differentiation for learners, and closure. Teacher educators support candidates in meeting these requirements while introducing creative curricular design using engaged pedagogy to integrate sustainability concepts.

Lesson planning can be a daunting task for fledgling teacher candidates. Candidates are used to teaching the way they were taught, within the lens of a single discipline. We agree with hooks' perception, "Teachers who are wedded to using the same teaching style every day, who fear any digression from the concrete lesson plan, miss the opportunity for full engagement in the learning process" (2002, p. 134). To move toward an expansive view of curriculum, we establish a workflow in a lesson writing workshop to accomplish the following: experience of multi-modal texts (video, imagery such as art or photography, web-based information, digital texts, print-based texts), model sustainability-based lesson plans, writing workshop time, and opportunities for peer teaching and reflection.

Texts, talk, and doing: cultivating a discourse of hope

Embodied and performative pedagogy acknowledges the experiences of the body within learning experiences. In considering the sensations crucial to understanding, Ellsworth, as cited by Perry and Medina (2011) "asserts that the notion of learning as experience pushes us to reconsider the practices that frame the work we do in pedagogy, and to question some of our taken for granted or invisible assumptions" (62). Engaged and performative pedagogies bridge both the sciences and the arts and humanities (Earth Charter, principle *IV. 14. b.*) by intersecting cultural and ecological issues. An activity such as "Peace Meditation Journaling" engages candidates in writing as a form of meditation using three modalities: narrative, sketching, and symbols. The goal is to cultivate an ethic of care and a pedagogy of hope (Noddings, 2003; hooks, b, 2003) by reflecting on our relational interdependence in the world. An ethic of care involves empathy for the issues plaguing both the earth and marginalized individuals, such as densely populated urban life, poverty, and scarcity of clean air, water, or interactions with nature. Candidates read the vignettes in Thich Nhat Hahn's (1991) *Peace is every step: The path of mindfulness in everyday life* during the journaling process. Hooks reminds us that Thich Nhat Hahn refers to the teacher as healer, offering "a way of thinking about pedagogy which emphasized wholeness, a union of mind, body, and spirit" (1994, p. 14). After reading, candidates synthesize a crystallized "nugget of wisdom," a wise saying, like a proverb, instructing action or interaction for the greater good. In a post-journaling dialogue, candidates share ways to lead peaceful and compassionate lives.

Aligned with ecocomposition, this pedagogy emphasizes taking time to internalize texts as a springboard for deeper discourse about being in the world and acting upon it. As Danvers notes, "Learning how to realize being-in-the-world, rather than thinking of ourselves as being-apart-from-the world, is not easy and takes time" (in Stibbe, 2009, p. 189). Aligned to Buddhist thought, "Mindfulness . . . is a way to take charge of the direction and quality of our own lives, including our relationships within the family, our relationship to work and to the larger world and planet" (Kabat-Zinn, 1994, p. 5). Although we cannot always change what we see occurring, we can make strides by being mindful of our daily actions and interactions with one another and the planet. Mindfulness nourishes spiritual and emotional well-being, an ethic embraced by the sustainability movement.

Focusing on the three areas of spiritual well-being, mental, and emotional well-being, as suggested by Richard Davidson, founder of The Center for Healthy Minds at the University of Wisconsin-Madison, we introduce practices such as "Yoga Calm," for centering and calming students. Arts-based and somatic approaches to knowing and learning, such as dramatic role-play and silent conversation encourage discourse. Hudspeth's chapter on sustainability stories emphasizes that "people are more likely to act reasonably and cooperatively, to communicate and work with others to solve problems," aligning with the ethic of engaged pedagogies. The power of storytelling supports students and teacher candidates in working together to envision and re-enact a just and sustainable world. ESD pedagogies as suggested by UNESCO (2012) include the art of storytelling as a way of critical and creative thinking, a key in solving wicked problems as we move into a complex future demanding innovation.

Candidates re-enact sustainability readings that provoke thinking about climate change aligned with UNESCO's (2017) Sustainable Development Goal 13.3, "The learner knows which human activities – on a global, national, local and individual level – contribute most to climate change" (36). After reading *The Collapse of Western Civilization* (Oreskes & Conway, 2014) for example, candidates construct a response using a Body Sculpture Theatre technique. This collaborative pedagogy developed in Boal's (1993) *Theatre of the Oppressed* invites students to use their bodies to create body sculptures as a platform for discussion about social inequalities. Discourse about the imminent threat of climate change and its mitigation is strengthened using somatic nuances of gesture and form, honoring intuited and embedded knowledge as candidates form sculptures to represent abstract emotions regarding ecological destruction or social devastation.

The art of teaching derives meaning from authentic engagement with the world. Through the process of participatory problem-solving, art-making, and reflection, students disrupt the ordered conventional ways of knowing producing knowledge that is personal, original, and valuable to the social community. Pedagogies are enacted both before and after sustainability readings embedded within candidate lesson plans. In a unit on alternative energy sources, for example, candidates support lessons with texts such as *Powering the future: How we will (eventually) solve the energy crisis and fuel the civilization of tomorrow* (Laughlin, 2011) or *Geothermal energy could provide all the energy the world will ever need* (Skoglund, 2010), to stimulate a discourse of hope. Immersing students in problem-solving experiences, creative and critical thinking is fostered, honing both little "c" and big "C" Creativity, which McWilliam & Dawson call skills valued in the new world of work, and essential for addressing sustainability issues (2008). Little "c" creativity involves everyday creative thinking skills which can be applied to solve big problems requiring big "C" creativity.

Exploring sustainability texts for lesson planning

Sustainability themes and multimodal texts support inquiry. Within the four walls of the classroom, the limited experiential realm can be expanded through strategic use of sustainability texts for sustainability education as recommended by the ESD Sourcebook (UNESCO, 2012), such as simulations, class discussion, issue analysis, and storytelling, A variety of credible sustainability-based children's and adolescent literature, websites, non-fiction, fiction, videos and YouTube clips, films and documentaries (Monsour, 2018) enrich lesson planning. After choosing a sustainability issue such as pollution or deforestation, candidates complete a sustainability issue using UNESCO's issue analysis guide, ". . . . a structured technique for exploring the environmental, social, economic, and political roots of problems that face communities (UNESCO ESD Sourcebook, p. 18).

This activity bridges the natural and social sciences, as candidates answer questions and research a sustainability issue grounded in a local context. For example, agriculture education candidates explored resources used to produce a dairy product (water, energy, space, etc.) as efficiently as possible, comparing differences in organic and conventional production. To create praxis as reflection-in-action (Zeichner & Liston, 1996), candidates form critical inquiry questions to frame the unit/lessons around essential understandings. Within the lesson, reflection-in-action occurs when candidates analyze their practice as they teach, problematizing assumptions, reflecting on how effectively choice of pedagogy enables essential understandings. The culminating project is directed to be collaborative and transdisciplinary, supported by a variety of texts. Next, candidates participate in a writing workshop approach to lesson planning.

The lesson plan writing workshop

At the start of the sustainability lesson plan writing workshop, we model lesson plans as an iterative process involving candidates working together in cooperative groups, writing goals, objectives, and framing the sustainability issue or problem with an essential question. Essential questions, (McTighe & Wiggins, 2005) clarify the lesson's "big idea" relating the relevance of the sustainability issue and interconnection with students' lives. Dialogue about what makes a good "essential question" occurs in small content area groups. Candidates envision the lesson objective and design formative assessments and conference with the instructor.

After practicing and modeling pedagogies, candidates begin lesson planning as a way to engage K-12 (early years and primary) and secondary (lower secondary and upper secondary) students in becoming change agents. According to Kemmis and Mutton (2012) praxis (action and practice) within sustainability curriculum involves three dimensions: language or literacy (cultural discursive dimension), the work students do (material economic dimension), and action in a realm outside of the classroom (the social/political dimension).

Another component of the lesson plan writing workshop involves considering ways the lesson could be improved. Students are encouraged to develop activities that foster higher order thinking skills using Bloom's taxonomy (1976), or Webb's (2009) Depth of Knowledge (DOK) levels. Bloom's taxonomy is a hierarchical categorization of educational goals, beginning with a simple and concrete base of knowledge, and becoming more complex and abstract as students move up the hierarchy: comprehension, application, analysis, synthesis, and evaluation. The DOK level framework measures how deeply a student understands concepts and categorizes the levels from simplest to most complex: recall and production, skills and concepts, strategic thinking, and extended thinking.

Candidates participate in peer teaching of at least one of the designed lesson plans to practice both teaching sustainability and giving constructive feedback.

The praxis achieved by collaborative problem-solving can be seen as candidates problematize sustainability issues such as soil erosion through a lab simulation, recording data while problem solving, and discussing issues in groups (Figure 14.1). Hypothetical questions guide the feedback loop for self-reflection: How did your lesson address the three pillars of sustainability (social, economic, and ecologic) (Purvis, Mao & Robinson, 2018)? Were the students engaged during the lesson?

FIGURE 14.1 Agriculture Education Candidate Analyzing Variables in Soil Erosion Lesson

What evidence do you have that students were successful or not in achieving the learning objective? What could you have done differently to improve the lesson? Do you need to go back and re-teach any parts of the lesson? What will you do tomorrow to build on this lesson? Did you anticipate student misconceptions and if so, how did you clarify them?

Lessons are taught both in and outdoors. For example, art candidates take a class outside to create sustainable nature sculptures to affirm a reverence for place, modeled by the ephemeral art of Andy Goldsworthy. Indoors, candidates create and use plant-based dyes for painting and writing about sustainability in hand-made books. Agriculture Education candidates direct a soil erosion lab experiment, engaging the class in testing sand plots using water, hay, sieves, and a blow dryer to determine how to approach soil erosion in different contexts. Curriculum designed by teacher candidates from various content areas provides many examples of meaningful sustainability lesson/unit construction. Former unit titles include: Science Education: *Wild Rivers Shape Their Courses*, Art Education: *Sustain a Sculpture*, Agriculture Education: *Erosion of Civilization*, Music Education: *Preserving our Culture: The Blues and Beyond*, Social Studies Education: *Immigration and Freedom of Expression*, Physical Education/Health: *School Lunches and Obesity*.

Concluding thoughts: prioritizing the quest to teach for change

Sustainability education prepares teacher candidates to educate and empower K-12, early years, primary, and secondary students to address challenging problems. In order to see the sustainability issues and problems of the future, students need to reflect critically on the present. Doll and Gough's (2002) *Curriculum Visions* provides a visionary look at curriculum as one that begins with an "embodied eye/I" (3), not only ". . . about hopes for the future but also about seeing the world otherwise *now* . . . The constructive "negativity" of critical vision can thus be manifested as the *avoidance* of some goals and the *refusal* of consensus" (4). This might mean avoiding or refusing to follow strict disciplinary curricular guidelines in favor of opening up curriculum to transdisciplinary sustainability understandings. As Sipos et al. (2008) assert, "The pedagogy of sustainability education is about creating spaces where disciplines are not piled on top of one another but instead integrated in new ways" (80).

Prioritizing sustainability education in our coursework demonstrates the intersection of an ethic of care, resilience, and regeneration, and advocacy for life's flourishing. The ethic of care is an integral part of sustainability teaching and learning, embedded in curriculum informed by engaged pedagogy, the arts, and self-expression. Working together in creative and collaborative ways, students are able to develop empathy for each other and the world they live in. Teaching K-12, early years, primary, and secondary sustainability lessons requires an experiential shift in nurturing critical thinking and compassionate understanding. Resilience and regeneration in sustainability pedagogy is inspired by presenting students with the skills to tackle contextually specific and challenging real-world problems, involving thinking and doing. Advocacy for life's flourishing is the praxis inherent in designing curriculum. Participatory and engaging curriculum includes pedagogies which guide students in becoming advocates for personal and institutional change.

To begin breaking down the complexity of the global sustainability dilemma, lesson planning must include creative and collaborative approaches to pondering and solving problems. Educators must stand for the freedom to create meaningful sustainability teaching and learning opportunities, even when teaching in a restricted environment which measures learning through standardized assessments. Teacher education programs strengthen sustainability education through engaged, performative, and place-based pedagogies with a focus on the triad of heads-on, hands-on, and hearts-on engagement (Sipos et al., 2008). Lesson planning for sustainability using ESD pedagogies supports transdisciplinary competencies and learning outcomes to fulfill the goal of preparing students for meaningful and productive lives in our world. Teacher educators who embrace sustainability education using engaged pedagogies provide hope for a future beyond.

Course Planning

In a Secondary Reading in the Content Area course and Elementary Educational Psychology course, teacher candidates create sustainability curriculum for content area teaching to K-12 (early years and primary and secondary students in schools). Secondary candidates work in content area groups (Agriculture, Music, Art, Language, Health and Physical Education) to choose a sustainability theme, and research a relevant sustainability issue to write curriculum for an "alternative text collection" unit plan. Groups explore the sustainability issue by completing an Aspects of Sustainability Guide and conduct an Issue Analysis (UNESCO, 2012). Candidates seek sustainability focused "alternative" texts representing diverse genres and perspectives to design meaningful curriculum and enrich teaching and learning. Elementary candidates write individual lesson plans based on a sustainability theme. The discourse of lesson plan writing reflects experiential ESD pedagogies using critical place-based and art-based activities to engage students in praxis. The secondary text collection unit includes a sustainability rationale, lesson plans, and a bibliography of alternative texts. The elementary lesson plan includes an interest approach, procedure, critical questions using Webb's (2009) Depth of Knowledge, and a variety of sustainability resources to support lesson design.

Procedure

Phase 1: planning for instruction

Content area secondary groups and elementary candidates choose a sustainability theme for curriculum integration.

TABLE 14.1 Sustainability Education Grounded in the Sustainable Development Goals and The Earth Charter

Conceptual Framework Dimensions	Project for Content Area Sustainability Education Curriculum	Learning Informed by the SDGs (Goals 1.1 to 17.19) and The Earth Charter (Principles I.1 to IV.16)
Ethic of Care – Values – Attitudes – Behaviors	**Lesson, Activity, or Project Title: Alternative Text Collection Unit Plan** Elementary candidates learn how service learning projects can create a sense of praxis within elementary lessons by giving back to the community. Secondary candidates seek supportive texts for lessons related to the sustainability issue to engage students in critical thinking and motivate action.	*Goal 13.3* Improve education, awareness raising, and human and institutional capacity on climate change mitigation, adaptation, impact reduction, and early warning
Resilience & Regeneration – Knowledge – Skills	Secondary and elementary candidates build knowledge and skills by participating in ESD pedagogies. Candidates explore activities such as touring organic farms or the university lab farm, walking along the riverbank to identify threatened plant species, calculating their carbon footprint, contributing to the local food shelf with vegetables grown at school, or participating in dramatic re-enactments or role play of texts. In-class activities involve role play of texts, creating collaborative body sculptures to initiate a dialogue about climate change, character role play, participating in Socratic seminar, and fishbowl discussions about sustainability issues.	*Goal 4.7.* By 2030, ensure that all learners acquire the knowledge and skills needed to promote sustainable development, including among others, through education for sustainable development and lifestyles, human rights, gender-equality, promotion of a culture of peace and nonviolence, global citizenship, and appreciation of cultural diversity and of culture's contribution to sustainable development. *Goal 13.3.* Improve education, awareness raising, and human and institutional capacity on climate change mitigation, adaptation, impact reduction, and early warning.

(Continued)

TABLE 14.1 (Continued)

Conceptual Framework Dimensions	Project for Content Area Sustainability Education Curriculum	Learning Informed by the SDGs (Goals 1.1 to 17.19) and The Earth Charter (Principles I.1 to IV.16)
Advocacy for Life's Flourishing – Action – Critique – Reflection	Elementary and secondary candidates compose lesson plans which engage students in praxis (reflection in action) related to the sustainability issue. A secondary lesson on soil erosion asks essential questions such as: "How does soil quality affect humans? What can I do to prevent erosion? Does it cost a significant amount of money? Why is soil erosion a problem for farmers?" as they participate in a soil erosion lab simulation. Students complete a write-up describing conservation practices, discussing the benefits to the farmland and the environment as well as how effective their conservation practices were at keeping the soil from the farmland out of the lake. In an elementary lesson on greenhouse gases, critical questioning guides inquiry, such as: "What is the importance of carbon in our life? How do humans use fossil fuels? What connection do food miles have with carbon footprint and greenhouse gases? Can someone diagram the greenhouse effect? Who can anticipate how climate change will impact the environment in the short and long term?" After lessons/units are written and shared with peers, candidates critically reflect on their practice through group and whole discussion, individual presentations, and exit slips.	*I.4.b.* Transmit to future generations values, traditions, and institutions that support the long-term flourishing of Earth's human and ecological communities. *IV.14.a.* Provide all, especially children and youth, with educational opportunities that empower them to contribute actively to sustainable development. *IV.14.b.* Promote the contribution of the arts and humanities as well as the sciences in sustainability education. *III.12.c.* Honor and support the young people of our communities, enabling them to fulfill their essential role in creating sustainable societies.

Source: Course Content Guide: (Secondary Content Area Reading, Dr. Mary Wright; Elementary Educational Psychology, Dr. Florence Monsour)

Planning for instruction: secondary groups research a sustainability issue related to their chosen theme using UNESCO'S (2012) Aspects of Sustainability and Issue Analysis guides. Elementary candidates conduct an inquiry on the sustainability topic or issue by viewing "The Story of Stuff" (2007) and "The Story of Solutions (2013)."

Phase 2: supporting sustainability issues within the unit/lesson

Each candidate in the secondary content area group finds supporting texts (rich, relevant sources that provide diverse perspectives), to plan a pre-reading, during-reading, vocabulary, or post-reading lesson within the sustainability text collection unit. Elementary candidates choose children's books to integrate in the sustainability lesson along with rich media (websites, videos, DVDs, movies) in order to plan activities for engaging the learner.

Phase 3: practicing ESD pedagogies

Each secondary content area group explores sustainability topics by participating in modeled ESD pedagogies as ways to engage students in critical and creative experiences. After reading texts, for example, The Collapse of Western Civilization (Oreskes & Conway, 2014) candidates re-construct meaning by creating collaborative body sculptures (Boal, 1993) as a launch for discussion. The pedagogies stimulate a discourse of hope as candidates, inspired by expressive dialogue, and artistic expression, are moved to praxis . Elementary candidates study various community needs related to sustainability lesson planning through a card-sorting activity.

Phase 4: sustainability instruction

Secondary content area groups write sustainability lesson plans to create a cohesive Alternative Text Collection Unit plan for teaching in schools. Sustainability infused lessons use immersive experiences with sustainability issues to engage students in discourse, affect change or action toward a solution. For example, in a unit on soil erosion, an activity is designed to simulate the problem. Students sketch their proposed idea for soil conservation efforts to implement on their inherited land and put their sketch into action on the model farm land they receive. Students complete a write-up at the end of the lesson explaining what went well, what didn't go as planned, where they could improve, and why this is important.

Elementary candidates write lesson plans with engaging activities, such as making a greenhouse experiment related to how greenhouse gases affect the environment. Non-fiction texts and videos support understanding of climate change issues, and how individuals can make a difference by changing their carbon footprint.

References

Apple, M. W., & Beane, J. A. (Eds.). (1995). *Democratic schools.* Alexandria, VA: ASCD.

Atwell, N. (1998). *In the middle: New understandings about writing, reading, and learning.* Portsmouth, NH: Heinemann.

Bloom, B. S. (1976). *Human characteristics and school learning.* New York: McGraw-Hill Book Company.

Boal, A. (1993). *Theatre of the oppressed.* New York: Theatre Communications Group.

Center for Healthy Minds. Retrieved from https://centerhealthyminds.org/

Danvers, J. (2014). Being-in-the world. In A. Stibbe (Ed.), *The handbook of sustainability literacy: Skills for a changing world* (pp. 185–191). Cambridge, UK: Green Books.

Dewey, J. (1934). *Art as experience.* New York: Perigree Books.

Dobrin, S. J., & Weisser, C. R. (2002). *Natural discourse: Toward ecocomposition.* Albany, NY: State University of New York.

Doll, W. E., & Gough N. (Eds.). (2002). *Curriculum visions.* New York: Peter Lang.

Earth Charter Commission. (2000). *The Earth Charter.* San Jose, Costa Rica: Earth Charter International. Retrieved from www.earthcharter.org.

Ellsworth, E. (1997). *Teaching positions: Difference, pedagogy and the power of address.* New York: Teachers College Press.

Ellsworth, E. (2005). *Places of learning: Media architecture pedagogy.* New York: Routledge Falmer.

Gould. S. J. (1993). Eight little piggies: *Reflections in natural history. New York: W. W. Norton & Company.*

Gould, S. J. (1991). Unenchanted evening. *Natural History, 100*(9), 4–9.

Greene, M. (1995). *Releasing the imagination: Essays on education, the arts, and social change.* San Francisco, CA: Jossey-Bass.

Gruenewald, D. A. (2003a). The best of both worlds: A critical pedagogy of place. *Educational Researcher, 32*(4), 3–12.

Gruenewald, D. A. (2003b). Foundations of place: A multidisciplinary framework for place-conscious education. *American Education Research Journal, 40*(3), 619–654.

Gruenewald, D. A. (2007). (Ed.). *Place-based education in the global age.* New York: Routledge.

Hensley, N. (2011). *Curriculum studies gone wild: Bioregional education and the scholarship of sustainability.* New York: Peter Lang.

hooks, b. (1994). *Teaching to transgress: Education as the practice of freedom.* New York: Routledge.

hooks, b. (2003). *Teaching community: A pedagogy of hope.* New York: Routledge.

Kabat-Zinn, J. (1994). *Wherever you go there you are: Mindfulness meditation in everyday life.* New York: Hyperion.

Kemmis, S., & Mutton, R. (2012). Education for sustainability (EfS): Practice and practice architectures. *Environmental Education Research, 18*(2), 187–207.

Laughlin, R. B. (2011). *Powering the future: How we will (eventually) solve the energy crisis and fuel the civilization of tomorrow.* New York: Basic Books.

Leonard, A. (2007). *The story of stuff project.* Retrieved from https://storyofstuff.org/movies/story-of-stuff/

Leonard, A. (2013). *The story of solutions.* Retrieved from https://storyofstuff.org/movies/the-story-of-solutions/

Leopold, A. (1949). *A Sand County almanac: And sketches here and there.* New York: Oxford University Press.

McTighe, J., & Wiggins, G. (2005). *Understanding by design.* Alexandria, VA: Association for Supervision and Curriculum Development.

McWilliam, E., & Dawson, S. (2008). Teaching for creativity: Towards sustainable and replicable pedagogical practice. *Higher Education, 56*, 633–643.

Monsour, F. A. (2018). *Sustainability based texts for children and adolescents.* Poster presented at the American Association of Sustainability in Higher Education. Pittsburgh, PA: AASHE.

Nhat Hahn, T. (1991). *Peace is every step: The path of mindfulness in everyday life.* New York: Bantam Books.

Noddings, N. (2003). *Caring: A feminine approach to ethics and moral education* (2nd ed.). Berkeley, CA: University of California Press.

Oreskes, N., & Conway, E. M. (2014). *The collapse of western civilization: A view from the future.* New York: Columbia University Press.

Orr, D. (1992). *Ecological literacy: Education and the transition to a postmodern world.* New York: State University of New York Press.

Perry, M. & Medina, C. (2011). Embodiment and performance in pedagogy research: Investigating the possibility of the body in curriculum experience. *Journal of Curriculum Theorizing, 27*(3), 62–75.

Pinar, W. F. (1975). *Curriculum theorizing.* Berkeley, CA: McCutchan.

Purvis, B., Mao, Y., & Robinson, D. (2018). Three pillars of sustainability: In search of conceptual origins. *Sustainability Science, 14*(3), 681–695. https://doi.org/10.1007/s11625-018-0627-5

Sipos, Y., Battisti, B., & Grimm, K. (2008). Achieving transformative sustainability learning: Engaging head, hands and heart. *International Journal of Sustainability in Higher Education, 9*(1), 68–86.

Skoglund, U. (2010, September 16). *Geothermal energy could provide all the energy the world will ever need.* Retrieved May 7, 2019 from www.renewableenergyworld.com/articles/2010/09/geothermal-energy is the-solution-for-the-future.html

Stibbe, A. (2009). (Ed.). The handbook of sustainability literacy: Skills for a changing world. London: UIT Cambridge Ltd.

Sterling, S. (2001). *Sustainable education; Revisioning learning and change.* Cambridge, UK: Green Books.

Stone, M. K., & Barlow, Z. (2005). *Eco-literate: Educating our children for a sustainable world.* San Francisco, CA: Sierra Club Books.

UNESCO. (2012). *The education for sustainable development sourcebook.* Retrieved from http://unesdoc.unesco.org/images/0021/002163/216383e.pdf

UNESCO. (2017). *Education for sustainable development goals: Learning objectives.* Paris: United Nations Educational, Scientific and Cultural Organization.

Webb's Depth of Knowledge Guide. (2009). Retrieved from www.aps.edu/sapr/documents/resources/Webbs_DOK_Guide.pdf

Wright, M. F., Cain, K., & Monsour, F. M. (2015). Beyond sustainability: A context for transformative curriculum development. *Transformative Dialogue: Teaching and Learning Journal, 8*(2), 1–19.

Yoga Calm. Retrieved from www.yogacalm.org/

Zeichner, K. M., & Liston, D. P. (1996). *Reflective teaching: An introduction.* Reflective teaching and the social conditions of schooling: A series for prospective and practicing teachers. Mahwah, NJ: Lawrence Erlbaum Associates.

15

SUSTAINABILITY ROLE MODELS FOR TRANSFORMATIVE CHANGE

A great turning in higher education

Thomas R. Hudspeth

Introduction

To work toward more sustainable futures and to seek solutions to complex, wicked, uncertain, and rapidly accelerating planetary-scale challenges requires transformative change. These challenges include loss of biodiversity, air and water pollution, population and material consumption growth that accelerates demands on Earth's ecosystems, grinding poverty made even worse by climate change, and rising inequality. Despite increasingly observable threats and advice from leading scientists, American and global societies have not taken appropriate action (Hudspeth, 2017, p. 407).

Through their roles in teaching, research, service, and outreach, higher education institutions (HEIs) have a crucial role to play in advancing the goal of a desirable, just, healthy, peaceful, and sustainable society (Barlett & Chase, 2013). HEIs in the US have witnessed a rapidly expanding response in recent decades, as many colleges and universities, recognizing their responsibility, have undertaken sustainability education (SE) initiatives dealing with curriculum (e.g., sustainability undergraduate majors, minors, and general education requirements; graduate programs and research initiatives; faculty scholars programs) and campus operations (establishing offices of sustainability to improve campus practices and link facilities operations and academics). For HEI educators who seek to embed SE into a course but lack background knowledge and skills to accomplish that shift, theoretically focused SE books abound. But there are relatively few with theory-to-practice applications, concrete examples of implementation strategies, and analyses in line with the theoretical framework on which a course is grounded.

This chapter tries to address the divide between theory and practice by focusing on Sustainability Stories – a term project with both a written paper and a videotape that students carry out in a course at the University of Vermont

(UVM) – through a description of the theoretical framework on which it is grounded and a detailed description of how I practically applied it to actively engage my students. It recognizes the need for transformative change, for telling a new story – of sustainability – to replace our current failing cultural story. And it emphasizes the power of exemplars, role models, champions (the terms are used interchangeably) to emulate for the successful transition to more sustainable communities, to a more sustainable and desirable future.

Creating environmentally sustainable communities course

For more than a quarter century, I have taught a capstone course in Environmental Studies at UVM, titled Creating Environmentally Sustainable Communities (CESC), for 25–30 senior majors and minors each spring semester. In developing the course, three main considerations influenced my choice of learning outcomes: inspiration, theoretical framework, and power of stories.

Inspiration for CESC

Over 30 years since the publication of the World Commission of Environment and Development report, *Our Common Future* (1987), critics at conferences where I present continue to claim – as they did when I first started teaching CESC in 1990 – that sustainability is too abstract to grasp and put into action. They argued that it was a vague and imprecise term; that is was an idealistic, utopian, theoretical concept but not something that is actually happening here and now and that it did not offer a positive vision of what is desired, but only decried the negative aspects of our present situation. There were also suggestions that technical solutions could mitigate climate change and related impacts by eco-engineering, for example, by placing iron filings into the ocean or by putting a screen in the atmosphere. In effect, these claims assumed a silver bullet that would allow people to continue their over-consumptive ways and environmental degradation.

I disagreed, aware of countless examples of individuals and groups from my own community who were already actively engaging with sustainability. I believed that sharing stories of their initiatives with others might help convince naysayers and skeptics. Books, journal articles, and videos convinced me that the same held true in other parts of the US and world. For my initial offering of CESC, I pulled together some of my own sustainability stories for the students to read, and also invited several sustainability champions to be guest speakers in the class, plus scheduled class field trips to Intervale Center to examine community food systems in Burlington and to Ten Stones Ecovillage in nearby Charlotte, Vermont. From students' responses to those activities, I developed the idea that they might undertake their own sustainability stories by focusing on a "champion" who had developed their own sustainability practice. That decision was reinforced when Ernest Callenbach, in his last letter before his death in 2012, emphasized a vision of sustainability coming into existence, promising developments and new ways of carrying out various activities as old institutions and habits broke down, and "experiments under way all over the world explor(ed) how sustainability can, in fact, be achieved locally" (p. 1). More recently, Paul Hawken and the Project Drawdown team (2017) point out that when they came up with the top 100 climate solutions with the greatest potential to reduce emissions or sequester carbon from the atmosphere, fully 80 of them were already in place (readily available, economically viable, and scientifically valid), but could have greater impact if scaled up.

Theoretical framework

The theoretical framework in which Simon (1957) explains why people behave as they do in our business-as-usual, dominant social paradigm is the "economic human ('rational man') theory of human behavior. This views humans as narrowly self-interested, rational, insatiable, and competitive; seeking to obtain the highest possible well-being for themselves given available information, to attain predetermined goals to the greatest extent with the least possible cost" (Hudspeth, 2017, p. 408). My CESC course based around sustainability stories offers an alternative theoretical framework, the Reasonable Person Model (RPM), in which R. and S. Kaplan (Kaplan & Basu, 2015) recognize that humans are social primates and "acknowledge humans' innate capacity and desire to be cooperative, altruistic, and empathic. Further, they offer insights into institutional design that builds on these new and different understandings of human behavior to achieve more effective, equitable, and – ultimately – sustainable outcomes" (Hudspeth, 2017, p. 408).

The Kaplans theorize that people are more likely to act reasonably and cooperatively, to communicate and work with others to solve problems, when their environments meet their informational needs. They posit that model building, being effective, and meaningful action provide a framework that can foster reasonableness by creating supportive environments for bringing out the best in people (Hudspeth, 2017, pp. 409–410).

The power of stories

Humans live by their stories, individually and collectively (Craven, 2010). Not only do stories entertain us, but also they help us to learn important concepts, skills, and values, and to transmit to others in our communities and societies our deepest beliefs about our human nature, origin, purpose, and what we hold sacred. Compelling narrative captures humans' imaginations and connects them to others and to their places "because we are storytelling animals who understand things better if they are told to us in a story" (Hudspeth, 2017, p. 411). Fien, Cox, and Calder (2010) remind us that stories were the primary way our ancestors transmitted knowledge and values. As they put it: "Since earliest times most of our stories have related to our earth, how it was created, the relationship between it and its human inhabitants, and problems that arise when we fail to remember the importance of living in harmony with it and each other" (p. 1).

Theologian and cultural historian Thomas Berry (1990), who insisted that the "great work" of our time is to transform from an industrial to an ecological civilization, claimed: "For people, generally, their story of the universe and the human role in the universe is their primary source of intelligibility and value. . . . The deepest crises experienced by any society are those moments of change when the story becomes inadequate for meeting the survival demands of a present situation" (p. xi). Korten (2016) builds on Berry's notion, asserting: "We are a self-reflective, storytelling, choice-making species gone astray for want of a sacred story adequate to the needs of our time. . . . a shared story reflecting our responsibility to. . . . bring ourselves into balance with the generative systems of a living Earth. . . . before the economic, social, environmental, and political system failure wrought by inadequate stories becomes irreversible" (p. 1). He believes we need to change the story in order to change the future.

Right now we are living at a time between stories. Our culture is unraveling, going through a crisis because its conventional-world, business-as-usual, industrial-growth-society story is rapidly losing credibility. Our failing story is a story of money and markets; of addiction to overconsumption, fossil fuels, and an economic paradigm predicated on continual economic growth in a finite world, focusing on the accumulation of more and better material goods – regardless of the toll this quest is taking on the environment, our personal happiness, public health, equity and social justice, and even our sense of citizenship and democracy – and emphasizing individualism and competition and independence over community and interdependence.

The failing story is being reconstructed, revised, and reimagined. Outdated and inappropriate notions and worldviews are being deconstructed and replaced with a new story that better describes what is going on in the world, which reflects our creation of positive and empowering possibilities and opportunities based on our envisioning. The new story that is emerging in its place is a story of sustainability, of humans who survive and thrive only as contributing, cooperative members of a living Earth community that recognizes the importance of a living democracy and an economy whose only legitimate purpose is to serve living communities (Korten, 2015). There is a Great Turning (Korten, 2015), a Great Transition (Great Transition Initiative, 2002), which represents a paradigm shift from domination of nature to a sense of humanity's place in the web of life and dependence on its health, sustainability, and bounty; from quantity of things to quality of life to define success and well-being; and toward solidarity. Similarly, systems-thinker Donella Meadows (1999), when considering leverage points, or places to intervene in a system to transform it for the better, claimed that the most effective one is to change the mindset or paradigm out of which the system – its goals, power structure, rules, and culture – arises. Relatedly, Frances Moore Lappe (2010) believes we can tell that story and create the world we want by aligning our mental maps with conditions that bring out the best in people and for which we evolved: cooperation, empathy, compassion, efficacy, being courageous and engaged rather than being fearful and feeling powerless, being active citizens instead of just consumers, and recognizing possibilities rather than decrying scarcity or lack. Wilson (1980) asserts: "The future is up for grabs. It belongs to any and all who will take the risk and accept the responsibility of consciously creating the future they want" (p. 1). And sustainability stories can certainly help with this important task.

CESC projects

Pre-term project learning

Prior to working on their term projects, students gain a strong background in sustainability by learning about:

- Definitions of sustainability;
- Principles of sustainability;
- Nature of numerous intersecting sustainability challenges and solutions;
- Promising practices (successful sustainability initiatives at the local, state, national, and international levels);
- Tools for sustainability (personal and community visioning, creating alternative futures, indicators such as ecological footprint analysis and carbon footprint analysis and Genuine Progress Indicator, life cycle analysis, full cost accounting, valuing ecosystem services, and unlearning consumerism).

Students also consider ideas about human nature, various models of change and transformation, and the importance of exemplars and role models. The power of storytelling and the need for a "new story" are another dimension. During this first part of the semester, readings are drawn from books and articles such as ones by Meadows (1999), Edwards (2010), Costanza and Kubiszewski (2014), McKibben (2010), De Young and Princen (2012), Hawken (2007), and Wessels (2006).

Students complete an entry in their journals related to the readings for each class. In addition, they complete several short papers focused on:

- Defining sustainability (some students prefer "thriveability" or "resilience") and developing a scorecard for assessing sustainability initiatives and including a visual representation (Mann, 2011) of their definition;
- Product origin as an element of footprint analysis that involves picking an item and tracing the materials and energy that went into its manufacture and transport from its place of origin to the consumer and to its ultimate demise;
- Visionary newspaper article written 20 years in the future describing conditions once their utopian vision for some aspect of the Burlington community has been fulfilled;

- Community and community-building, including reacting to Putnam's (2000) ideas on those topics;
- "Ad-buster spoof advertisement" to convince people to consume less or, at least, practice more mindful and less environmentally harmful consumption.

CESC term project

During the portion of the semester that students work on their own sustainability stories papers and videos, they read others' stories from articles posted on Blackboard as well as from four fiction and more than a dozen nonfiction books (collectively over the years, but not all of them during any one semester), most notably: Callenbach (2004), Porritt (2013), Estill (2013), Lappe and Lappe (2003), Lerner (1997), McKibben (2007), and Walljasper, Spayde, and The Editors of Utne Reader (2001). I begin each class with a quote related to what students are doing in their term projects. Most emphasize the importance of envisioning a sustainable world, sharing that vision with other people, and identifying the importance of prophets who can see the seeds of the future and maps of the world to come. Some of the desirable attributes for a sustainability champion which the students identify include:

> "has a positive vision of a sustainable future and acts to achieve it, to turn it into reality; inspires, encourages, and empowers others; offers courageous, creative, innovative approaches; solves sustainability problems; takes action at the local grassroots level to deal with, or minimize the impacts of, global sustainability challenges; is a catalyst for change, a pioneer, a leader, a risk-taker; informs others of beneficial actions that can be taken; initiates real change out of concern for the earth and fellow human beings; and through her/his actions, demonstrates the power of the individual, illustrates how one person can make a difference."
>
> *(Hudspeth, 2015)*

Students select the champion they feature in their papers and videos, usually by emphasizing a sustainability challenge about which they are especially concerned or by choosing an analogue in the Greater Burlington area (Vermont portion of the Lake Champlain Basin Bioregion) of an individual or group featured in their readings that particularly interests them. They then conduct background research on their champion (analysis of documents and materials) and arrange for one or more semi-structured interviews with her/him.

CESC sustainability story videos

Students who do not have their own iPhone or video camera are able to check out flipcams or other video cameras from the university Media Services in the library. Staff there and at the Center for Teaching and Learning offer valuable assistance in videography and video-editing for those without previous video experience, as does my videotape of expert videographer Victor Guadagno when he presented to one of my classes. Some students are able to learn more about interviewing skills from the Vermont Folklife Center and some from participating in storytelling skill-building labs offered by the Vermont Story Lab. Students benefit from my handouts on "Pointers for Developing an Engaging Video that Tells Your Subject's Story in a Compelling Way" and "Videography and Video-editing Tips."

Almost all the videos are taken in the field, where the subject works or lives. Students are expected to have their champions sign an interview release form once the interview is completed, but a few students always fail to do so. I highly recommend using a professional video camera, a directional microphone (lavalier or external), and a tripod; however, most students use their own iPhones. Admittedly, the lenses and other features of the video function on the phones continue to improve appreciably. I emphasize the importance of paying American Society of Composers, Authors, and Publishers (ASCAP) a licensing fee if they use copyrighted music in their videos, and almost all students do so; if any do not, I am not able to place their videos on the website for the course. Students show their videos in the classroom near the end of the semester. The champions of videos are invited to the presentations, as are students' friends, roommates, and relatives. Cider, cheese and crackers, and doughnuts are provided to make the occasion more festive.

Observations and reflections

From 1990–2010, students' stories focused on any sustainability topic they chose; from 2011–2015, all the stories dealt with climate change or sustainable agriculture or both. The subjects or topics of the several hundred stories fell into eleven major categories (See Table 15.1). Brief descriptions of a few of the stories are included below.

Sustainable agriculture was, by far, the largest category. This related to such topics as community-based agriculture, food systems, food security, food justice, nutrition, agroecology, and permaculture. It included numerous farmers (many of them ENVS alumni/ae), brewers, and composters; farmer's markets, food cooperatives, CSAs (community supported agriculture is a food production and distribution

TABLE 15.1 Students' Sustainability Stories Fell Into Eleven Main Categories As Shown Below

Sustainable agriculture	Sustainable transportation
Sustainability education	Indigenous leaders and wisdom keepers
Climate change	Ecovillages/cohousing/intentional community
Sustainable business and enterprise	Faith communities
Sustainable building and design	University students, alumni, faculty, programs
	Events

system that directly connects farmers and consumers), and pick-your-owns; and planters of pollinator gardens (including in solar fields), forest gardens, rain gardens (often as part of green stormwater infrastructure projects), wildlife-friendly yards, or schoolyards (often replacing grass lawns with native plants).

On 360 acres of farmland close to downtown Burlington and UVM, Intervale Center works to foster a local food economy that is good for people and the planet. Its pioneering initiatives, like CSA, large-scale composting, food hubs, and farm incubators, help transform the food system from one that is degrading, anonymous, and industrial to one that is restorative, familiar, and human-scale. It implements innovative, replicable, and place-based solutions to address some of global agriculture's most pressing problems.

Approximately 1500 migrant workers who typically work 60–80 hours per week and endure extreme isolation on dairy farms that sustain Vermont's iconic working landscapes formed Migrant Justice to build the voice, capacity, and power of the farmworker community and engage community partners to organize for economic justice and human rights.

Another very popular topic was sustainability education. This included public and private school teachers; educators and interpreters at environmental education centers, nature centers, science centers, museums, and farms; authors, storytellers, and musicians; Crow's Path, which offers nature-connection programs to build relationships to human and more-than-human ecosystems; and a filmmaker who explores nature's powerful role in children's health and development. Burlington's Sustainability Academy is the only public elementary magnet school in the US using sustainability as a lens and integrative tool to teach all academic disciplines. Shelburne Farms is nationally recognized for its Sustainable Schools Project, professional learning programs for K-12 educators, field trips for schools to its 1400-acre working farm, and numerous partnerships with other SE providers.

The climate change category related to climate change adaptation and mitigation, climate justice/just transition, and renewable energy. In 2014, Burlington became the first city in the country to source 100% of its electricity from renewables (hydro, wind, solar, and biomass); its next ambitious target is to become a "net zero energy" city in the thermal (heating and cooling) and transportation sectors, which will involve sourcing more renewables while transitioning the city off fossil fuels.

Not surprisingly, some students chose fellow students who were active in pushing for a Sustainability General Education requirement, banning on-campus sale of plastic water bottles and use of paper products made from old growth forests, taxing themselves $10 per semester for a Clean Energy Fund, and urging Sodexho to join the Real Food Challenge.

Several students featured the LEED Platinum renovated Aiken Building, home of UVM's Rubenstein School of Environment and Natural Resources, which has an ecomachine designed by John Todd for treating human wastes, a green roof with experimental watersheds, wood from 17 species harvested from UVM's Forest Stewardship Council-certified Jericho Research Forest, waterless and low-flow fixtures, environmental/energy dashboard monitoring system, and interpretation of its sustainability features.

Several students also featured the Greater Burlington Sustainability Education Network, which is a Regional Center of Expertise in Education for Sustainable Development recognized by the United Nations University to help operationalize sustainability at the regional level, using collective impact to connect research and practice and link across sectors and disciplines to work on the 17 U.N. Sustainability Development Goals (SDGs) (2015).

A notable event which a few students featured was "For Love of Earth," a daylong Earth Charter (2000) celebration at Shelburne Farms by more than 2000 participants in 2001, in which Satish Kumar led a pilgrimage and spoke, along with Jane Goodall and Earth Charter Commission member Steven Rockefeller and several local sustainability leaders, and Paul Winter played music. After being treated to dance, music, and paintings of several Vermont artists, participants joined hands and offered a prayer of reverence and commitment to Mother Earth.

Just as the course evolved over time, so did the types of champions. Throughout the years, there were large numbers of farmers and sustainability educators. In the early years, the preponderance of champions were white males and nongovernmental organizations (NGOs) related to initiatives such as conservation, protection of biodiversity, or water quality. Over time, there were more women, indigenous leaders, and people of color with more emphasis on social justice and equity aspects of sustainability. After several ecological economists came to UVM, students' projects placed more emphasis on economic feasibility aspects of sustainability. Not surprisingly, as climate change became more pronounced, it created a sense of urgency. There were more marches, protests, and demonstrations in the US (Step it Up, Occupy, etc.), and a marked increase in topics focused on advocacy, social action, climate change, and renewable energy.

No empirical evaluations of the students' sustainability stories have been conducted, so it is difficult to make any conclusive statements about their impact. However, I carried out my own formative evaluations during the semester and administered UVM's standardized end-of-semester course evaluation instruments along with several open-ended questions about particular elements of the course. There were many responses, many of them excellent. Students enjoyed getting out in the real world and meeting real people who are doing exciting things and affecting change, and sharing their stories with others. They felt good about being part of the bridge between UVM and the community, sharing with the larger community the insights, knowledge, and skills they had gained from their undergraduate education, and learning not just for the sake of learning but to communicate with and serve others, and to work as change agents. A few students mentioned that they had obtained internships or been hired by the person or group they had featured in their story. One student said that the course had influenced her to go to graduate school to learn about videography for social change; a couple of others to study journalism. A few students thought there were too many journal assignments. Several students suggested I tried to fit too much into one course, claiming they devoted far more time in total to this course than most other three-credit courses and reminding me that most students enrolled in it were seniors simultaneously completing their six-credit senior thesis project. Most, but not all, students reported that their term project inspired them with hope, empowered them, helped them to consider alternatives to our current unsustainable practices, and showed them that they – and the people and groups they interviewed and celebrated – can make a difference. They liked focusing on positive solutions to the daunting sustainability problems we face and featuring champions' success stories.

Conclusion

Prioritizing sustainability education by telling sustainability stories about positive role models helps cultivate a sense of place and builds community. These stories bring out humanity's best efforts and demonstrate positive, practical solutions to today's daunting sustainability problems, thereby providing hope, inspiration, optimism, and empowerment to counter despair and doom-and-gloom. They offer a way by which HEIs can play a central role in sustainability education by partnering with stakeholders from various sectors and offering active, creative, engaged, authentic, hands-on learning opportunities for students. All the stories collected can help humanize and concretize the concept of sustainability. These success stories of individuals and groups working at various levels to ensure a sustainable future benefit from using engaged pedagogies. Writing elsewhere in this volume (see chapter 14), Wright and Monsour emphasize these in their work with teacher candidates in Wisconsin.

It is heartening to note that others from HEIs recognize the power of sustainability stories (Miller, 2010; Nichols, Dernikos, & Morphis, 2017). Heretofore, there has been far more attention devoted to the topic in popular publications than academic presses and SE- and sustainability-related professional journals. The environmental challenges we face are daunting, as is the challenge of changing people's mindsets, habits, and political and economic systems (Next Systems Project, 2019) on a large scale. But what people and groups have already done and are doing right now all around the world, even in the little corner featured in this chapter, is remarkable, exciting, and hopeful. But time is not on our side, and we must pick it up and create opportunities for new thinking, as Albert Einstein (1946) is reputed to have reminded us that "We cannot solve our problems with the same thinking we used when we created them." We must collaborate even more, including with unlikely allies, to achieve the greatest impact, continue to balance the message of urgency with hope, and tell sustainability stories to inspire others.

Course Planning

This course considers the process of creating communities which are environmentally sound, economically successful, and socially just; and then examines

TABLE 15.2 Sustainability Education Grounded in the Sustainable Development Goals and The Earth Charter

Conceptual Framework Dimensions	Project	Learning Informed by the SDGs (Goals 1.1 to 17.19) and The Earth Charter (Principles I.1 to IV.16)
Ethic of Care – Values – Attitudes – Behaviors	**Title:** Create a Sustainability Story (paper and video) about an individual or group in the Greater Burlington area (Vermont portion of the Lake Champlain Basin Bioregion) who serves as a sustainability exemplar or role model or champion (the terms are used interchangeably) for others to follow or emulate in bringing about the transition to more environmentally sustainable communities – related to local aspects of climate change or sustainable agriculture. Demonstrate your ability to research (using semi-structured interviews and analysis of documents and materials) and tell a compelling story, to communicate ideas about a sustainability champion clearly and persuasively in writing and in video.	*Goal 2.* End hunger, achieve food security and improved nutrition, and promote sustainable agriculture *Goal 13.* Take urgent action to combat climate change and its impacts *II.7* Adopt patterns of production, consumption, and reproduction that safeguard Earth's regenerative capacities, human rights, and community well-being. *III.10* Ensure that economic activities and institutions at all levels promote human development in an equitable and sustainable manner.
Resilience & Regeneration – Knowledge – Skills	**Phase 1: Paper** Write your paper in the same fashion as each story in our readings by Lerner, Lappe & Lappe, McKibben, etc. in that it both tells your champion's story and how what s/he is doing fits in with sustainable solutions; and demonstrates how s/he offers a viable alternative to conventional ways of doing business, to the dominant social paradigm, and in so doing, outline how business-as-usual or the conventional ways are not sustainable. Trace your champion's values, attitudes, and behaviors that cultivate an ethic of care. Trace your champion's knowledge and skills that foster resilience and regeneration. Trace your champion's actions that advocate for life's flourishing.	

Conceptual Framework Dimensions	Project	Learning Informed by the SDGs (Goals 1.1 to 17.19) and The Earth Charter (Principles I.1 to IV.16)
Advocacy for Life's Flourishing – Action – Critique – Reflection	**Phase 2: Video** The video should be on the same subject as your written paper. It should follow the example of Douglas Gayeton in his Lexicon of Sustainability project (2009) in developing an engaging video that tells your champion's story in a compelling way (that is, not just "talking heads," but also including "b rolls" that make what your subject is talking about come alive visually, etc.).	

Source: Course Content Guide: Creating Environmentally Sustainable Communities, Dr. Hudspeth

sustainability in action, where the concept comes alive, going beyond identifying sustainability challenges to focusing on actual solutions. After gaining an understanding of sustainability from conceptual and operational points of view and becoming familiar with some tools for sustainability and successful sustainability initiatives at the local, state, national, and international levels, students complete a term/research project for which they write a paper and produce a video that tells a Sustainability Story, which helps operationalize sustainability, make it more concrete, put a face on it, humanize it, and make it come alive by emphasizing positive role models who can inspire and empower others, creating hope versus despair.

References

Barlett, P., & Chase, G. (Eds.). (2013). *Sustainability in higher education: Stories and strategies for transformation*. Cambridge, MA: MIT Press.

Berry, T. (1990). *The dream of the earth*. San Francisco, CA: Sierra Club.

Callenbach, E. (2004). *Ecotopia: The notebook and reports of William Weston*. Berkeley, CA: Banyan Tree.

Callenbach, E. (2012). *Live within contradictions: Ernest Callenbach's last message*. Retrieved from www.yesmagazine.org/planet/live-within-contradictions-ernest-callenbachs-last-message

Costanza, R., & Kubiszewski, I. (Eds.). (2014). *Creating a sustainable and desirable future: Insights from 45 global thought leaders*. Hackensack, NJ: World Scientific.

Craven, J. (2010). *Importance of narrative*. Vermont Public Radio commentary, November 29, 2010.

De Young, R., & Princen, T. (Eds.). (2012). *The localization reader: Adapting to the coming downshift*. Cambridge, MA: MIT Press.

The Earth Charter. (2000). Retrieved from earthcharter.org

Edwards, A. (2010). *Thriving beyond sustainability: Pathways to a resilient society*. Gabriola Island, BC: New Society.

Einstein, A. (1946). *Did Albert Einstein ever say/write that "We can't solve problems by using the same kind of thinking we used when we created them"? If so, where and when did he say/ write so?* Retrieved from www.quora.com/Did-Albert-Einstein-ever-say-write-that-We-cant-solve-problems-by-using-the-same-kind-of-thinking-we-used-when-we-created-them-If-so-where-and-when-did-he-say-write-so

Estill, L. (2013). *Small stories, big changes: Agents of change on the frontlines of sustainability.* Gabriola Island, BC: New Society.

Fien, J., Cox, B., & Calder, M. (2010). *Storytelling.* UNESCO. Retrieved from www.unesco.org/education/tlsf/mods/theme_d/mod21.html

Gayeton, D. (2009). *Lexicon of sustainability videos.* Retrieved from www.lexiconofsustainability.com

Great Transition Initiative. (2002). Retrieved from www.greattransition.org/

Hawken, P. (2007). *Blessed unrest: How the largest movement in the world came into being and why no one saw it coming.* New York: Viking.

Hawken, P. (Ed.). (2017). *Drawdown: The most comprehensive plan ever proposed to reverse global warming.* New York: Penguin.

Hudspeth, T. (2015). *Course description for creating environmentally sustainable communities.* Burlington, VT: Environmental Program, University of Vermont.

Hudspeth, T. (2017). Reimagining sustainability education to address Anthropocene challenges: Envisioning, storytelling, community scenario planning. In P. B. Corcoran, J. P. Weakland, & A. E. J. Wals (Eds.), *Envisioning futures for environmental and sustainability education.* Wageningen, The Netherlands: Wageningen Academic Publishers.

Kaplan, R., & Basu, A. (Eds.). (2015). *Fostering reasonableness: Supportive environments for bringing out our best.* Ann Arbor, MI: Michigan Publishing.

Korten, D. (2015). *Change the story, change the future: A living economy for a living earth.* Oakland, CA: Berrett Koehler.

Korten, D. (2016). *The new economy: A living earth system model.* Retrieved from https://thenextsystem.org/the-new-economy-a-living-earth-system-model

Lappe, F., & Lappe, A. (2003). *Hope's edge: The next diet for a small planet.* New York: Tarcher/Putnam.

Lappe, F. (2010). *Why are we creating a world that no one wants?* TEDx Talks. Retrieved from http://tinyurl.com/z8zo4dz

Lerner, S. (1997). *Eco-pioneers: Practical visionaries solving today's environmental problems.* Cambridge, MA: MIT Press.

Mann, S. (2011) *Sustainable lens: A visual guide.* Retrieved from http://computingforsustainability.wordpress.com/2009/03/15/visualising-sustainability/

McKibben, B. (2007). *Hope, human and wild: True stories of living lightly on the earth.* Minneapolis, MN: Milkweed Editions.

McKibben, B. (2010). *Earth: Making a life on a tough new planet.* New York: Henry Holt and Company.

Meadows, D. (1999). *Leverage points: Places to intervene in a system.* Hartland, VT: The Sustainability Institute.

Miller, M. (2010). Storytelling for sustainability. *Ometeca,* XIV–XV, 320–341.

Next System Project. (2019). Retrieved from https://thenextsystem.org/

Nichols, B., Dernikos, B., & Morphis, E. (2017). Green stories of the future: Leveraging standards-based narrative techniques to guide student storytelling for sustainability. In P. B. Corcoran, J. P. Weakland, & A. E. J. Wals (Eds.), *Envisioning futures for environmental and sustainability education.* Wageningen, The Netherlands: Wageningen Academic Publishers.

Porritt, J. (2013). *The world we made: Alex Mckay's story from 2050.* London: Phaidon Press.

Putnam, R. (2000). *Bowling alone: The collapse and revival of American community.* New York: Simon & Schuster.

Simon, H. (1957). *Models of man: Social and rational.* New York: Wiley.

Sustainable Development Goals. (2015). Retrieved from www.un.org/sustainabledevelopment/sustainable-development-goals/

Walljasper, J., Spayde, J., & The Editors of Utne Reader. (2001). *Visionaries: People and ideas to change your life.* Gabriola Island, BC: New Society.

Wessels, T. (2006). *The myth of progress: Toward a sustainable future.* Burlington, VT: UVM Press.

Wilson, R. A. (1980, November). Interview by Neil Wilgus from *Science Fiction Review, 37*(9), 4. Retrieved from http://rawilsonfans.org/1980/11/

World Commission on Environment and Development. (1987). *Our common future.* Oxford: Oxford.

16

EDUCATION FOR SUSTAINABILITY AND THE SEARCH FOR NEW STORIES TO LIVE BY

Arran Stibbe

Introduction

If asked what three questions are the most important for educators to ask ourselves in the current conditions of the world, I would say that the first is *'Who am I?'* The second is *'Who am I within an unjust and unsustainable society?'* And the third is *'Who do I need to become?'*

To answer these questions for myself: 'Who am I?' I am, among other things, an educator who teaches English. 'Who am I within an unjust and unsustainable world?' The answer to this is painful, but unavoidable. I am someone who reproduces, entrenches and perpetuates injustice and unsustainability through my teaching practices, partly through specific actions but mostly through inaction. With the pain faced, the third question brings hope: 'Who do I need to become?' My answer is someone whose teaching allows students to challenge the foundations of the unjust and unsustainable society around them – the stories we live by – and helps empower them to convey new stories to live by, stories that work better in the conditions of the world we face.

This chapter describes how I have responded to the significant challenge of being an educator within an unsustainable society and integrated sustainability into my teaching. My journey started with completing a Ph.D. in linguistics at Lancaster University in the U.K., comparing Chinese and Western ideas of illness. The next step was working as a linguistics lecturer in South Africa, then as an English lecturer in the mountains of Japan, where I first gained ecological awareness. It continued back to the U.K. where I studied human ecology at the Centre for Human Ecology, Edinburgh, and then to the University of Gloucestershire where I am now Professor in Ecological Linguistics. For fourteen years now at Gloucestershire, I have been surprising students with modules which focus on social justice and 'sustainability' as the overarching goals. Two modules I teach are particularly focused on sustainability: *The Stories We Live By* (first year), and *The Search for New Stories to Live By* (second year). I also run the free online course *The Stories We Live By* (Stories, 2019), which provides videos, notes, readings and discussion groups for students across the world. It offers free tuition over email in 12 languages thanks to volunteer tutors, and more than 1500 students have enrolled.

Although I say that these modules focus on 'sustainability', I use the word with mixed feelings and scare quotes. The terms 'sustainability' and its counterpart 'sustainable development' have a long history of use and abuse since sustainable development came to prominence with the *Our Common Future* (Brundtland, 1987). In Stibbe (2015a) I document how the term 'development' originally referred to an altruistic goal of poverty reduction in poor countries through helping their economies to grow (p. 54). It then became 'equitable development' to emphasize contributing to a fairer society, then 'sustainable development' to ensure that the environment was protected, too. However, the term 'sustainable development' was co-opted by rich countries to refer to maximising *their own* economic growth while reducing damage to the environment. More recently the term 'sustained growth' was coined, with the environment forgotten and the focus on international competition to build the wealth of already-rich countries at the expense of poorer ones. This description is, of course, a simplification, but illustrates a general process where altruistic attempts to benefit the world (intrinsic values) are twisted to serve the dominant goals of wealth for the few at the expense of other people, other species and the ecosystems that support life.

My own way of characterizing sustainability, therefore, refers only to intrinsic goals, i.e., goals that are valuable in themselves, as opposed to extrinsic goals, such as profit or economic growth, which are at best a means to an end and never an end in themselves:

> Sustainability is the pursuit of intrinsically valuable goals such as human health, wellbeing, poverty reduction, peace, social justice, and the survival and wellbeing of other species, underpinned by care for the ecosystems that life depends on.
>
> *(Crompton, 2010, p. 10)*

Ecosystems, although crucial in keeping us alive, can feel very distant from the English curriculum – a matter for environmental science students, not English students. Nothing could be further from the truth, however. The foundations of the unsustainable society we live in are built through discourses, and English students are in a key position to use their knowledge to expose and challenge those discourses. It is not just English students, however, who could benefit from close attention to language and the way it forms the stories we live by: it is a fundamental sustainability skill for students in any discipline.

The stories we live by

It is often hard for people to see a connection between language and sustainability. For me, though, the connection is clear. Quite simply, increasing ecological destruction and social injustice calls into question the fundamental stories our society is built on, and we can use the tools of linguistic analysis to reveal those stories and contribute to the search for new ones. Students are confused by this at first, which is unsurprising since it is a 'threshold concept' (Meyer & Land, 2005). Understanding this will require a fundamental rethinking of the power of language to shape reality, rethinking what it means to be a student in an unsustainable society and rethinking what the goal of education is.

To help students over the threshold, I start the *Stories We Live By* module with a practical analysis of texts. I hand out printouts from websites which sell artificial grass, i.e., plastic lawns. What stories do the visual images and linguistic features in the texts tell? The following are some extracts from the websites:

- The crème de la crème of artificial grasses
- Makes gardening a pleasure
- Enjoy the luxury of your garden
- Enjoy your garden, enjoy life
- Make your garden fit for a king
- His artificial grass garden helped him overcome Afghan bomb blast wounds
- Lifestyle Elite Premium – luxurious alternative to natural grass
- Mayfair Supreme Lawn

Heads down in conversation, occasionally passing advertisements on to another group, some laughter, moving around the room to see what other groups have found. They've found a lexical set across the texts: *elite, luxury, royal, rich, crème-de-la-crème, (fit for a) king*. It fits the common story of PURCHASING GOODS IS A PATH TO HIGH SOCIAL STATUS and matches the competitive framing that another group has found: *rich realistic results to wow the neighbours*. There are presuppositions embedded in sentences that imply that artificial grass is beautiful and enhances enjoyment not only of the garden but also of the changing seasons. This fits a general story of PRODUCTS AS A PATH TO HAPPINESS, where enjoyment of nature (which could potentially be free) is substituted by the consumption of products. And then, across all of the advertisements, manifesting in a range of ways, is the simple story that CONVENIENCE IS GOOD. Classroom discussion moves on to the potential impact of stories such as PRODUCTS ARE A PATH TO HAPPINESS on people's behavior; do they encourage people to protect the ecosystems that support life through reducing their consumption, or damage them further by fuelling even more consumption? The discussion starts by examining the small technical details of the text and images and widens out to the larger context of the stories that lie behind them, and how they encourage us to protect or destroy the ecosystems that life depends on.

This is the first class in *The Stories We Live By* module. The concept of 'story' as the basis of a society or culture has a long history. Chara Armon (this volume) draws from the work of Thomas Berry, who as far back as 1978 described the environmental crisis as a question of story:

It's all a question of story. We are in trouble just now because we do not have a good story. We are in between stories. The old story, the account of how we fit into it, is no longer effective. Yet we have not learned the new story.

(Berry, 1978, p. 1)

Each week in the *Stories We Live By* module, we focus on one particular way that linguistic features convey the stories we live by. We start with *ideologies*, drawing on Critical Discourse Analysis. One of the key ideologies we investigate is HUMANS ARE FUNDAMENTALLY SELFISH, which is embedded in many of the main economics textbooks, and promotes the building of a society based on greed. Then we look at *frames* and *metaphors*, using cognitive linguistics (e.g. Lakoff & Wehling, 2012). Then *evaluations*, using appraisal theory (Martin & White, 2005). Evaluations are stories about whether an area of life is good or bad, and we investigate the dangers of the story ECONOMIC GROWTH IS GOOD, which is deeply embedded in our society and commits us to unending increases in consumption.

We move on to *identities*, using identity theory (Benwell & Stokoe, 2006) and look at how consumerist identities in lifestyle magazines set up ideals of masculinity and femininity that associate owning particular items with being a particular kind of person. Then we look at *convictions*, using facticity theory (Potter, 1996), and consider linguistic techniques used by climate change deniers and ways to resist them. Finally, we explore *erasure* and *salience*, drawing from van Leeuwen's (2008) work. We consider how the ecosystems that support life have been erased in so many texts that surround us in everyday life, and we search for inspiring discourses which can help give the natural world salience by representing it prominently, as something important and worthy of attention. Each week I give input on linguistic theory, but always in the context of the larger picture of critiquing the unjust and unsustainable society around us, and searching for new stories to live by (see Stibbe, 2015b for a more detailed case study of this module).

The feedback from students shows how learning about the stories we live by inspires not only critical awareness of how everyday texts encode the stories we live by, but practical changes in lifestyle. The following are examples of comments from students:

- Very enlightening in terms of igniting awareness.
- Increased my understanding of how society and the media influence the world around me.
- I am more conscious of my own impact on the environment.
- I will be more aware of what products I am buying in the future.
- Made me look at the world very differently in relation to ecology and my place in the world.
- I now view advertisements and texts in different ways.
- I will take more care in everything, start a more sustainable lifestyle.

Developing an ecosophy

It's important that the classes do not attempt to force particular values or world-views onto students. Students are sensitive to indoctrination and need to accept new ideas through their own process of critically evaluating alternative view-points. If they do this, then the ideas will lodge far deeper in their minds than if they accept them at a surface level to please the lecturer and get high marks. One way to avoid imposing values would be to have a course which focused entirely on technical details of language structure without considering the larger social and ecological context at all. This, however, is also a political stance because it implicitly endorses the stories we currently live by through leaving them unchallenged. It assigns to education the role of reproducing an unjust and unsustainable society rather than changing it.

My way of addressing the issue of values and worldview is to ask students to develop their own ecosophy (or ecological philosophy) which they use to judge stories against. An ecosophy is a values framework which considers not just humans but also other species, the physical environment, and the ecosystems that life depends on (Naess, 1995, p. 8). Each student is expected to come up with their own ecosophy, based on their reading and experience, and develop this on an ongoing basis over the three years of the course (and throughout their lives).

In developing their own ecosophies, students investigate a wide spectrum of ecosophies from the most conservative (i.e., the least challenge to dominant political structures) to the most transformative. At the most conservative end of the spectrum is *Ecological Modernization*, as exemplified in many of the UN's Sustainable Development Goals (SDGs). This ecosophy relies on technological progress, industrialization, and economic growth to reduce poverty, and puts the brunt of sustainability onto resource efficiency ("doing more and better with less" as SDG12 put it). Ecological modernization also tends to treat other species and the physical environment as resources for human use (e.g., SDG14, *Life Below Water*, speaks of "sustainable use of marine resources" and SDG15 of "utilization of genetic resources"). As Hickel points out, the SDGs are conservative in terms of the economy because they fail to challenge the dominant economic model:

> the goals are not only a missed opportunity, they are actively dangerous: they lock in the global development agenda for the next 15 years around a failing economic model that requires urgent and deep structural changes . . . the core of the SDG programme for development and poverty reduction relies precisely on the old model of industrial growth – ever-increasing levels of extraction, production, and consumption.
>
> *(2015, n.p.)*

A more transformative ecosophy is *Social Ecology* (Bookchin, 2005),. which insists not only on reducing poverty, but also challenging the system of hierarchy and domination which allows a small group of people to consume vast resources at the expense of other people and the planet. *Deep Ecology* challenges the dominant paradigm in another way by recognizing the intrinsic value not only of humans but of other species and the ecosystems that life depends on (Naess, 1995). The Transition Movement (Hopkins, 2008) calls for social change based on a philosophy of 'resilience' at a time when climate change and resource depletion are leading to an inevitable decline in the ability of the Earth to support human life. The movement is localist in encouraging communities to regain the bonds and skills to look after each other and fulfil their own needs in turbulent times. By contrast, The Dark Mountain Project (Kingsnorth & Hine, 2009) is less optimistic than Transition. It recognizes that with the globally dominant political focus on economic growth and consumerism, the collapse of industrial civilization is inevitable. The aim, therefore, is to lay the foundations for a new, more ecologically-focused form of civilization to emerge for those who survive the collapse. Deep Green Resistance (McBay et al., 2011), at the radical end of the spectrum, sees industrial civilization as evil due to the damage and suffering it causes both humans and other species. Rather than waiting for industrial civilization to destroy itself, Deep Green Resistance aims to hasten its end through direct action against strategic infrastructure, combined with rebuilding just and sustainable human communities. Perhaps the most radical of all is the semi-serious VHMT (Voluntary Human Extinction Movement), which believes that only the extinction of the human species through a worldwide agreement not to have children can prevent the destruction of the ecosystems that all life depends on.

Figure 16.1 maps these ecosophies on a chart for the purpose of illustration and discussion. Of course, the exact position of the different ecosophies is open to debate. The 'optimistic' and 'pessimistic' boxes refer to whether the collapse of industrial civilization is seen as inevitable, although from a different perspective

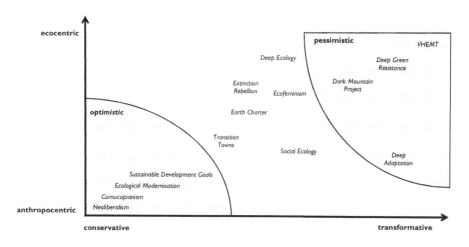

FIGURE 16.1   An Illustrative Mapping of Ecosophies to Stimulate Discussion

these boxes could be labelled 'unrealistic' and 'realistic'. It is exactly this kind of discussion which it is useful to have with students (see Hopwood et al., 2005 for a chart along similar lines).

To help students develop an ecosophy, the Earth Charter (ECI, 2017) is a useful document to examine since it contains a mixture of ecosophies towards the centre of the spectrum, including deep ecology, "Care for the community of life with understanding, compassion, and love" (Principle 2), and social ecology, "Promote social and economic justice" (Principle 3b). Although the Earth Charter does not directly challenge the dominant paradigm of economic growth, it does subtly resist consumerism: "when basic needs have been met, human development is primarily about being more, not having more" (Introduction).

It is not just reading which helps students develop their own ecosophy, but also their own direct experience of interacting with communities and the natural world. A key question that they are encouraged to ask themselves through this process is *who and what do I care about*? It is impossible for educators to force students to care about others, but I have found that students do find themselves caring about continuation of life on the planet, about the welfare of other people, particularly oppressed groups, and about other species. It is not that they did not care about these before the process of reflection; it's more that their care comes into the forefront of their minds where it can be put into action.

The students I teach tend to reject ecosophies at both ends of the spectrum – both those at the conservative end that promote unlimited economic growth and treat other species as resources for exploitation, and those which aim to hasten the end of industrial civilization. Although they show some variation in their ecosophy, the following statements sum up the most common values that they align with:

- *Valuing life:* The life and well-being of all species, not just humans, should be valued, celebrated, respected and affirmed.
- *Now and the future:* Life and well-being are important not just in the present but also into the future, including the ability of future generations to live and live well.
- *Environmental limits:* If human consumption exceeds the ability of natural resources to replenish themselves then this damages the ability of ecological systems to support life into the future. To keep within environmental limits, an immediate and large-scale reduction of total global consumption is necessary.
- *Social justice:* Currently, large numbers of people do not have the resources to live, or to live with high well-being. As global consumption levels drop (either voluntarily or through resource exhaustion), resources will need to be redistributed from rich to poor if all are to live with high well-being.

Once they have established their ecosophy, students can use it to judge the underlying stories and hidden messages in texts. So, for example, if they find that advertisements encode a story that PURCHASING PRODUCTS IS A PATH TO HAPPINESS then they can criticize this story on the grounds that it encourages excess consumption, which threatens environmental limits. Or if they analyse discourses of the meat industry which represent animals as objects or machines, they could criticize them based on the principle of respecting all life.

The theoretical foundation for these activities is Critical Discourse Analysis (Fairclough 2003), which uses linguistic analysis to expose the role of language in reproducing oppressive power relationships (e.g., racism, and sexism). This framework needs extending in two directions, however, to deal effectively with the issues that humanity is currently facing. Firstly, it needs to not only critique oppressive discourse, but also to search for positive ways of using language that can inspire people to create more equal societies. I therefore found it useful to use Positive Discourse Analysis (Martin, 2004; Bartlett, 2012) to help students contribute to the search for positive new stories to live by. Secondly, there is little point in creating an equal society if it is unsustainable and on a path towards ecological collapse. It is therefore necessary to consider not just relationships of humans with other humans but of humans with other species and the physical environment. The theoretical framework is therefore based primarily on ecolinguistics (Fill & Penz, 2017), an approach which considers the impact of discourse on other species and the ecosystems that support life.

The search for new stories to live by: resilience, regeneration and reduction

Revealing and critiquing the stories we live by is an important step towards sustainability awareness, but only a first step. The next step is to search for new stories to live by, ones which resonate with the ecosophy of the students. As Ben Okri puts it, "Stories are the secret reservoir of values: change the stories that individuals or nations live by and you change the individuals and nations themselves" (1996, p. 21).

If a student's ecosophy is based on Transition, then they would look for stories that promote resilience, both of human and natural systems. If their ecosophy is based on Deep Ecology, then they may look towards regeneration and restoration of the ecosystems that all life depends on. For students whose ecosophy recognizes environmental limits and the limits of what resource efficiency can achieve, then stories that promote reduction in consumption are of central importance (e.g., "being more rather than having more").

In the second-year module, *The Search for New Stories to Live By*, students begin by exploring the discourse of New Economics. They discover how the language of the New Economics Foundation (NEF, 2015) and Bhutan's Gross National Happiness project (CBS, 2012) challenge the story that ECONOMIC GROWTH IS THE MAIN GOAL OF SOCIETY, and instead use language in innovative ways to tell new stories, such as WELL-BEING IS THE MAIN GOAL OF SOCIETY or HAPPINESS IS THE MAIN GOAL OF SOCIETY. These new stories resonate with an ecosophy that calls for a reduction of consumption to remain within environmental limits since they break the mental connection between social progress and material accumulation. Students explore how the Gross National Happiness project in Bhutan not only tells new stories about the goal of society, but also tells new stories about happiness itself, to shift the concept away from self-centred gratification:

> We have now clearly distinguished the 'happiness' . . . in GNH from the fleeting, pleasurable 'feel good' moods so often associated with that term. We know that true abiding happiness cannot exist while others suffer, and comes only from serving others, living in harmony with nature, and realising our innate wisdom.
>
> *(CBS, 2012, p. 7)*

Another place that students search for new stories to live by is in traditional cultures from around the world which have ways of representing humans as interconnected with and dependent on the natural world. This engagement with worldwide cultures is essential if students are to find stories which radically differ from the mainstream stories of an unsustainable civilization. A simple example is the following metaphor, attributed to Chief Seattle:

> Humankind has not woven the web of life. We are but one thread within it. Whatever we do to the web, we do to ourselves. All things are bound together. All things connect.
>
> *(in CIE, 2017)*

This metaphor overcomes the split between 'humans' and 'environment' that is prevalent in a lot of environmental discourse and promotes *relational awareness*. Humans are very much part of the natural world, and the story HUMANS ARE A THREAD IN THE WEB OF LIFE is useful in emphasizing that concern for the environment is not just for the sake of exotic and beautiful species which are endangered, but for the survival of humans, too (Stibbe, 2017a). It helps promote an ecosophy that calls for protecting the well-being of all species into the future since it shows how short-term gain for the few at the expense of the environment leads to long-term destruction for everyone.

The students also explore Japanese Haiku poetry, which encodes stories that the ordinary plants and animals that surround us are important and worthy of observation, attention and appreciation. The haiku poems achieve this by representing animals and plants as beings who are actively involved in leading their own lives in ways consistent with their nature, whether that is flying, slithering or blooming. And they represent animals as beings with mental lives who know, feel and have desires (Stibbe, 2012, p. 153). This is in complete contrast to the discourse of animal product industries, where animals are objects or machines, and even to some discourses of conservation and nature documentaries, where animals are valued only for being rare or spectacular in some way. Importantly, haiku tell the story that PLANTS AND ANIMALS ARE WORHTY OF APPRECIATION through the linguistic features which convey this message between-the-lines in vivid and powerful ways, rather than a direct and dry statement. It is not just the stories that students are searching for, but the creative linguistic features which tell those stories.

There are many other places to search for new stories to live by, e.g., the Romantic poetry of William Wordsworth or John Clare, the imaginative naturalist writings of Rachel Carson or Aldo Leopold, the 'new nature writing' of Richard Mabey or Kathleen Jamie, the contemporary ecopoetry of Helen Moore or Susan Richardson and traditional literary schools such as the Shan-Shui writers of China (see Stibbe, 2015b, 2017a, 2017b). For their assignment, students seek out their own sources to search for new stories to live by, transforming how they see their place in the world in the process. Feedback comments from students include:

- I always walk away from lessons glowing with happiness because of appreciation of the world around us.
- It opened my eyes – I started to see things in a different light.
- It enhances interest in nature making me appreciate things I would have previously not noticed.
- Incredibly interesting and is opening my eyes, very engaging.
- Really encourages me to think outside the box.
- Helped me to be more open minded about my surroundings.

Conclusion: advocacy for life's flourishing

I teach in a society which is unsustainable, which means that because of the levels of inequality, resource use and waste, the society cannot continue into the future in its current form. There are only two possibilities: either the society changes at a deep, fundamental level, or it fails to change and collapses. I believe that teaching within an unsustainable society places certain demands on educators – it is no longer sufficient just to teach disciplinary conventions which were forged at a time when environmental limits were not a consideration. And it is not sufficient to teach students as if the society around them will exist in its current form in the future.

As an educator, I have therefore been using ecolinguistic techniques to help students reveal and question the stories we live by – the cognitive structures shared across cultures which influence how we think, talk and act. When students find that those stories are not working – are contributing to unsustainability and ecological destruction – then ecolinguistics provides the tools to help them search for new stories to live by. I hope that they will use these tools to rethink society and contribute to the changes needed to build a sustainable society. But I realise that the current direction humanity is heading in will be hard to change in time, and that collapse is a more likely outcome. With collapse, however, comes the possibility of the survivors building a new civilisation, and

TABLE 16.1 Sustainability Education Grounded in Students' Own Ecosophy

Context: The course *The Search for New Stories to Live By* is a second-year undergraduate module where students explore the stories that underpin the unsustainable society they are part of, question these stories from an ecological perspective, and explore literature in the search for new stories. Students are free to create their own learning outcomes, which could be drawn from mainstream documents such as the SDGs, or alternative sources such as the *Deep Ecology Platform* (DE, 2018), the *Dark Mountain Manifesto* (DM, 2018), or *Theses for the People's Ecology* (PE, 2018), which present a stronger challenge to the dominant stories that underpin industrial civilization. Various exercises connected with this task are available to teachers as part of the free online course *The Stories We Live By* (Stories, 2019).

Conceptual Framework Dimensions	Lesson, Activity, or Project
Ethic of Care – Values – Attitudes – Behaviors	**Lesson, Activity, or Project Title: Positive Discourse Analysis to Reveal New Stories to Live By** *Phase 1: Ecosophy.* Students create their own ecological philosophy (ecosophy) that they will use to judge whether stories are positive or negative. They do this by examining a range of philosophical positions and considering these positions in relation to their direct experience of communities and natural systems. In class they formulate the ecosophies in brief statements, discuss them with other students and refine them into a practically applicable framework.
Resilience & Regeneration – Knowledge – Skills	*Phase 2: Analysis.* Students analyze a range of texts that shape the dominant stories of our culture, from newspapers, magazines and advertisements to economics textbooks. They reveal the underlying stories and critique them by comparing them with their ecosophy. Where stories are found not to be working, i.e., to be contributing to the destruction of the systems that life depends on, then they begin a search for new stories. This involves analysis of a wide range of literature from countries around the world, selected because it has the potential to inspire people to care about each other, other species and the physical environment. The students analyze these texts, revealing the linguistic features which make them inspiring (Stibbe, 2012, 2015a).

Conceptual Framework Dimensions	Lesson, Activity, or Project
Advocacy for Life's Flourishing – Action – Critique – Reflection	*Phase 3: Action.* In this final phase students identify actions that they can take to resist destructive stories and promote beneficial ones. Firstly, they could engage in personal resistance of the discourses of consumerist society by adjusting their purchasing patterns to focus on seeking well-being rather than material accumulation. Secondly, they could resist dominant stories by publicly criticizing discourses which promote consumerism and unlimited economic growth or treat other species as resources to be exploited. This could include obvious discourses, such as advertising or industrial farming, but also mainstream discourses of sustainable development or environmentalism, which sometimes reproduce rather than challenge dominant stories (Stibbe, 2012, 2015a). Thirdly, they could employ linguistic devices in their own writing to encode new stories to live by, using words in inspiring ways that promote care towards other people and the ecosystems that life depends on. Fourthly, they could do consultancy work, helping charities and businesses convey inspiring messages in their communication practices. A final form of action is in sharing the concepts and tools of ecolinguistics to help others become critical of the stories that underpin our unequal and unsustainable industrial civilisation and contribute to the search for new stories to live by.

Source: Course Content Guide: The Search for New Stories to Live By, Arran Stibbe

for that it becomes essential that new stories to live by are found. There is no time to lose in searching for these new stories.

References

Bartlett, T. (2012). *Hybrid voices and collaborative change: contextualising positive discourse analysis*. London: Routledge.

Benwell, B., & Stokoe, E. (2006). *Discourse and identity*. Edinburgh: Edinburgh University Press.

Berry, T. (1978). New story. In *Teilhard Studies No. 1*. New York: Anima.

Bookchin, M. (2005). *The ecology of freedom: The emergence and dissolution of hierarchy*. Oakland, CA: AK Press.

Brundtland, G. (1987). *Our common future*. Oxford: Oxford University Press.

CBS. (2012). *A short guide to gross national happiness*. Centre for Bhutan Studies. Retrieved from www.bhutanstudies.org.bt

CIE. (2017). *Chief Seattle*. Californian Indian Education. Retrieved from www.califor niaindianeducation.org/famous_indian_chiefs/chief_seattle/

Crompton, T. (2010). *Common cause: The case for working with our cultural values*. WWF-UK. Retrieved from http://assets.wwf.org.uk/downloads/common_cause_report.pdf.

Dark Mountain. (2018). *The Dark Mountain manifesto*. The Dark Mountain Project. Retrieved from https://dark-mountain.net/about/manifesto/

Deep Ecology. (2018). *The deep ecology platform*. Foundation for Deep Ecology. Retrieved fromwww.deepecology.org/platform.htm

ECI. (2017). *The Earth Charter*. Retrieved from http://earthcharter.org/discover/the-earth-charter

Fairclough, N. (2003). *Analysing discourse: Textual analysis for social research*. London: Routledge.

Fill, A., & Penz, H. (Eds.). (2017). *The Routledge handbook of ecolinguistics* (1st ed.). New York: Routledge.

Hickel, J. (2017). *Five reasons to think twice about the UN's sustainable development goals*. Retrieved from http://blogs.lse.ac.uk/southasia/2015/09/23/five-reasons-to-think-twice-about-the-uns-sustainable-development-goals/

Hopkins, R. (2008). *The transition handbook: From oil dependency to local resilience*. Dartington: Green Books.

Hopwood, B., Mellor, M., & O'Brien, G. (2005.) Sustainable development: Mapping different approaches. *Sustainable Development*, *13*(1), 38–52.

Kingsnorth, P., & Hine, D. (2009). *The Dark Mountain Project manifesto*. Retrieved from http://dark-mountain.net/about/manifesto/

Lakoff, G., & Wehling, E. (2012). *The little blue book: The essential guide to thinking and talking Democratic*. New York: Free Press.

Martin, J., & White, P. (2005). *The language of evaluation: Appraisal in English*. New York: Palgrave Macmillan.

Martin, J. (2004). Positive discourse analysis: solidarity and change. *Revista Canaria de Estudios Ingleses*, *49*, 179–200.

McBay, A., Keith, L., & Jensen, D. (2011). *Deep green resistance: Strategy to save the planet*. New York: Seven Stories Press.

Meyer, J., & Land, R. (2005). Threshold concepts and troublesome knowledge (2): Epistemological considerations and a conceptual framework for teaching and learning. *Higher Education*, *49*(3), 373–388.

Naess, A. (1995). The shallow and the long range, deep ecology movement. In A. Drengson & Y. Inoue (Eds.), *The deep ecology movement: An introductory anthology* (pp. 3–10). Berkeley, CA: North Atlantic Books.

NEF. (2015). *People powered money: Designing, developing and delivering community currencies*. London: New Economics Foundation.

Okri, B. (1996). *Birds of heaven*. London: Phoenix.

People's Ecology. (2018). *Theses for the people's ecology in the twenty-first century*. Retrieved from http://new-compass.net/articles/21-theses-peoples-ecology

Potter, J. (1996). *Representing reality: Discourse, rhetoric and social construction*. London: Sage.

Stibbe, A. (2012). *Animals erased: Discourse, ecology, and reconnection with the natural world*. Middletown, CT: Wesleyan University Press.

Stibbe, A. (2015a). *Ecolinguistics: language, ecology and the stories we live by*. London: Routledge.

Stibbe, A. (2015b). *Innovative pedagogies series: The search for new stories to live by*. HigherEducation Academy. Retrieved from www.heacademy.ac.uk/system/files/arran_stibbe_-_final2.pdf

Stibbe, A. (2017a). Critical discourse analysis and ecology: The search for new stories to live by. In J. Richardson & J. Flowerdew (Eds.), *The Routledge handbook of critical discourse analysis*. London: Routledge.

Stibbe, A. (2017b). Positive discourse analysis: Re-thinking human ecological relationships. In A. Fill & H. Penz (Eds.), *The Routledge handbook of ecolinguistics*. London: Routledge.

Stories. (2019). *The stories we live by: A free online course*. Retrieved from www.storieswe liveby.org.uk

van Leeuwen, T. (2008). *Discourse and practice*. Oxford: Oxford University Press.

VHMT. (2019). *The voluntary human extinction movement*. Retrieved from www.vhemt.org

CONCLUSION

Joan Armon

As environmental degradation, climate change, and associated challenges esca-late, it is crucial for educators to accelerate sustainability education initiatives, as authors in this volume express. A key step is to involve students in the holis-tic approaches that shift unsustainable mindsets and behaviors into sustainable thinking and living on campuses and in communities. This is a complex pro-cess, which will involve a comprehensive readjustment of current practices and economically-driven, industrialized, and technological ways of thinking. But it is a challenge which has to be confronted. A path to this shift appears through key themes that are developed in this book.

Cultivating an *Ethic of Care* is foundational to comprehensive sustainability education in which educators and students:

- Situate teaching and learning not only in classrooms but also in natural envi-ronments and communities to develop relational awareness accompanied by a commitment to the harmony and well-being of the natural world and the lives within it.
- Dialogue regarding the intrinsic value of the natural world, human, and other-than-human lives; of lives lived in moderation, sufficiency, humility, and gratitude; and of ethical decision-making and action informed by spiri-tual or existential perspectives.
- Establish reciprocal relationships with places, people, and other-than-human lives.
- Pursue sustainable, compassionate, and just ways to distribute wealth more equitably and promote the well-being of all sectors of the human community.
- Honor and learn from the values, traditions, beliefs, and experiences of oth-ers who have developed sustainable ways of living, particularly those from marginalized groups, such as indigenous and traditional cultures, alternative

communities that combine ancient and contemporary practices, and women, elders, farmers, and others who work with and care for the natural world.
• Develop multi-dimensional perception of the natural world, its qualities, and its needs by summoning not only scientific analysis and evaluation but also intuition, playfulness, imagination, compassion, and love.

Fostering *Resilience and Regeneration* involves not only *learning about* but also *engaging in* comprehensive sustainability education to develop vital knowledge and skills as educators and students:

• Select conducive contexts for engaging in authentic transdisciplinary, transformative, and participatory teaching and learning experiences.
• Acquire knowledge of Earth's systems and become adept at systems thinking.
• Engage in transdisciplinary teaching and learning that calls upon students to contribute knowledge and skills from their disciplinary backgrounds, and then to synthesize contributions to create novel pathways for addressing authentic challenges.
• Expose, and create alternatives to, the thinking and practices of root causes of environmental destruction and climate change such as anthropocentrism, consumerism, individualism, corporatization, and the quest for economic gain above the well-being of the commons and the lives that inhabit them.
• Draw upon varying cultures' histories, traditions, stories, and values to develop resilience in times of environmental, social, political, and economic turbulence and unpredictability.
• Value features of the natural world that constitute the commons; evaluate evidence of their health or degradation; explore implications; and, if necessary, propose, participate in, and advocate for regenerative change.

Advocating for *Life's Flourishing* is an essential dimension of comprehensive sustainability education that includes:

• Transformational learning in which students experience disequilibrium between long-held values, beliefs, assumptions, and practices and those that are based on alternative data, whether scientific, experiential, or humanities-based stories, myths, and visions, that motivate them to reframe thought and action.
• Collaboration with community members to identify local problems worthy of study, solicit multiple perspectives regarding the problems, engage in dialogue, and, as appropriate, experience the problem in its authentic setting – all with the aim of proposing, implementing, and advocating for approaches that contribute to beneficial change.
• Confrontation of conditions that animals and people experience as they interact with corporate mindsets and practices, proposing alternative approaches, and advocating for their well-being.

- Study of climate change and environmental science balanced by humanities approaches that are integrated into all higher education coursework and experiential education.
- Creation of cross-generational solidarity focused on the recognition that environmental, social, political, technological, and economic flourishing require acquisition of resilient and regenerative mindsets and skills in the context of likely turbulence and instability.
- Listening to and advocating for disregarded voices of children, youth, young adults, and others who have awakened to the depth of environmental crises in which we find ourselves, who call for immediate prioritization of these crises in every arena, and who envision paradigms not yet perceived by others.

Challenges for comprehensive sustainability educators

Four notable and pressing challenges confront educators who are prioritizing comprehensive sustainability education in their courses and programs. One challenge is how to dilute or transform powerful controls that higher education disciplines exert on curricula, pedagogies, hiring and promotion practices, policies, space allocation, scheduling, operations, and funding. Disciplinary controls are too often out-of-date or irrelevant as humanity confronts massive threats to its existence. What is required now is for educators to collectively assert the urgency of directing substantive attention to sustainability education, continually request shifts in their departments and institutions, and creatively discern how their own courses and leadership can incorporate deep and meaningful sustainability education, as the authors featured in this book model in their chapters.

A second challenge is how to elevate the significance of transdisciplinary courses that are designed to develop systems thinking and driven by environmental and climate change information from both humanities and science sources and experiences. Such courses may involve co-planning and/or co-teaching with colleagues in other disciplines, disrupting existing scheduling, space allocations, and salary structures. We recommend that educators identify how they can partner with colleagues to craft transdisciplinary learning experiences for the students at their institution.

A third challenge is how to re-conceptualize teaching and learning so that courses occur in contexts conducive not only to acquisition of knowledge, but also skills. Such teaching and learning might become project-based with significant portions of time and experience devoted to identifying campus and community sustainability problems that educators and students then address in innovative ways. Through project-based learning, students gain experience in conceptualizing and implementing sustainability-oriented change that may involve compassionate relationship, humor, and a sense of harmony and hope in the face of unpredictable challenges that lie ahead. We advocate that comprehensive sustainability educators build coalitions that advocate for and create meaningful project-based learning opportunities that make comprehensive sustainability education a reality.

A final challenge is to overcome hesitation and inertia and to begin. We urge a summoning of our individual and collective capacities for humility, fearlessness, and fortitude to sustain us as we create planetary thriving. Most importantly, we must now act together in communities steered by vision, love, and resolve. How we reach this point of resolve requires what Sterling terms anticipative learning (2019). It begins with acknowledging, owning, and engaging with misdirected illusions, such as our disregard for and separateness from nature and our unbridled quest for economic gain at the expense of life. It reflects on the sorrow we feel for that which we have carelessly destroyed and continue to destroy, yet it arouses love and gratitude for that which still lives and must be protected. It beckons us to imagine alternative pathways that create and safeguard life-honoring economic, political, and social systems and ways of living and being that are embedded in environmental care. It requires fearless action and change on behalf of current and future generations. Similarly, Leonardo Boff points humanity toward change that is revolutionary:

> A sustainable way of life is humankind's new ethical and cultural dream. It entails another way of conceiving the common future of Earth and humankind and, accordingly, it demands a true revolution in minds and hearts, values and habits, forms of production, and relationship with nature.
>
> *(2008, p. 130)*

This revolution calls for a new education on the side of life. On the side of life, this is the time for unwavering commitment to future generations' prospects for not only surviving, but also thriving.

References

Boff, L. (2008). The ethic of care. In P. Corcoran and J. Wohlpart (Eds.), *A voice for earth: American writers respond to the earth charter* (pp. 129–145). Athens, GA: University of Georgia Press.

Sterling, S. (2019). Planetary primacy and the necessity of positive dis-illusion. *Sustainability, 12*(2), 60–67.

INDEX